MLA Handbook for Writers of Research Papers

MLA Handbook for Writers of Research Papers

Sixth Edition

Joseph Gibaldi

THE MODERN LANGUAGE ASSOCIATION OF AMERICA
New York   2003

The Modern Language Association publishes two books on its documentation style: the *MLA Handbook for Writers of Research Papers* (for high school and undergraduate students) and the *MLA Style Manual and Guide to Scholarly Publishing* (for graduate students, scholars, and professional writers). These volumes provide the most accurate and complete instructions on MLA style.

If updates of the information in this handbook become necessary, they will be posted at the MLA's World Wide Web site (http://www.mla.org/).

For information about obtaining permission to reprint material from MLA book publications, send your request by mail (see address below), e-mail (permissions@mla.org), or fax (646 458-0030).

Library of Congress Cataloging-in-Publication Data

Gibaldi, Joseph, 1942–
    MLA handbook for writers of research papers / Joseph Gibaldi. — 6th ed.
        p.   cm.
Includes bibliographical references and index.
    ISBN 0-87352-986-3 (alk. paper)
    1. Report writing—Handbooks, manuals, etc.   2. Research—Handbooks, manuals, etc.   I. Title: Handbook for writers of research papers.   II. Modern Language Association of America.   III. Title.
    LB2369.G53   2003
    808'.027—dc21   2002156363

Second printing 2004

Book design by Charlotte Staub. Set in Melior and Avenir Book. Printed on recycled, acid-free paper

Published by The Modern Language Association of America
26 Broadway, New York, New York 10004-1789
www.mla.org

Contents

Foreword

The *MLA Handbook for Writers of Research Papers* is designed to introduce you to the customs of a community of writers who greatly value scrupulous scholarship and the careful documentation, or recording, of research. Read from beginning to end, the *MLA Handbook* provides a comprehensive picture of how research papers are created. Once you are familiar with the contents, you can use the book as a reference tool. Chapter 1 suggests some of the educational and intellectual purposes of research and describes the first steps in a scholarly project: choosing a topic; using a library and the Internet; evaluating electronic sources; and producing a working bibliography, notes, outlines, and drafts. Chapter 2 explains why plagiarism is an important concern and how to avoid unintentional plagiarism. Chapter 3 gives practical advice on such matters as spelling, punctuation, and the presentation of names, numbers, titles of works, and quotations. This chapter is meant to help you craft writing that is clear, consistent, and stylistically authoritative. Chapter 4 gives guidelines on the physical format of the paper. The next two chapters cover the MLA's system, or style, of documenting print and electronic sources: chapter 5 explains how to list sources at the end of a paper, while chapter 6 shows how to cite them in the text of a paper. Chapter 7 describes abbreviations that are useful in documentation and in certain other contexts. Appendix A lists notable reference works in specialized fields; appendix B presents some systems of documentation other than the MLA's. Finally, there are sample pages of a research paper that illustrate MLA style.

Learning the rules the *MLA Handbook* outlines will help you become a writer whose work deserves serious consideration. Similarly, your study of these rules can make you a more discerning reader: knowing how an author is supposed to use sources is essential to judging a text's reliability.

The *MLA Handbook* was developed by the Modern Language Association of America (MLA), an organization of teachers and scholars founded in 1883, when the modern languages were just beginning to gain a place in the college curriculum alongside the classical languages—ancient Greek and Latin. The MLA now has about thirty thousand members and supports a variety of publications and activities designed to strengthen teaching and scholarship in languages and literature. One of the association's best-known publications, the *MLA Handbook* has been widely used by generations of students at high schools, colleges, and universities throughout the United States and in other countries. The documentation style the book outlines is preferred by a substantial majority of scholarly journals in languages and literature.

The *MLA Handbook* originated over fifty years ago. Convinced that commonly agreed-on rules for documenting quotations, facts, opinions, and paraphrases would simplify the task of preparing a manuscript for publication, William Riley Parker, the MLA executive director, compiled and published the "MLA Style Sheet" in 1951 in the association's journal, *PMLA*. The "Style Sheet" gained almost immediate acceptance among MLA members and scholarly publishers both because Parker codified uniform practices among journal editors and university presses and because he encouraged consensus on matters about which there was less agreement. The "Style Sheet" continued to respond to the changing needs of scholars, editors, and publishers and, in time, also addressed the needs of undergraduate students, becoming in 1977 the *MLA Handbook for Writers of Research Papers*. Over the years John Hurt Fisher, Joseph Gibaldi, Walter S. Achtert, Judith Altreuter, Martha Evans, Elizabeth Holland, and Eric Wirth contributed to successive editions of the publication.

The second edition of the *MLA Handbook*, which appeared in 1984, introduced the current simplified set of rules for documentation that allow citations to be placed in the text within parentheses. The third edition, produced in 1988, covered some aspects of electronic publication, and the editions that followed kept up with technological changes and their effects on research and writing. The book you hold, the sixth edition, not only encompasses recent technological changes but also includes guidelines for doing research on the Internet and for evaluating the reliability of Web sites. A new chapter on plagiarism responds to requests from MLA members for more information about this difficult problem.

Because the MLA is a membership association, all its projects are communal efforts. The collaborative work on the *MLA Handbook* is particularly far-reaching; the various editions have benefited for over forty years from the contributions of MLA committee and staff members, editors, scholars, librarians, teachers, and students. The members of two *MLA Handbook* committees contributed to the development of the rules for citing electronic material: Wayne C. Booth, Marshall J. Brown, Wendy Chun, Anne Ruggles Gere, Joel D. Goldfield, James L. Harner, Susan Kallenbach, John W. Kronik, Ian Lancashire, and Cynthia L. Selfe. The members of the MLA Committee on Computers and Emerging Technologies in Teaching and Research also participated in the discussion of the best ways to cite electronic publications. Among the many teachers, librarians, and students who suggested ideas for this edition are Marsha Cummins, Frank Duba, Matthew Goldie, Gail Green-Anderson, Deborah Landau, Maria de Vasconcelos, Linda Westervelt, Mark Bobrow, Robert Cirasa, Robert Friedman, Caroline Pari, Andrew Rubenfield, Susan Bachman, Melissa Bergin, Melba Cuddy-Keane, Julia Jerles, Dan Linehan, Chris Michalski, Bob Nestor, Barbara Rugeley, Pat Sazy, and Ellen Strenski.

Many MLA staff members provided advice and direction during the planning of this edition of the *MLA Handbook*. Members of the book publications department, headed by David G. Nicholls, lent support to Joseph Gibaldi as he prepared the manuscript. Members of the editorial department, headed by Judy Goulding, contributed to changes in the new edition.

Phyllis Franklin
Executive Director
Modern Language Association
July 2002

1 Research and Writing

1.1. THE RESEARCH PAPER AS A FORM OF EXPLORATION

Personal Essays and Research Papers

During your school career you have probably written many personal essays that presented your thoughts, feelings, and opinions and that did not refer to any other source of information or ideas. Some subjects and assignments, however, require us to go beyond our personal knowledge and experience. We undertake research when we wish to explore an idea, probe an issue, solve a problem, or make an argument that compels us to turn to outside help. We then seek out, investigate, and use materials beyond our personal resources. The findings and conclusions of such an inquiry appear in the research paper. The term *research paper* describes a presentation of student research that may be in a printed, an electronic, or a multimedia format.

Types of Research

The research paper is generally based on primary research, secondary research, or a combination of the two. *Primary research* is the study of a subject through firsthand observation and investigation, such as analyzing a literary or historical text, a film, or a performance; conducting a survey or an interview; or carrying out a laboratory experiment. Primary sources include statistical data, historical documents, and works of literature or art. *Secondary research* is the examination of studies that other researchers have made of a subject. Examples of secondary sources are books and articles about political issues, historical events, scientific debates, or literary works.

Using Secondary Research

Most academic papers depend at least partly on secondary research. No matter what your subject of study, learning to investigate, review, and productively use information, ideas, and opinions of other researchers will play a major role in your development as a student. The sorts of activities that constitute a research paper—identifying, locating, assessing, and assimilating others' research and then developing and expressing your own ideas clearly and persuasively—are at the center of the educational experience.

Combining Research and Original Ideas

Research increases your knowledge and understanding of a subject. Sometimes research will confirm your ideas and opinions; sometimes it will challenge and modify them. But almost always it will help to shape your thinking. Unless your instructor specifically directs you otherwise, a research paper should not merely review publications and extract a series of quotations from them. Rather, you should look for sources that provide new information, that helpfully survey the various positions already taken on a specific subject, that lend authority to your viewpoint, that expand or nuance your ideas, that offer methods or modes of thought you can apply to new data or subjects, or that furnish negative examples against which you wish to argue. As you use and scrupulously acknowledge sources, however, always remember that the main purpose of doing research is not to summarize the work of others but to assimilate and to build on it and to arrive at your own understanding of the subject.

Different Approaches to Research and Writing

A book like this cannot present all the profitable ways of doing research. Because this handbook emphasizes the mechanics of preparing effective papers, it may give you the mistaken impression that the process of researching and writing a research paper follows a fixed pattern. The truth is that different paths can and do lead to successful research papers. Some researchers may pursue a more or less standard sequence of steps, but others may find themselves working less sequentially. In addition, certain projects lend themselves to a standard approach, whereas others may call for different strategies. Keeping in mind that researchers and projects differ, this book discusses activities that nearly all writers of research papers perform, such as selecting a suitable topic, conducting research, compiling a working bibliography, taking notes, outlining, and preparing the paper.

An Intellectual Adventure

If you are writing your first research paper, you may feel overwhelmed by the many tasks discussed here. This handbook is designed to help you learn to manage a complex process efficiently. As you follow the book's advice on how to locate and document sources, how to format your paper, and so forth, you may be tempted to see doing a paper as a mechanical exercise. Actually, a research paper is an adventure, an intellectual adventure rather like solving a mystery: it is a form of exploration that leads to discoveries that are new—at least to you if not to others. The mechanics of the research paper, important though they are, should never override the intellectual challenge of pursuing a question that interests *you* (and ultimately your reader). This quest or search should guide your research and your writing. Even though you are just learning how to prepare a research paper, you may still experience some of the excitement of pursuing and developing ideas that is one of the great satisfactions of research and scholarship.

Research Papers and Professional Writing

Skills derived from preparing research papers are by no means just academic. Many reports and proposals required in business, government, and other professions similarly rely on secondary research. Learning how to write a research paper, then, can help prepare you for assignments in your professional career. It is difficult to think of any profession that would not require you to consult sources of information about a specific subject, to combine this information with your ideas, and to present your thoughts, findings, and conclusions effectively.

1.2. THE RESEARCH PAPER AS A FORM OF COMMUNICATION

A research paper is a form of written communication. Like other kinds of nonfiction writing—letters, memos, reports, essays, articles, books—it should present information and ideas clearly and effectively. You should not let the mechanics of gathering source materials, taking notes, and documenting sources make you forget to apply the knowledge and skills you have acquired through previous writing experiences.

This handbook is a guide for the preparation of research papers. It is not a book about expository writing. (See 1.11 for a selected list of useful books on usage, language, and style.) Nonetheless, no set of conventions for preparing a manuscript can replace lively and intelligent writing, and no amount of research and documentation can compensate for a poor presentation of ideas. Although you must fully document the facts and opinions you draw from your research, the documentation should only support your statements and provide concise information about the sources cited; it should not overshadow your own ideas or distract the reader from them.

1.3. SELECTING A TOPIC

1.3.1. Freedom of Choice

Different courses and different instructors offer widely varying degrees of freedom to students selecting topics for research papers. The instructor of a course in a specific discipline (e.g., art, history, literature, science) may supply a list of topics from which to choose or may, more generally, require that the paper relate to an important aspect of the course. If you are given the latter option, review course readings and class notes to find topics that particularly interest you. Discuss possibilities with other students and with your instructor. If your choice is limited to a set list of topics, you will probably still need to decide which aspect of a topic to explore or which approach to use.

In a writing class, you may have more freedom to select a topic. The instructor may assign a general problem that can generate many kinds of responses—for example, you might be asked to choose a modern invention and show what benefits and problems it has brought about. If you have complete freedom to choose a topic, consider using a personal interest that lends itself to research (e.g., education, the environment, movies, new technologies, nutrition, politics, the business of sports) or an issue that has recently generated public interest or controversy (e.g., cloning, global warming, biological warfare, terrorism).

Teachers understand the importance of choosing an appropriate topic for a research paper. When freedom of choice is permitted, students are commonly required to submit topics to the instructor for approval early in the research project.

1.3.2. Finding an Appropriate Focus

As you choose a topic, remember the time allotted to you and the expected length of the research paper. "International politics in the modern age" would obviously be too broad a subject for a ten-page term paper. You may prefer to begin with a fairly general topic and then to refine it, by thought and research, into a more specific one that can be fully explored. Try to narrow your topic by focusing on an aspect of the subject or an approach to it. A student initially interested in the general subject of "violence in the media" might decide, after careful thought and reading, to write on "the effects of cartoon violence on preschool children." Likewise, an interest in architecture could lead to a focus on the design and construction of domes, which could in turn be narrowed to a comparison between the ancient Roman dome and the Byzantine dome.

Preliminary reading is essential as you evaluate and refine topics. Consult, in print or electronic form, general reference works, such as encyclopedias, as well as articles and books in the areas you are considering (see 1.4 on conducting research). You can also refine your topic by doing subject searches in reference databases (see 1.4.4d) and in online catalogs (see 1.4.5a) and through Internet search tools (see 1.4.8e). Such preliminary reading and searches will also let you know if enough work has been done on the subject to permit adequate research and whether the pertinent source materials are readily accessible.

Selecting an appropriate topic is seldom a simple matter. Even after you discover a subject that attracts your interest, you may well find yourself revising your choice, modifying your approach, or changing topics altogether after you have begun research.

1.3.3. SUMMING UP

- Give yourself plenty of time to think through and rethink your choice of a topic.
- Look for a subject or an issue that will continue to engage you throughout research and writing.
- Consult library materials and other print and electronic information resources to refine the topic and to see if sufficient work has been done on the subject to make it a viable topic for the research paper.

- Before settling on a final topic, make sure you understand the amount and depth of research required and the type and length of paper expected.
- If you encounter problems at any point in the project, do not hesitate to consult your instructor, whether to clarify the assignment or to get help in choosing, developing, or researching a topic or in preparing the paper.

1.4. CONDUCTING RESEARCH

1.4.1. The Modern Academic Library

The library will generally be your most reliable guide as you conduct research for papers that draw on the published work of experts. Librarians evaluate resources for authority and quality before acquiring them for use in research. You should therefore become thoroughly acquainted with the libraries available to you and take full advantage of the resources and services they provide on-site and over the Internet.

Resources and Services

The modern academic library typically offers resources in print and electronic forms and in other nonprint media (e.g., films, sound recordings), as well as computer services, such as word processing, high-quality printers, and access to the Internet. Whereas some important resources are available only in the library building (e.g., most books and other publications solely in print form, microfilm materials, special collections), your library probably provides a number of electronic resources, such as bibliographic and full-text databases, that are accessible not only through computer terminals in the library but also over the Internet through the library's Web site.

Orientation and Instruction

Most academic libraries have programs of orientation and instruction to meet the needs of all students, from beginning researchers to graduate students. Ask about introductory pamphlets or handbooks and guided tours as well as lectures and classes on using the library and on related subjects like developing research strategies and

searching the World Wide Web. The library's Web site likely contains scheduling information on such classes as well as descriptions
of available resources and services. The site may also offer a virtual
tour of the library.

Professional Reference Librarians

Nearly all public and academic libraries have desks staffed by professional reference librarians who can tell you about available
instructional programs and help you locate sources. Specialist librarians often prepare and distribute, in print and electronic forms,
research guides to specific fields of study. Consulting a librarian at
key points in your research may save you considerable time and
effort.

1.4.2. Library Research Sources

Touring or reading about your library will reveal the many important
sources of information it makes available to researchers. Information
sources fall into four general categories.

Books and Similar Publications

The library typically houses a vast number of books as well as similar publications such as pamphlets and perhaps dissertations. Books
are essential sources for many projects, and some instructors require
that students use books—in addition to articles, Internet sites, and
other materials—during research. Relatively few books are available
electronically over the Internet, but you can usually borrow most
books from the library. A common exception is the library's collection of reference works (see 1.4.4). Although reference works usually
cannot be borrowed, many important ones are likely available to you
through the library's Web site. (See 5.6 on citing books and other
nonperiodical publications in the list of works cited.)

Articles and Other Publications in Print Periodicals

The library gives access to numerous articles and similar writings
(e.g., reviews, editorials) published in print periodicals such as
scholarly journals, newspapers, and magazines. (See 5.7 on citing
articles and other publications in print periodicals in the list of
works cited.)

Miscellaneous Print and Nonprint Sources

Most libraries also provide nonprint sources such as sound recordings and video recordings and possibly also unpublished writings (e.g., manuscripts or private letters in special collections). (See 5.8 on citing these sources in the list of works cited.)

Electronic Sources

Your library probably offers reference works in electronic form (see 1.4.4) and full-text databases (see 1.4.6) and may also recommend useful Internet sites (see 1.4.8). Your library may also subscribe to journals available only in electronic form. (See 5.9 on citing electronic sources in the list of works cited.)

1.4.3. The Central Information System

Most academic libraries provide an online central information system to guide students and faculty members to research sources. The system ordinarily includes

- **the library's catalog of holdings** (books, periodicals, electronic sources, audiovisual materials, etc.; see 1.4.5)
- **bibliographic databases**, such as *Readers' Guide to Periodical Literature*, *Business Periodicals Index*, *Humanities Index*, *Social Sciences Index*, and *General Science Index*
- **other electronic resources**, including reference works (see 1.4.4), full-text databases to which the library subscribes (see 1.4.6), and recommended Internet sites to which the library provides links (see 1.4.8)

The central information system might also be part of a network linking the catalogs of a number of libraries. For instance, the system in your school might permit you to search the holdings of local public libraries or of other schools. If your library is part of a network such as the Center for Research Libraries (CRL), the Online Computer Library Center (OCLC), or the Research Libraries Information Network (RLIN), you may be able to locate sources recorded in the catalogs of thousands of other libraries. (The central information system has almost completely replaced the card catalog in academic libraries. Card catalogs are sometimes still used for materials such as special collections that have not yet been incorporated into the information system.)

1.4.4. Reference Works

A useful way to begin a research project is to consult relevant reference works. Some reference works, like indexes and bibliographies,
categorize research materials by subject and provide data that permit
you to locate sources—author, title, date of publication, and so forth.
Other reference works, like encyclopedias, dictionaries, and biographical sources, give basic information about subjects. This section
provides a brief introduction to the range of general and specialized
reference works you should know about, many of which are available in print and electronic forms. For a more comprehensive listing
by subject area, see appendix A.

a. Reference Works That Provide Data about Research Materials

Indexes guide you to material in newspapers, magazines, and journals as well as to writings in book collections.

- *The New York Times Index, The Wall Street Journal Index,* and
  The Washington Post Index list news stories and feature articles in
  three major newspapers.
- *Readers' Guide to Periodical Literature* indexes the contents of
  popular magazines.
- *Essay and General Literature Index* lists essays and articles pub-
  lished in books.
- Most subject areas have their own specialized indexes, such as *Art
  Index, Business Periodicals Index, Education Index, General
  Science Index, Humanities Index, Index to Legal Periodicals and
  Books, The Philosopher's Index,* and *Social Sciences Index.*

Bibliographies are lists of related publications and other materials.

- Bibliographies in specific disciplines include *Bibliography of
  Agriculture, Bibliographic Guide to Art and Architecture, Bibliography and Index of Geology,* and *MLA International Bibliography*
  (for the field of language and literature).
- *Bibliographic Index* contains citations of bibliographies that are published as books or pamphlets, as parts of books, or in periodicals.

Collections of abstracts present summaries of journal articles and
other literature.

- *Newspaper Abstracts* covers the *Atlanta Constitution,* the *Boston
  Globe,* the *Chicago Tribune,* the *Christian Science Monitor,* the *Los*

Angeles Times, the *New York Times*, *USA Today*, the *Wall Street Journal*, and the *Washington Post*.

- *Periodical Abstracts* treats a wide range of English-language academic journals and newsmagazines.
- Collections of abstracts in specific disciplines include *Art Abstracts, Biological Abstracts, Business Abstracts, Chemical Abstracts, Historical Abstracts, Humanities Abstracts, Linguistics and Language Behavior Abstracts, Physics Abstracts, Psychological Abstracts*, and *Sociological Abstracts*.
- Summaries of doctoral dissertations are available in *Dissertation Abstracts International*.

Guides to research seek to direct you to the most important sources of information and scholarship in the area you are researching. Unlike indexes, bibliographies, and collections of abstracts, which tend to strive for comprehensiveness and objectivity in presenting information, guides to research are usually selective and evaluative.

- Some research guides cover entire fields, such as James L. Harner's *Literary Research Guide* (4th ed. [New York: MLA, 2002]); other, similar works have titles like *Art Information: Research Methods and Resources, A Guide to the Literature of Pharmacy and the Pharmaceutical Sciences*, and *Philosophy: A Guide to the Reference Literature*.
- Some guides to research are devoted to specific subjects within fields (e.g., *Reference Guide to Mystery and Detective Fiction*).

To learn of any guides that might be useful to your project, consult the latest edition of the American Library Association's *Guide to Reference Books*, your instructor, or a librarian.

b. Reference Works That Give Basic Information about Subjects

Dictionaries are alphabetically arranged works that provide information, usually in concise form, about words or topics.

- Among the most authoritative dictionaries for English words are *Webster's Third New International Dictionary of the English Language* and, especially for the history of a word's meanings and usages, *The Oxford English Dictionary*.
- More concise English-language dictionaries often recommended for student writers are *The American Heritage College Dictionary, Merriam-Webster's Collegiate Dictionary*, and *Random House Webster's College Dictionary*.

- Foreign language dictionaries typically present words in one language followed by translations of those words into another language—for instance, *The New World Spanish-English, English-Spanish Dictionary* (also titled *El New World diccionario español-inglés, inglés-español*). Some language dictionaries in specialized fields are in a multilingual format, such as *Elsevier's Dictionary of Environment in English, French, Spanish, and Arabic.*
- A thesaurus lists groups of synonyms—words with similar meanings. It is useful for writers who wish to find the most precise word for a particular context or to vary their choice of words. Examples are *The Merriam-Webster Collegiate Thesaurus* and *Roget's International Thesaurus.*
- Major fields of study have specialized dictionaries, such as *The Dictionary of Art, Dictionary of Computing, Black's Law Dictionary, Dorland's Illustrated Medical Dictionary, The New Grove Dictionary of Music and Musicians, A Dictionary of Philosophy, The Anchor Bible Dictionary,* and *The Penguin Dictionary of Sociology.*

Encyclopedias are works, usually alphabetically arranged, that give introductory information about subjects.

- Popular general encyclopedias are *Academic American Encyclopedia, The Columbia Encyclopedia, The Encyclopedia Americana,* and *The New Encyclopaedia Britannica.*
- Specialized encyclopedias include *Encyclopedia of Architecture, The Film Encyclopedia, Encyclopedia of American History, The New Princeton Encyclopedia of Poetry and Poetics, The Corsini Encyclopedia of Psychology and Behavioral Science,* and *McGraw-Hill Encyclopedia of Science and Technology.*

Biographical sources present information on the lives of prominent persons.

- Information on living persons is collected in *Current Biography, The International Who's Who, The Canadian Who's Who,* and *Who's Who in America.* Similar books exist for other countries as well: *Who's Who in Australia, Who's Who in Italy, Who's Who in Latin America, Who's Who in the Arab World,* and so forth.
- Sources for persons no longer living are *American National Biography* (for the United States), *Dictionary of Canadian Biography, Dictionary of National Biography* (for Great Britain), and *Webster's New Biographical Dictionary.*

Yearbooks present information about specific years in the past. Examples are *The Americana Annual, Britannica Book of the Year,* and *The Europa Yearbook.*

Almanacs are annual publications containing data, especially statistics, about many subjects. Examples are *The World Almanac and Book of Facts* and *The World Factbook.*

Atlases are collections of maps. *The National Atlas of the United States of America* is the official atlas of the United States; *The Times Atlas of the World* covers regions and nations of the entire world.

Gazetteers provide geographic information. Examples are *The Columbia Gazetteer of the World* and *Merriam-Webster's Geographical Dictionary.*

Statistical resources provide numerical or quantitative information.

- Collections of statistics are often published by government agencies. Such works include the following annual publications: *Statistical Abstract of the United States,* issued by the United States Bureau of the Census, and *Statistical Yearbook* and *Demographic Yearbook,* both published by the United Nations.
- The United States government has also created a number of Internet sites that provide statistical data. *American FactFinder,* produced by the Census Bureau, is a source for population, housing, economic, and geographic data. *FedStats,* published by the Federal Interagency Council on Statistical Policy, gives access to statistics and other information produced by more than seventy United States government agencies. The Congressional Information Service's *CIS Statistical Universe* provides comprehensive United States statistical information, including an index to over 100,000 statistical publications.

c. Publication Forms of Reference Works: Print and Electronic

Your library probably has reference works in print and electronic forms.

Print. Print works may be located in a reference room. General reference books, like dictionaries, encyclopedias, biographical sources, yearbooks, atlases, and gazetteers, may all be shelved together in one place, while specialized reference books may be grouped according to subject area—biology, business, literature, psychology, and so forth. The volumes of reference works published annually—indexes, bibliographies, and abstracts collections—are likely lined up in chronological order.

Electronic. Reference works available as electronic databases are usually online or on CD-ROM. Searching and drawing material from the library's databases can be done in the library building and probably from outside as well, over the Internet.

Print versus electronic. Online and CD-ROM databases have a number of advantages over print versions of reference works.

- Much more information is generally available in a database. Whereas the print version of an annual bibliography covers research and scholarship for only one year, the electronic version of the work typically covers several years. Let us say, then, that you want to find out what was written on a subject during the last five years. With the print version of an annual bibliography, you would need to consult five volumes—in effect, conduct five searches—to identify what you want. With the electronic version, you would need to do just one search.
- Information is usually more current in electronic formats. The printed volume of an annual reference work, for example, is published once a year. A CD-ROM version of the same work is commonly updated and issued to subscribers several times a year. An online database is normally an ongoing, continually updated project and is therefore the most up-to-date of the three forms.
- Electronic databases generally allow you to print out or download any information you wish to record, whereas you need to write out information when using printed sources. You can transfer downloaded data from your computer diskette to your research paper without the risk of introducing errors through copying by hand. Since compilers of bibliographic reference works sometimes make errors, however, you need to verify the information derived from a database (author's name, title, etc.) against the source itself when you consult it.
- Some bibliographic databases provide hypertextual links that can take you directly from a reference to a full-text electronic version of the source.
- Most important of all, you can search electronic versions of a reference work in many more ways than you can the printed version (see 1.4.4d).

d. Searching a Reference Database

Every field of study has standard reference works. One such work is the *MLA International Bibliography*, which lists studies in the fields of language and literature. This work is published in print and electronic formats.

VERSIONS

- **Print.** The printed library edition of this work is published annually in two clothbound books. The first contains listings in five areas: literature in English, literature in other languages, linguistics, general literature and related topics, and folklore. The second book provides a subject index to the first.
- **Electronic.** The *MLA International Bibliography* is also published in online and CD-ROM versions, which contain all citations published in annual volumes of the bibliography from 1963 to the present. Therefore, while an annual print volume of the *MLA International Bibliography* lists around sixty thousand titles, the electronic versions offer information on more than 1.5 million titles. Using these electronic editions, which are available from different vendors, involves searching techniques common to most databases. The standard ways of searching this database and similar ones are by author, title, and subject. Each vendor's system has help screens to guide you through its software interface.

TYPES OF SEARCHES

- **Author searches.** By entering the name of a scholar, you can obtain a list of the titles by the author that are collected in the database. For example, if you want to know what studies by the writer Deborah Tannen have been published in the fields covered by this bibliography, you can enter her name and receive a list of titles.
- **Title searches.** If you know only the title of a work—like the essay "Black Matter(s)" or the book *Talking Voices*—you can call forth complete bibliographic information about the work from the database by entering the title. If you remember only part of the title (e.g., "city"), you can request a listing of all titles containing that term (e.g., "Fun City: TV's Urban Situation Comedies of the 1990s," "The City in Modern Polish and Hungarian Poetry," "The London Scene: City and Court," "Japanese Adolescent Speech Styles in Hiroshima City: An Ethnographic Study").
- **Subject searches.** Since every work added to this bibliography is accompanied by at least one descriptor—a term that describes the

work's subject matter—you can also search the database by subject. Thus, if you ask for studies that discuss, for instance, "detective fiction," the system will search through its files and present you with all titles that have "detective fiction" as a descriptor. If you want studies of Toni Morrison's novels, you can search for records with "Toni Morrison" as a descriptor.

- **Expanded searches.** Databases like the *MLA International Bibliography* also permit you to expand or narrow your searches usefully. While you are trying to decide on a topic, you may want to do expanded searches to get a broad sense of possibilities. An expanded subject search of this database can be particularly helpful when you are developing a suitable research topic. If you have a general idea that you want to write on detective fiction, you can find related subjects by entering the word "detective" in your expanded subject search. The following is a sampling of the related topics you will receive, with links to relevant bibliographic listings:

detective comics	female detective
detective drama	French detective
detective fiction	hard-boiled detective
detective film	American detective fiction
detective magazines	Egyptian detective fiction
detective novel	English detective fiction
detective story	paranormal detective fiction
detective television	Senegalese detective fiction

Also useful for expanded searches is the truncation (or wild card) feature. By using a truncated, or shortened, term—for example, a word root—followed by an asterisk (or the symbols : or $, depending on the vendor's software interface), you can retrieve all variants of it. If you wish, for instance, to do a paper on feminism but cannot decide what aspect to focus on, you can enter as a search term "femini*" and receive records on, among other subjects, "feminine discourse," "femininity," "feminist literary theory and criticism," "feminist movement," and "feminist writers."

- **Boolean searches.** The electronic *MLA International Bibliography* also permits searching according to Boolean logic—named after the nineteenth-century British mathematician and logician George Boole. In this kind of searching, you customize your search request with the operators *and*, *or*, and *not* (see fig. 1, on the next page). For example, you can use the Boolean operator *or* to expand your search. The following search expression will furnish

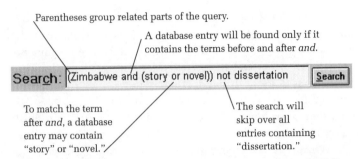

Parentheses group related parts of the query.

A database entry will be found only if it contains the terms before and after *and*.

Search: (Zimbabwe and (story or novel)) not dissertation   [Search]

To match the term after *and*, a database entry may contain "story" or "novel."

The search will skip over all entries containing "dissertation."

Fig. 1. Boolean searching. When using the *MLA International Bibliography* through the *WinSPIRS* software, you can enter this search phrase to find scholarship about short stories or novels relating to Zimbabwe. The search will exclude PhD dissertations.

---

more titles than either "Arthur Conan Doyle" or "Sherlock Holmes" by itself would:

Arthur Conan Doyle or Sherlock Holmes

If you want to perform narrower searches, the Boolean operators *not* and *and* can limit the field of titles accessed. If you are interested in finding studies on, say, versions of the story of Othello other than Shakespeare's, enter the following:

Othello not Shakespeare

Or if you would like to identify studies that compare Shakespeare's play with *Otello*, Verdi's operatic adaptation of it, keying the following rather than just "Othello" will result in a shorter, more focused list of sources:

Othello and Otello

• **Other advanced searches.** The *MLA International Bibliography* in its electronic versions offers other ways to restrict your search. It allows you to retrieve titles from a single publication source—for instance, articles on *Othello* that have appeared in *Shakespeare Quarterly* over the last several decades. The database also allows you to limit your search according to language of publication (e.g., Japanese, Spanish), publication type (e.g., book, journal article), and publication year. You can obtain a list, for example, of books on Goethe's *Faust* that were written in German and published in 2000 or later.

BIBLIOGRAPHIC INFORMATION PROVIDED

The database allows you to print out and download bibliographic information. It also gives you a choice of how to view, print, or download data. The display style varies among the interfaces through which the *MLA International Bibliography* is offered. Figures 2 and 3 present two ways in which the bibliographic information may appear. The complete record (fig. 2) includes title, author, source, international standard serial number (ISSN), language of publication, publication type, publication year, subject descriptors, sequence number, update code, and accession number. The shortened citation (fig. 3) usually gives only title, author, and source.

TITLE: Gender in Research on Language: Researching Gender-Related Patterns in Classroom Discourse

AUTHOR(S): Tannen,-Deborah

SOURCE: TESOL-Quarterly (TESOLQ) Alexandria, VA. 1996 Summer; 30(2): 341-44.

INTERNATIONAL STANDARD SERIAL NUMBER: 0039-8322

LANGUAGE: English

PUBLICATION TYPE: journal-article

PUBLICATION YEAR: 1996

DESCRIPTORS: language-; sociolinguistics-; social-dialects; role of gender-; in classroom-discourse

SEQUENCE NUMBER: 1996-3-2795

UPDATE CODE: 199601

ACCESSION NUMBER: 1996090615

Fig. 2. A complete citation from a bibliographic database.

TI: Gender in Research on Language: Researching Gender-Related Patterns in Classroom Discourse

AU: Tannen,-Deborah

SO: TESOL-Quarterly (TESOLQ) Alexandria, VA. 1996 Summer; 30(2): 341-44.

Fig. 3. A shortened citation from a bibliographic database.

The advantage of the short form is that it saves time and space while providing the information necessary for locating the material and for creating a preliminary entry for your works-cited list. You can easily convert the bibliographic data in figure 3 to MLA documentation style (see ch. 5):

Tannen, Deborah. "Gender in Research on Language: Researching Gender-
Related Patterns in Classroom Discourse." TESOL Quarterly 30 (1996):
341-44.

1.4.5. The Online Catalog of Library Holdings

An important part of a library's central information system is the online catalog of holdings (e.g., books, journals, electronic publications, audiovisual materials). There is no standard system for online catalogs. Systems differ, for example, in how users access information and in what appears on the screen. All systems, however, permit searching.

a. Searching an Online Catalog

When using an online catalog, you can locate a work in a number of ways. The most common are by author, by title, and by subject.

- **Author searches.** If you enter the author's full name—whether a personal name (e.g., Maxine Hong Kingston) or a corporate name (e.g., United States Central Intelligence Agency)—the screen displays a list of all the works the library has by that author. If you know only an author's last name (e.g., Kingston), you can obtain a list of all authors with that last name.
- **Title searches.** Entering the title produces a list of all works the library has with that title. The online catalog contains not only book titles but also titles of other works in the system, including journals (e.g., *Psychology and Marketing*), databases (e.g., *Sociofile*), and book series. If you enter the name of a book series, such as "Approaches to Teaching World Literature" or "Loeb Classical Library," you will receive a list of all book titles in the series. If you know only the beginning of a title—for example, only *Advertising, Competition*, instead of *Advertising, Competition, and Public Policy: A Simulation Study*—you can enter what you know, and the screen will display all titles that begin with those words.

- **Subject heading searches.** If you have no author or title in mind, you can enter a subject heading to produce a list of works about the subject. Most academic libraries exclusively use the subject headings that appear in the *Library of Congress Subject Headings*. Many headings have more specific subheadings. For example, you can enter "Mass media and the environment" and receive a list of all works assigned that general subject heading, or you can obtain a more specialized list by entering one of the following:

  Mass media and the environment—Great Britain
  Mass media and the environment—India
  Mass media and the environment—Latin America
  Mass media and the environment—United States

- **Call number searches.** If you know a work's call number, the designation by which the work is shelved in the library, you can enter it and receive bibliographic information about the work. For example, if you enter "PA817.B43 1992," you will learn that it applies to the book *An Introduction to New Testament Greek*, written by Frank Beetham and published in London by Bristol Classical Press in 1992.

- **Keyword searches.** An online catalog also helps you to initiate more sophisticated searches. A keyword search looks for individual words regardless of their location in a name, title, or subject heading. You can, for example, call up a list of all works that contain "competition" anywhere in their titles, such as

  Information Agreements, Competition, and Efficiency
  Conglomerate Mergers and Market Competition
  Competition and Human Behavior

  A subject heading search using the keyword "competition" will produce the titles of all works whose subject descriptions include the word, such as *Europe versus America? Contradictions of Imperialism*, one of whose subject headings is "Competition, International," or *Unequal Freedoms: The Global Market as an Ethical System*, one of whose subject headings is "Competition—Moral and ethical aspects."

- **Boolean searches.** Online catalogs also typically permit searching according to Boolean logic—that is, using the operators *and, or,* and *not*. For instance, suppose you are interested in studies on the relation between nutrition and cancer. A search using "nutrition" alone or "cancer" alone would yield a list of all works having anything to do with the subject of each search, and you would have to pick out the items dealing with the two subjects together. In contrast, a Boolean search using "nutrition *and* cancer" excludes all works not about both subjects. Likewise, if you want to see which authors besides Goethe wrote about the Faust theme, you can enter "Faust *not* Goethe." In addition to narrowing lists of titles, Boolean searching is useful for expanding them. For example, if you wish to research solar heating, you might enter "solar *or* sun *and* heating," which will produce more titles than would just "solar *and* heating." (On using Boolean logic in searching a reference database, see 1.4.4d.)

- **Other advanced searches.** Online catalogs allow you to limit your search in various ways. You may ask for titles published during a certain range of years (e.g., 2000 to the present) or titles located only in one specific part of your library (e.g., the main collection). You may be able, too, to limit your search to specific media (e.g., books, serials, electronic publications, archives, manuscripts, musical scores, films, video or sound recordings). This feature will permit you, say, to request a list of books that were published in Spanish between 1990 and 2000 about cave paintings in Spain, or it will let you find out if your library has any video recordings about mythology or the Civil War.

b. Bibliographic Information Provided

When you access a title, the screen shows something like the example in figure 4. The top lines of the screen image contain the author's name (McCann, Sean), the full title of the book (*Gumshoe America: Hard-Boiled Crime Fiction and the Rise and Fall of New Deal Liberalism*), and complete publication information (the book was published by Duke University Press in Durham, North Carolina, in 2000). Then follows the call number. The next section tells you that the library possesses one copy of the work, which is located on an open shelf (the "stack"), and that the copy is in the library and not on loan to anyone. The following lines describe the physical characteristics of the book (it has 8 pages of front matter—material before the main text—and 370 pages of text and measures 23 centimeters in height); indicate that it contains a bibliography and an index; show the subject headings under which the book is cataloged; and give the international standard book numbers (ISBNs) for the cloth and paperback versions of the book.

c. Information Needed for Research and Writing

For the purposes of researching and writing your paper, you normally will not use most of the information that appears in the catalog entry. You need to know the call number, of course, to locate the work in the library (see 1.4.5d); and, for your paper's works-cited list, you also need to know the author, title, and full publication information (see ch. 5 on information needed for compiling the list of works cited). Following is the entry in the works-cited list for the title given above:

> McCann, Sean. Gumshoe America: Hard-Boiled Crime Fiction and the Rise and Fall of New Deal Liberalism. Durham: Duke UP, 2000.

Transcribe this information carefully. Online catalog systems typically give the option of printing out or downloading the bibliographic data displayed on the screen. This feature saves you the effort of copying the information and eliminates the possibility of

---

AUTHOR: McCann, Sean
TITLE: Gumshoe America: Hard-Boiled Crime Fiction and the Rise and Fall of New Deal Liberalism
IMPRINT: Durham [N.C.]: Duke University Press, 2000
CALL NUMBER: PS374.D4 M38 2000

LOCATION	COPY	STATUS
Stack	#1	In Library

PHYSICAL FEATURES: viii, 370 p.: 23cm.
NOTES: Includes bibliographical references (p. 349-64) + index
SUBJECTS:
      Detective and mystery stories, American--History and criticism
      Politics and literature--United States--History--20th century
      American fiction--20th century--History and criticism
      Liberalism--United States--History--20th century
      Political fiction, American--History and criticism
      New Deal, 1933-39
      Crime in literature
ISBN: 0822325802 (cloth) * 0822325942 (pbk.)

Fig. 4. An entry from an online catalog.

transcription errors. You should, of course, verify the information you derive from the catalog against the source itself; errors sometimes occur during cataloging.

d. Call Numbers

The call numbers in your library probably follow one of two systems of classification: the Library of Congress system or the Dewey decimal system. Learning your library's system will not only help you to find works and know their contents from their call numbers but also guide you to sections of the library in which to browse.

The Library of Congress system divides books into twenty major groups:

A   General works
B   Philosophy, psychology, and religion
C   General history
D   World history
E–F   American history
G   Geography and anthropology
H   Social sciences
J   Political science
K   Law
L   Education
M   Music
N   Fine arts
P   Language and literature
Q   Science
R   Medicine
S   Agriculture
T   Technology
U   Military science
V   Naval science
Z   Bibliography and library science

The Dewey decimal system classifies books under ten major headings:

000   General works
100   Philosophy and psychology
200   Religion
300   Social sciences
400   Language
500   Natural sciences and mathematics

600   Technology and applied sciences
700   Fine arts
800   Literature
900   Geography and history

e. Location of Library Materials

The library catalog normally indicates not only the call number for a title but also the section in which to find the work, whether in the main collection or in a different location. It may also indicate if a title is checked out, missing, at the bindery, or on order. Check with the circulation desk to see if it is possible to recall or search for a missing book.

- **Open shelves and closed stacks.** Most library holdings are kept on open shelves, to which the public has direct access. To obtain a work in closed stacks, you usually have to present a call slip to a library staff member, who will locate the work for you.
- **Sections for reserved works and reference works.** If the word *Reserved* appears in a catalog entry, it indicates that the work is required in a course and stored in a special section, at the instructor's request, so that the work may not be borrowed but stays available for students in the course. A work shelved in the reference section, designated in the catalog entry by *R* or *Ref*, is too widely used to be borrowed and thus must also remain in the library.
- **Other sections.** Libraries also commonly set aside areas for other types of materials—current periodicals, pamphlets, and nonprint materials, like CD-ROMs, films, and audio and video recordings. Some libraries have additional special collections, such as rare books or government documents, that are similarly kept separate from the main collection. Consult the library directory or a librarian for locations.

1.4.6. Full-Text Databases

Modern academic libraries subscribe to and make generally available a wide variety of databases: not only those containing bibliographic citations and abstracts (see 1.4.4a), which guide researchers to relevant sources, but also full-text databases, which offer complete texts of many sources. Your library likely subscribes to full-text databases of reference works and other book-length texts as well as of articles from periodicals (newspapers, magazines, scholarly journals). Some of these databases may be limited to use in the library, but many probably can also be accessed from outside, through the library's Web site. Virtually all full-text databases are searchable by author, title, and subject and through more sophisticated strategies (e.g., keyword searching, Boolean searching), as discussed in 1.4.4d and 1.4.5a.

a. Reference Works and Other Book-Length Texts

- **Online reference works** to which libraries typically subscribe include *The Oxford English Dictionary*, *The New Encyclopaedia Britannica*, *American National Biography*, *The Grove Dictionary of Art Online*, and *Routledge Encyclopedia of Philosophy*.
- **Other book-length texts** may also be available to you through library subscriptions. One ambitious project is the University of Chicago's Project for American and French Research on the Treasury of the French Language (or the ARTFL Project), which is a collection of nearly two thousand French texts from the seventeenth to the twentieth century, ranging from classic works of French literature to nonfiction prose and technical writing. Similarly, the Digital History Books Project, a collaboration among the University of Pennsylvania Library, Oxford University Press, and Cambridge University Press, includes over four hundred books in its database.

b. Articles in Periodicals

Many full-text databases to which academic libraries subscribe comprise articles from periodicals—newspapers, magazines, and especially scholarly journals.

- **Major newspapers**, like the *New York Times* and *Wall Street Journal*, are available individually through library subscription.
- **Major scholarly journal publishers**—those that issue numerous journals, often in different fields—permit libraries to subscribe to databases containing all journals that each press publishes. Such publishers include Academic Press, American Chemical Society, American Mathematical Society, Cambridge University Press, Elsevier, Oxford University Press, University of Chicago Press, and Wiley. Thus, a subscription to, for example, American Mathe-

matical Society Journals gives access to all journals published by that society.

- **A scholarly journal archive** collects articles from journals published by different presses. *JSTOR*, for instance, is a collection of articles from over one hundred scholarly journals in such fields as the humanities, the social sciences, the natural sciences, and business.

c. Database Subscription Services

Information service companies, such as EBSCO, Gale, and Lexis-Nexis, amass huge numbers of bibliographic and full-text materials, organize these materials into different kinds of databases, and offer these databases, often in different combinations, by subscription to academic libraries. Some typical packages of databases follow:

- **EBSCO.** Your library may subscribe to a number of EBSCO's bibliographic databases as well as to its full-text databases, such as *Academic Search Premier* (articles from over three thousand scholarly publications in all major disciplines), *Business Source Premier* (articles from over two thousand scholarly business journals), *Health Source* (articles from over five hundred scholarly medical journals), *Newspaper Source* (articles from some two hundred United States and international newspapers), and *Masterfile Premier* (articles from nearly two thousand periodicals on a variety of subjects, including general reference, business, and health).
- **Gale.** The following is a typical package of Gale databases to which a library might subscribe: *Custom Newspapers* (articles from, e.g., the *New York Times*, the *Wall Street Journal*, and local newspapers selected by the library), *General Reference Center* (articles from reference books, magazines, and newspapers on topics of general interest—e.g., current events, popular culture, arts, sciences), *Health Reference Center* (articles on topics related to health—e.g., medicine, nutrition, diseases, public health, occupational health and safety), *Business and Company Resource Center* (company profiles, brand information, investment reports, etc.), *Contemporary Authors* (biographical and bibliographic information on thousands of authors), and *Contemporary Literary Criticism* (critical introductions to modern authors).
- **Lexis-Nexis.** *Lexis-Nexis Academic Universe*, one of many products and services provided by this company, collects material from over five thousand publications and organizes information

under the following topics: news, business, legal research, medicine, and general reference.

d. Information Needed for List of Works Cited

Most documents in databases were previously or simultaneously published in print form. Therefore, most bibliographic citations of database sources begin with the publication information the database supplies for the print version of the source (see 5.9.1). The citation then continues with facts about the electronic publication. Subscription databases vary considerably in the amount and kind of electronic publication information they furnish, and bibliographic citations of these sources vary accordingly. For some sources, a URL (uniform resource locator, or network address) of the specific document is available; for others, a URL of only a search page must be given; and for still others, no URL can be cited.

- **URL of specific document.** Some databases connect you to an Internet site, give relatively short and logical URLs for each document, and even provide full documentation information for each document. For example, the information in figure 5 appears at the end of an entry in the electronic database for *American National Biography.* Such information makes it easy to create a bibliographic entry for the source using MLA style (see 5.9.1):

Malleck, Daniel J. "Leavitt, Mary Greenleaf Clement." American National
   Biography Online. Oxford UP, 2000. Amer. Council of Learned Socs. 14
   Jan. 2002 <http://www.anb.org/articles/15-00398.html>.

- **URL of search page.** Sometimes the URL of a document is so long and complicated that reproducing it would invite transcription

---

Citation:
Daniel J. Malleck. "Leavitt, Mary Greenleaf Clement."
http://www.anb.org/articles/15-00398.html
American National Biography Online February 2000
Access date: Monday, January 14, 2002
Copyright © 2000 American Council of Learned Societies.
Published by Oxford University Press. All rights reserved.

Fig. 5. Bibliographic information provided by a database publisher.

errors or would at least cause inconvenience. In such instances, it is preferable to give instead the URL of the site's search page, if such a page exists. Once there, the reader can readily access the document by keying in other publication facts recorded in the citation (e.g., author's name, title). For example, *JSTOR* assigns the following URL to a 1998 article by Nancy Tolson in *African American Review*:

http://links.jstor.org/sici?sici=1062-4783%28199821%2932%3A1%3C9%3AM
BATRO%3E2.0.CO%3B2-2

Rather than try to reproduce such a URL, simply give the URL of the database's search page.

Tolson, Nancy. "Making Books Available: The Role of Early Libraries,

Librarians, and Booksellers in the Promotion of African American

Children's Literature." African American Review 32 (1998): 9-16. JSTOR.

1 Oct. 2002 <http://www.jstor.org/search>.

- **No URL.** Some database subscription services assign no apparent URLs to documents or assign URLs that are unique to the subscribing institution or to the current research session. Such URLs are useless to the general reader. For example, an article that Sami Youakim published in 2001 in *American Family Physician* is included in Gale's database *Health Reference Center*. When you access this article from the Bergen County Cooperative Library System in New Jersey, you find that its URL contains over 130 characters and concludes with the suffix "sw_aep=bergen_main," which is unique to this library system. Consequently, the URL of the article has no value for anyone without access to the system and has virtually no value for anyone who does, for you can locate the article much more easily by using the search page of the database than by typing in the URL. When writing the bibliographic citation for this source, then, you may conclude not with the URL of the document but rather with the URL of the home page of the service, if you know it, or you may simply end with the date of access (see 5.9.7):

Youakim, Sami. "Work-Related Asthma." American Family Physician 64

(2001): 1839-52. Health Reference Center. Gale. Bergen County

Cooperative Lib. System, NJ. 12 Jan. 2002 <http://

www.galegroup.com/>.

1.4.7. Other Library Resources and Services

Besides knowing about the print and nonprint materials discussed above, you should become familiar with the library's other resources and services.

a. Microforms

Microform designates printed matter greatly reduced in size by microphotography; common types are microfilm, microfiche, and microcard. Libraries use microforms to store such materials as back copies of periodicals (newspapers, magazines, scholarly journals) and rare books (see fig. 6). Microforms are usually kept in a special section of the library. To use them, you need a reader that magnifies them; a special photocopier can reproduce microform pages. Library staff members are usually on hand to assist researchers in locating microform materials and operating the readers and photocopiers.

Fig. 6. An enlargement of part of a microfiche containing pages from the journal *PMLA*.

b. Media Center

Many libraries have a special section devoted to audio recordings (e.g., compact discs, audiotapes, long-playing records), video recordings (e.g., on VHS or DVD), and multimedia materials. These resources are generally kept in closed stacks and used only in the library, although there may be exceptions, such as for use in the classroom.

c. Electronic and Other Resources

Photocopying machines are typically located at various sites in the library, as are computer terminals that give access to the central catalog and other databases and to the Internet. Your school may also permit students to borrow laptop computers, with Internet connections, for use in the library. Some schools have electronic-resource centers in the library as well. Such centers provide, for student use, a variety of software applications for tasks such as word processing, spreadsheet analysis, database management, desktop publishing, drawing, image processing, and drafting. Output services might include high-quality printing, CD mastering, and image and text scanning. Some schools have facilities for photographic, audio, and video production.

d. Interlibrary Loans

Most libraries have agreements for the exchange of research materials on a regional, statewide, national, or even international basis. If your library does not have the materials you need, ask whether it can borrow them from another library. If it can, ask your librarian for help in initiating an interlibrary loan. Finding the source in a nearby library rather than a faraway one will save considerable time. To discover which libraries own your title, you may search other library catalogs included in your library's central information system or consult such databases as the Online Computer Library Center (OCLC) or the Research Libraries Information Network (RLIN), if they are available to you. Or you can consult such print sources as *National Union Catalog*, for book holdings at other libraries, or *Union List of Serials* and *New Serial Titles*, for periodicals.

1.4.8. Internet Sources

a. Range of Sources

Researchers regularly use facts and ideas from Internet sources to complement those derived from traditional print sources. Through the World Wide Web, a researcher can read and transfer material from library catalogs and millions of other useful sites, created by professional organizations (e.g., American Chemical Society, American Philosophical Association), government agencies (e.g., Library of Congress, Bureau of the Census), commercial enterprises (e.g.,

publishers of encyclopedias, news organizations), educational enti-
ties (e.g., universities, libraries, academic departments, research centers, scholarly projects), and individual scholars. These sites provide
not only information sources but also the full texts of documents—
such as historical papers, literary and religious works, and articles in
periodicals (e.g., journals, magazines, newspapers)—and audiovisual
materials (e.g., photographs, paintings, sound and video recordings).

b. Using Recommended Sites

Even those who are familiar with the World Wide Web find that
using it to do research requires practice and training just as using a
library does. Therefore, whenever possible, follow the guidance of
an instructor, an academic department, or a librarian in selecting
Internet sites for research. In addition to online databases available
through subscription (see 1.4.6), your library may recommend
important Internet sources that were likely selected after careful
evaluation and consultation. Check the library's Web site for links to
such resources. A librarian might also be able to advise you about
sites relevant to your research. Similarly, you may find sites recommended by academic departments and individual instructors on
Web pages for the department, the instructor, or the course.

c. Gateway Sites

Your librarian or instructor might direct you to a "metapage" or
"gateway" that provides links to other sites. Examples of gateway
sites follow (the URLs shown may change):

- *Voice of the Shuttle* (Univ. of California, Santa Barbara; http://
  vos.ucsb.edu/) offers on its home page a menu of subjects in the
  humanities—anthropology, archaeology, architecture, history, literature, philosophy, and so forth. Selecting "media studies," for
  example, gives you a list of specific fields (e.g., journalism, television, film and video, popular music, comics, cyberculture). The
  choice of "media history and theory" presents links to numerous
  resources in this area: professional organizations, bibliographies,
  chronologies, journals, articles and papers, course descriptions,
  and other related sites, including some created and maintained by
  scholars in media studies. The home page also provides general
  links to libraries and museums, reference works, journals, publishers and booksellers, e-mail discussions and news groups, conferences, and travel resources.

• *Social Science Information Gateway* (Univ. of Bristol; http://
sosig.esrc.bris.ac.uk/) likewise presents a menu of subjects—business, economics, education, psychology, sociology, and so forth. If
you click on "sociology," you receive a list of specific subject
areas (the sociology of, e.g., adolescence, children, gender, law
and crime, medicine, race and ethnicity, religion, sport, work).
Selecting one of these areas yields links to relevant articles,
papers, reports, bibliographies, data, educational materials, government publications, journals, discussion groups, professional
organizations, research projects, and resource guides.
• *Women's Studies Database* (Univ. of Maryland; http://www.mith2
.umd.edu/WomensStudies/) allows the researcher to choose from
such categories as the following: conferences, announcements,
bibliographies, syllabi, film reviews, gender issues, other Web
sites, and reference room. If you choose the last of these, you
receive links to academic papers, book reviews, fiction, history,
nonfiction, and poetry.

d. Peer-Reviewed Sites

Some gateway sites are refereed (see 1.6.1 on refereed publications).
Argos (Univ. of Evansville; http://argos.evansville.edu/), for example, is a "peer-reviewed, limited-area search engine" designed for
students, teachers, and scholars of the "ancient and medieval
worlds." An editorial board of specialists reviews and approves each
site before it is included in this search engine. The home page of
Argos contains a list of these "associate sites," such as the following:

• *Abzu: Guide to Resources for the Study of the Ancient Near East
Available on the Internet* (Univ. of Chicago)
• *Byzantium: Byzantine Studies on the Internet* (Fordham Univ.)
• *Diotima: Materials for the Study of Women and Gender in the
Ancient World* (Univ. of Kentucky)
• *The Labyrinth: Resources for Medieval Studies* (Georgetown Univ.)
• *The Perseus Digital Library* (Tufts Univ.)

e. Searching the Internet

Search tools. If you are working without professional guidance,
whether developing a research topic or looking for research sources,
use the search tools created to help locate Internet materials.
Common ways to conduct searches with these tools are by subject
and by keyword. Some search tools, such as *Google* and *Yahoo!*,

offer hierarchically arranged subject directories through which you can navigate until you find specific topics you wish to explore.

- **Google.** If you click on the subject "arts" on the directory page for *Google*, you might receive a list of categories like architecture, art history, classical studies, humanities, and literature. Choosing "humanities" would lead you to a list containing anthropology, history, languages, philosophy, and so on. The subject "history" might offer such selections as "by region," "by time period," and "by topic." If you choose "sixteenth century" from the list of periods, you could receive a choice of two topics: "Reformation" and "Renaissance." Selecting the latter would result in a list of relevant Web sites, including *Plague and Public Health in Renaissance Europe* (Univ. of Virginia). If you click on the prompt "Similar pages" next to this link, you are directed to other relevant sites, such as *The Black Death: Bubonic Plague* (Brigham Young Univ.) and *Plague* (Virginia Polytechnic Inst. and State Univ.). In ranking a Web site, *Google* takes into account the number of links there are to the site as well as the importance and quality of the linking sites.
- **Yahoo!** Similarly, if you select "humanities" among the categories listed in the *Yahoo!* directory, you might receive a list of such categories as classics, critical theory, cultural studies, history, literature, medical humanities, philosophy, and theology. The selection "medical humanities" would lead you to "biomedical ethics," which would prompt another set of subtopics (abortion issues, animal experimentation, cloning, euthanasia, genetic engineering). Your eventual choice of a specific subject (e.g., human cloning) will yield a listing of documents and files devoted to the subject.

Specific searches. If you know at the outset the exact topic you wish to research, you can perform a keyword search, which produces a listing of files containing the word or words you specify. To avoid long lists containing many irrelevant sites, be as specific as possible in your commands—thus, "human cloning" will yield a shorter, more unified list than "cloning" alone would (see fig. 7). Most search tools offer instructions on how to phrase search requests for the best results. You can often use Boolean and other operators to make searches precise (see 1.4.4d and 1.4.5a).

Current issues and current events. The Internet is particularly helpful when you want to find materials related to current issues

and current events. The Web site *NewsDirectory.com* (http://www
.newsdirectory.com/) provides thousands of links to online newspapers, magazines, television stations, and other media. Examples
follow (the URLs shown may change):

- **Newspapers**
  New York Times (http://www.nytimes.com/)
  Wall Street Journal (http://www.wsj.com/)
  Washington Post (http://www.washingtonpost.com/)
- **Magazines**
  Atlantic Monthly (http://www.theatlantic.com/)
  Harper's (http://www.harpers.org/)
  Newsweek (http://www.newsweek.com/)
  Time (http://www.time.com/)
  U.S. News and World Report (http://www.usnews.com/)
- **Television and radio news and information organizations**
  CNN (http://www.cnn.com/)
  C-Span (http://www.c-span.org/)
  Discovery (http://www.discovery.com/)
  The History Channel (http://www.historychannel.com/)
  National Public Radio (http://www.npr.org/)
  Public Broadcasting System (http://www.pbs.org/)

Bookmarking and recording the URL. Whenever you discover what
seems a useful document or site, be sure to add it to your bookmark
or favorites list. In so doing, you can easily return to the source for
further information or clarification. If you cannot use a bookmark—

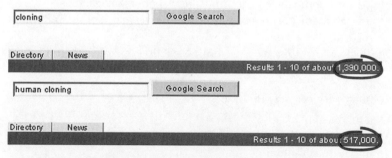

Fig. 7. Narrowing an Internet search. Changing the searching term from
"cloning" to "human cloning" reduced the results by more than half at
Google.

perhaps because you share a computer—keep a precise record of the URL. In any event, you may want to keep a log of all sites you visit, whether or not you initially bookmark them, since a site you originally passed over may seem more useful later.

Recording the date of access. Always make note of the date or dates on which you consult a source. The date of access is important because the material could be revised after you visit the site. The URL and the date of access are items of information you will need for your working bibliography and your list of works cited.

Internet sources among other sources. Whereas many instructors encourage using Internet sources, few consider a search of the World Wide Web alone adequate research for most research papers. Instructors generally require that other materials, including print publications, be sought. Similarly, e-mail discussion lists and online "chat rooms" are helpful for sharing ideas but are rarely deemed acceptable resources for research papers. (See 1.6 on evaluating source materials.)

1.4.9. SUMMING UP

Your school library is likely to be your most reliable guide when you conduct research. You should therefore become as familiar as possible with the library's print and electronic resources and its various services. Library resources include

- books and similar publications (e.g., pamphlets)
- print periodicals (e.g., journals, newspapers, magazines)
- miscellaneous print and nonprint sources (e.g., sound and video recordings)
- electronic resources (e.g., online catalog of holdings, reference works, bibliographic and full-text databases)

Library services may include

- a media center
- photocopying machines
- access to computers
- use of software applications, printers, scanning devices, and other hardware
- interlibrary loans

Useful Internet sources are

* sites recommended by instructors and librarians
* gateway sites
* peer-reviewed sites

1.5. COMPILING A WORKING BIBLIOGRAPHY

1.5.1. Keeping Track of Sources

As you discover information and opinions on your topic, you should keep track of sources that you may use for your paper. A record of such sources is called a *working bibliography*. Your preliminary reading will probably provide the first titles for this list. Other titles will emerge when you consult reference works and the library's central catalog and when you explore the Internet. If you read carefully through the bibliography and notes of each work you consult, more often than not you will discover additional important sources. Your working bibliography will frequently change during your research as you add titles and eliminate those that do not prove useful and as you probe and emphasize some aspects of your subject in preference to others. The working bibliography will eventually evolve into the list of works cited that appears at the end of the research paper.

1.5.2. Creating a Computer File for the Working Bibliography

A computer is particularly useful for compiling the working bibliography. Create a computer file for this purpose, and enter full information about sources into the file as you proceed with your research. Whenever you wish to add new works to the list, to remove works you no longer think helpful, or to correct entries already stored, you retrieve the file, make the changes, and save the revised file for future use. As you research, you can arrange and rearrange your sources however you wish (e.g., in alphabetical order, in chronological order by date of publication, in order of relevance to your topic); you can also divide sources into groups (e.g., those already consulted and those not yet consulted, those most useful and those less so). At any point, you can print the file to review it or to use it for research. Since bibliography files are essential to researching and writing the paper, be certain to save these files and to keep copies of them on paper and on a backup disk.

1.5.3. Recording Essential Publication Information

When you add sources to your working bibliography, be sure you enter all the publication information needed for the works-cited list. The information to be recorded depends on the kind of source used. Following are typical examples of citations for a book, an article in a scholarly journal, a newspaper or magazine article, and an Internet source. The sources you encounter might require more information. See chapter 5 for complete guidelines on compiling the works-cited list of the research paper.

BOOK (see 5.6)

1. Author's full name (last name first)
2. Full title (including any subtitle)
3. Edition (if the book is a second or later numbered edition or a revised edition)
4. Number of the volume and the total number of volumes (if the book is a multivolume work)
5. City of publication
6. Shortened form of the publisher's name (see 7.5)
7. Year of publication

Budden, Julian. The Operas of Verdi. Rev. ed. 3 vols. Oxford: Clarendon, 1992.

ARTICLE IN A SCHOLARLY JOURNAL (see 5.7.1–4)

1. Author's name
2. Title of the article
3. Title of the journal
4. Volume number
5. Year of publication
6. Inclusive page numbers of the article (i.e., the number of the page on which the article begins, a hyphen, and the number of the page on which the article ends)

Frith, Simon. "The Black Box: The Value of Television and the Future of Television Research." Screen 41 (2000): 33-50.

NEWSPAPER OR MAGAZINE ARTICLE (see 5.7.5–6)

1. Author's name
2. Title of the article
3. Title of the periodical
4. Date of publication
5. Inclusive page numbers of the article

Hoover, Eric. "New Attacks on Early Decision." Chronicle of Higher
    Education 11 Jan. 2002: A45-46.

INTERNET SOURCE (see 5.9.1–4)

1. Author's name
2. Title of the document
3. Full information about any previous or simultaneous publication
   in print form
4. Title of the scholarly project, database, periodical, or professional
   or personal site
5. Name of the editor of the scholarly project or database
6. Date of electronic publication or last update
7. Name of the institution or organization sponsoring or associated
   with the site
8. Date when you accessed the source
9. Network address, or URL

**A document previously or simultaneously published
in print form**

Mistral, Gabriela. "Silueta de Sor Juana Inés." Abside 15 (1951) : 501-06.
    The Sor Juana Inés de la Cruz Project. Ed. Luis M. Villar. Feb. 1998.
    Dartmouth Coll. 23 Jan. 2002 <http://www.dartmouth.edu/~sorjuana/
    Commentaries/Mistral/Mistral.html>.

A document published only in electronic form

Bitel, Lisa M. "St. Brigit of Ireland: From Virgin Saint to Fertility Goddess."
    Matrix. Ed. Katherine Gill and Bitel. Feb. 2001. Boston Coll. 23 Jan.
    2002 <http://matrix.bc.edu/commentaria/bitel01.html>.

1.5.4. Noting Other Useful Information

Besides the data needed for the works-cited list, it is useful to add other information to items in the working bibliography. For example, if you derive a source from a bibliographic work, record where you found the reference, in case you need to recheck it. Always also note the library call number, the network address (URL), or other identifying information required to locate each work.

The following entry in a working bibliography contains not only all the facts needed for the final bibliography (author's name, full title, and relevant publication information) but also information useful for research: the origin of the reference (the electronic database of the *MLA International Bibliography*) and the call number (PS374.D4 M38 2000). You will delete reference origins and call numbers when you convert your working bibliography into the list of works cited.

> McCann, Sean. Gumshoe America: Hard-Boiled Crime Fiction and the Rise and Fall of New Deal Liberalism. Durham: Duke UP, 2000. [MLA Bib.; PS374.D4 M38 2000]

1.5.5. Verifying Publication Information

Whenever you consult a source, carefully verify the publication facts against your records—even if you have printed out or downloaded the data. Add any missing information that you will need for the works-cited list, and correct any part of your records that does not match the data obtained from the work itself. Recording and verifying all the information about your sources when you first consult them will spare you many last-minute problems and frustrations.

1.5.6. Converting the Working Bibliography to the Works-Cited List

Eventually, you will transform your working bibliography into a works-cited list. If your working bibliography is in a computer file, edit the entries to remove unnecessary information (e.g., origin of reference, call number), arrange them alphabetically by author (see 5.5 on the arrangement of entries), and title the list "Works Cited" (see 5.3 on titles for other kinds of source lists). When you have finished the final draft of your paper, transfer the edited bibliography file to the end of the file containing the paper (see 5.4 on the format of the list).

1.5.7. SUMMING UP

If compiled with care and attention, the working bibliography will be invaluable to you throughout the preparation of your paper. It will, on the one hand, function as an efficient tool for finding and acquiring information and ideas and, on the other, provide all the data you will need for your list of works cited.

1.6. EVALUATING SOURCES

All researchers, students as well as professional scholars, need to assess the quality of any work scrupulously before using and citing it. Students writing their first research papers often find it difficult to evaluate sources. Not all sources are equally reliable or of equal quality. In reading and evaluating potential sources, you should not assume that something is truthful or trustworthy just because it appears in print or is on the Internet. Some material may be based on incorrect or outdated information or on poor logic, and the author's knowledge or view of the subject may be biased or too limited. Weigh what you read against your own knowledge and intelligence as well as against other treatments of the subject. Focus particularly on the *authority, accuracy,* and *currency* of the sources you use. Following are some criteria to keep in mind when you evaluate sources. If you have doubts about a source, your instructor or a librarian can probably help you.

1.6.1. Authority

Peer Review

Most scholarly journals and academic book publishers are committed to a policy of consultant review—commonly referred to by scholars as "peer review." In peer review, publishers seek the advice of expert readers, or referees, before considering a manuscript for publication. Each consultant reads the work and sends the publisher a report evaluating the manuscript and, in general, either recommending or not recommending it for publication. Readers comment on such matters as the importance of the subject, the originality and soundness of the argument, the accuracy of the facts, and the currency of the research. At most scholarly journals and presses, moreover, there is also an editorial board that similarly reviews the manuscript, along with the readers' reports, before deciding whether to publish the work. Thus, a manuscript submitted to a refereed publication must undergo rigorous scrutiny before it is published.

Internet Sources

Assessing Internet resources is a particular challenge. Whereas the print publications that researchers depend on are generally issued by reputable publishers, like university presses, that accept accountability for the quality and reliability of the works they distribute, relatively few electronic publications currently have comparable authority. Some Internet publications are peer-reviewed, but many are not. Online materials are often self-published, without any outside review.

What to Look For

In evaluating any source, print or electronic, look especially for information on the following aspects. Figure 8 shows how these considerations apply to a specific Web site.

- **Author.** When we consult a printed book or article, we expect to find prominently displayed the name of the author of the work. Whenever you consult a source, print or electronic, make sure that the author of the document or the person or group responsible for the publication or site is identified. Once you establish authorship, consider the authoritativeness of the work. Publications sometimes indicate an author's credentials in the field by including relevant biographical information (e.g., professional title or affiliation, list of publications or other accomplishments). On the Web, you may find the author's credentials by following a link to a home page or to a page (labeled, e.g., "About Us") that lists personnel responsible for the site. You can also search the Internet and other sources to find information about an author. For example, if you are evaluating a book, you might consult *Book Review*

Index and *Book Review Digest* to see how experts in the field of study received this book and any others by the author.

- **Text.** If you are working with historical documents or literary texts that exist in various versions, make certain you use reliable editions. For example, versions of Shakespeare's plays published during his lifetime and shortly after his death sometimes differ drastically. The task of a modern scholarly editor is to compare,

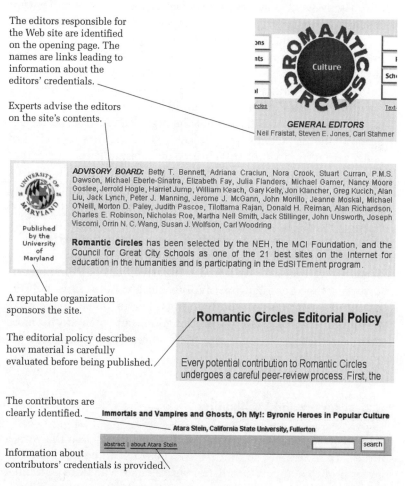

Fig. 8. Evaluating the authority of an Internet source. The Web site *Romantic Circles* (http://www.rc.umd.edu/) has the characteristics of an authoritative source suitable for scholarly research.

analyze, and evaluate these variations and produce an edition that is as historically authoritative as possible. Therefore, if you want to use, say, an electronic text of a Shakespeare play, look for one that, at a minimum, clearly states who the editor of the text is and when the electronic edition was published or identifies the printed source that was the basis for the electronic version.

- **Editorial policy.** Take note of the entire work or site you are using even if you are interested only in a particular document within it. In a journal or at a Web site, look for a statement of mission or purpose as well as for evidence that the document underwent consultant review (e.g., the listing of an editorial board, for a journal, or of a moderator, for a discussion group).

- **Publisher or sponsoring organization.** Like the name of the author, the name of the publisher is normally evident in print publications. Similarly, the name of the publisher or sponsoring organization of an Internet site should be clearly stated, preferably with access to information about the organization (e.g., through a prompt such as "About the Project"). To determine the kind of organization from which a Web site emanates, note the last part of the domain name (e.g., the *.org* in "www.npr.org"). This suffix identifies where the source originates from—for example, a commercial enterprise (*.com*), an educational institution (*.edu*), a government agency (*.gov*), or a not-for-profit organization (*.org*). There is no guarantee that material from, say, an *.edu* site is reliable; such a site probably includes students' unsupervised personal pages as well as peer-reviewed scholarly projects. Nonetheless, knowing the organization involved might help you evaluate potential usefulness or shortcomings. For instance, many sites ending in *.com* offer helpful information, but some are no more than advertisements, such as a book company's lavish praise for books that it publishes.

1.6.2. Accuracy and Verifiability

If you are evaluating scholarly material, check to see that the work's sources are indicated, so that its information can be verified. The sources probably appear in a list of works cited. The titles in the list might also tell you something about the breadth of the author's knowledge of the subject and about any possible bias. The author of a Web publication might supply hypertextual links to the sources.

Note, too, if the document or site gives an e-mail address or otherwise tells how you can ask the author or sponsoring organization for further information or clarification.

1.6.3. Currency

The publication date of a print source suggests how current the author's scholarship is. Although online documents and sites have the potential for continual updating, many remain in their original states and, depending on the subject, may be out-of-date. When considering any resource, be sure at least one date is assigned to it. Several dates are sometimes listed for an electronic publication. For example, if a document on the Internet had a previous print existence, there could be the date of print publication as well as the date of electronic publication. In addition, there might be the date when the material was last revised or updated. Ideally, a document should record all dates of publication and revision (see 5.9.1 on including all relevant dates in works-cited-list entries). Finally, scrutinizing the publication dates of works cited in the text also reveals the currency of its scholarship.

1.6.4. SUMMING UP

Evaluate all sources you use for your research. Focus on the authority, accuracy, and currency of the sources. Consider such questions as the following:

- Who is the author of the work, and what are the author's credentials for writing and publishing this work?
- When judged against your previous reading and your understanding of the subject, is the information furnished by the author correct? Is the argument presented with logic and without bias?
- Are the author's sources clearly and adequately indicated, so that they can be verified?
- Are the author's sources current, or are they outdated?
- Who is the publisher, or what is the sponsoring organization, of the work?
- Is the work peer-reviewed—that is, has it been read and recommended for publication by experts?

1.7. TAKING NOTES

When you determine that material is reliable and useful, you will want to take notes on it.

1.7.1. Methods of Note-Taking

Although everyone agrees that note-taking is essential to research, probably no two researchers use exactly the same methods. Some prefer to take notes by hand on index cards or sheets of paper. Using a computer might save you time and should improve the accuracy with which you transcribe material, including quotations, from your sources into the text of your paper. However you take notes, set down first the author's full name and the complete title of the source—enough information to enable you to locate the source easily in your working bibliography. If the source is not yet in the working bibliography, record all the publication information you will need for research and for your works-cited list (see 1.5.3–4), and add the source to the working bibliography.

1.7.2. Types of Note-Taking

There are, generally speaking, three types of note-taking:

- **Summary.** Summarize if you want to record only the general idea of large amounts of material.
- **Paraphrase.** If you require detailed notes on specific sentences and passages but do not need the exact wording, you may wish to paraphrase—that is, to restate the material in your own words.
- **Quotation.** When you believe that some sentence or passage in its original wording might make an effective addition to your paper, transcribe that material exactly as it appears, word for word, comma for comma. Whenever you quote verbatim from a work, be sure to use quotation marks scrupulously in your notes to distinguish the quotation from summary and paraphrase. Using electronic materials calls for special vigilance. If you download a text and integrate quotations from it into your paper, check to see that you have placed quotation marks around words taken from the source.

1.7.3. Recording Page Numbers

In summarizing, paraphrasing, or quoting, keep an accurate record of the pages or other numbered sections (e.g., numbered paragraphs in an electronic text) that you use. When a quotation continues to another page or section, carefully note where the page or section break occurs, since only a small portion of what you transcribe may ultimately find its way into your paper.

1.7.4. Using a Computer for Note-Taking

Using a word processor to store notes is handy, but while you are doing research, you may find yourself in a situation—for example, working in the library—where you do not have access to a computer. Then you will need to write your notes by hand and transfer them into a computer later. Strategies of storing and retrieving notes vary (see 1.9 for using note files during writing). A few common strategies follow:

- For a short paper for which you have taken few notes, you may place all notes in a single file and draw material from it whenever you want.
- For a longer paper that makes use of numerous sources, you may create a new file for each source.
- Another strategy is to write out summaries and paraphrases of the source by hand and to enter into computer files only quotations, which you can electronically copy into your text as you write. At the least, this strategy will eliminate the time and effort and, more important, the possibility of error involved in transcribing quoted words more than once.
- By downloading quotations from a database to your computer disk, you of course do not need to transcribe them at all.

When you use a computer for note-taking, be certain to save all note files on your working disk and to keep copies of them on paper and on a backup disk.

1.7.5. Amount and Accuracy of Note-Taking

In taking notes, seek to steer a middle course between recording too much and recording too little. In other words, try to be both thorough and concise. Above all, strive for accuracy, not only in copying words for direct quotation but also in summarizing and paraphrasing authors' ideas.

1.7.6. SUMMING UP

The three main types of note-taking are *summary*, *paraphrase*, and *quotation*. There are, however, varying methods and strategies for note-taking. You may take notes by hand or use a computer. If you are using a computer, you can type in or download material, you can create one file for all sources or separate files for different sources, and so forth. Whichever method or strategy you follow, be sure to save and back up all computer files, to set down or verify publication information you will need for research and writing, to keep a careful record of page numbers, and, most important of all, to take accurate notes. Precise note-taking will help you avoid the problem of plagiarism (see ch. 2).

1.8. OUTLINING

1.8.1. Working Outline

A Useful Intermediate Activity

Some writers like to work from an outline; others do not. For research papers, outlining can be a particularly useful intermediate activity between research and writing. In fact, some instructors require each student to hand in an outline with the final draft. Others require a draft outline earlier, asking the student to submit not only a topic for the paper but also a tentative list of subtopics for research. They then suggest that this working outline be continually revised—items dropped, added, modified—as the research progresses. Instructors who require submission of a research project portfolio (see 1.9.4) sometimes ask that at least one version of the working outline be included in the portfolio in addition to the final outline (see 1.8.3).

An Overall View of the Paper

You may find a series of outlines helpful, whether or not your instructor requires them, especially if you are a beginning writer of research papers. An outline will help you to get an overall view of your paper and, perhaps more important, to figure out how each section of the paper relates to the others. Thus, developing an outline can help you to see the logical progression of your argument. A working outline will also make it easier to keep track of all important aspects of your subject and to focus your research on relevant topics. Continual revision of the working outline, moreover, will encourage you to change your thinking and your approach as new information modifies your understanding of the subject.

Creating a Computer File for Each Version

Word processing is useful for preparing a working outline, which may well pass through many and sometimes quite different versions. Word-processing programs commonly have an outlining feature that offers several formats with automatic numbering and lettering. It is probably best to create a different computer file for each version of an outline. For example, assign the first version a name like "outline1," and save the file when it is finished. When you are ready to revise the outline, create a new file for the second version ("outline2"), copy the first-draft file into the new file, and revise. If you become dissatisfied with the way the second or a subsequent one is progressing, you can discard it, return to an earlier draft, which is stored untouched on the disk, and begin revising in another direction. Printing out each new version will let you compare it more easily with other versions.

1.8.2. Thesis Statement

An Answer to a Question or Problem

As you get closer to writing, you can begin to shape the information you have at hand into a unified, coherent whole by framing a thesis statement for your paper: a single sentence that formulates both your topic and your point of view. In a sense, the thesis statement is your answer to the central question or problem you have raised. Writing this statement will enable you to see where you are heading and to remain on a productive path as you plan and write. Try out different possibilities until you find a statement that seems right for your purpose. Moreover, since the experience of writing may well alter your original plans, do not hesitate to revise the thesis statement as you write the paper. Word processing, through its storage and retrieval capabilities, can help you build effectively on previous drafts of a thesis statement.

Purpose and Audience

Two factors are important to the shaping of a thesis statement—your *purpose* and your *audience*:

- What *purpose* will you try to achieve in the paper? Do you want to describe something, explain something, argue for a certain point of view, or persuade your reader to think or do something?
- What *audience* are you writing for? Is your reader a specialist on the subject? someone likely to agree or disagree with you? someone likely to be interested or uninterested in the subject?

The answers to these questions should to a large extent give your research the appropriate slant or point of view not just in your thesis statement but also in the final outline and the paper itself.

Requirements and Assistance of the Instructor

Many instructors require students to submit thesis statements for approval some two or three weeks before the paper is due. The statement is often included in a research project portfolio (see 1.9.4). If you have difficulty writing a thesis statement, talk with your instructor about the research you have done and about what you want to say; given this information, your instructor can probably help you frame an appropriate thesis statement.

Sample Thesis Statement

The following sample is a thesis statement for section 1.4 ("Conducting Research") of this book:

> Students who wish to write successful research papers must know as much as possible about the modern academic library—its central information system, reference works, online catalog of holdings, full-

text databases, and other resources and services—and must be knowl-edgeable about finding useful Internet sources.

1.8.3. Final Outline

From Working Outline to Final Outline

After you have a satisfactory thesis statement, you can begin trans-forming your working outline into a final one. This step will help you organize your ideas and the accumulated research into a logical, fluent, and effective paper. Again, many instructors request that final outlines be submitted with papers or included in a research project portfolio (see 1.9.4).

Deleting Irrelevant Material

Start by carefully reviewing all your notes to see how strongly they will support the various points in the working outline. Next, read over your working outline *critically* and delete everything that is ir-relevant to the thesis statement or that might weaken your argument.

Eliminating material is often painful since you might have a nat-ural desire to use everything you have collected and to impress your readers (especially teacher readers) with all the work you have done and with all you now know on the subject. But you should resist these temptations, for the inclusion of irrelevant or repetitive mate-rial will lessen the effectiveness of your paper. Keep your thesis statement and your audience in mind. Include only the ideas and information that will help you accomplish what you have set out to do and that will lead your readers to care about your investigation, your presentation, and your conclusions.

Shaping a Structure for the Paper

As you continue to read, reread, and think about the ideas and infor-mation you have decided to use, you will begin to see new connec-tions between items, and patterns of organization will suggest themselves. Bring related material together under general headings, and arrange these sections so that one logically connects with another. Then order the subjects under each heading so that they, too, proceed logically. Finally, plan an effective introduction and a conclusion appropriate to the sequence you have worked out.

Organizing Principles

Common organizing principles include

- **chronology** (useful for historical discussions—e.g., how the Mexican War developed)
- **cause and effect** (e.g., the consequences a scientific discovery will have)
- **process** (e.g., how a politician got elected)
- **deductive logic**, which moves from the general to the specific (e.g., from the problem of violence in the United States to violence involving handguns)
- **inductive logic**, which moves from the specific to the general (e.g., from violence involving handguns to the problem of violence in the United States)

Methods of Development

As you choose an organizational plan, keep in mind the method or methods you will use in developing your paper. For example, which of the following do you plan to accomplish?

- to define, classify, or analyze something
- to use descriptive details or give examples
- to compare or contrast one thing with another
- to argue for a certain point of view

The procedures you intend to adopt will influence the way you arrange your material, and they should be evident in your outline.

Integrating Quotations and Reference Sources

It is also a good idea to indicate in the outline, specifically and precisely, the quotations and reference sources you will use. All this planning will take a good deal of time and thought, and you may well make several preliminary outlines before arriving at the one you will follow. But the time and thought will be well spent. The more planning you do, the easier and more efficient the writing will be.

Types of Outlines

If the final outline is only for your use, its form will have little importance. If it is to be submitted, your instructor will probably discuss the various forms of outline and tell you which to use. Whatever the form, maintain it consistently. The two most common forms are

- **the topic outline** (which uses only short phrases throughout)
- **the sentence outline** (which uses complete sentences throughout)

Labeling Parts of an Outline

The descending parts of an outline are normally labeled in the following order:

I.
  A.
    1.
      a.
        (1)
          (a)
          (b)
        (2)
      b.
    2.
  B.
II.

Logic requires that there be a *II* to complement a *I*, a *B* to complement an *A*, and so forth.

Sample Outline

The following sample is a topic outline of section 1.4 of this book. Next to each major topic, in brackets, is the number of the subsection in 1.4 to which the topic in the outline corresponds. These numbers are added so that you can easily compare the outline with the corresponding text.

Conducting Research

I. The modern academic library   *[compare with subsection 1.4.1]*
  A. Resources and services
    1. Print, electronic, and other nonprint resources
    2. Computer services
    3. Availability of resources: on campus and off campus
  B. Orientation and instruction
    1. Introductory pamphlets and handbooks
    2. Orientation tours, lectures, classes
  C. Professional reference librarians
II. Library research sources   *[cf. 1.4.2]*
  A. Books and similar publications (pamphlets, dissertations)

B. Articles and other publications in print periodicals (scholarly journals, newspapers, magazines)
C. Miscellaneous print and nonprint sources (sound recordings, video recordings, manuscripts, private letters)
D. Electronic sources (reference works, full-text databases, Internet links)

III. The central information system   *[cf. 1.4.3]*
A. Library's catalog of holdings
B. Bibliographic databases
C. Other electronic resources
D. Links to other library catalogs

IV. Reference works   *[cf. 1.4.4]*
A. Reference works that provide data about research materials
   1. Indexes
   2. Bibliographies
   3. Collections of abstracts
   4. Guides to research
B. Reference works that give basic information
   1. Dictionaries
   2. Encyclopedias
   3. Biographical sources
   4. Yearbooks
   5. Almanacs
   6. Atlases
   7. Gazetteers
   8. Statistical data sources
C. Publication forms of reference works
   1. Print
   2. Electronic (online databases, CD-ROM databases)
   3. Print versus electronic
D. Searching a reference database (example: *MLA International Bibliography*)
   1. Versions (print and electronic)
   2. Types of searches (author, title, subject, expanded, Boolean, other advanced searches)
   3. Bibliographic information provided

V. The online catalog of library holdings   *[cf. 1.4.5]*
A. Searching an online catalog (author, title, subject heading, call number, keyword, Boolean, etc.)
B. Bibliographic information provided
C. Information needed for research and writing

D. Call numbers
  1. Library of Congress system
  2. Dewey decimal system
E. Location of library materials
  1. Main collection (open shelves, closed stacks)
  2. Sections for reserved works and reference works
  3. Other sections (e.g., periodicals, nonprint materials, special collections)
VI. Full-text databases   *[cf. 1.4.6]*
A. Reference works and other book-length texts
B. Articles in periodicals
  1. Newspapers
  2. Scholarly journals
  3. Scholarly journal archive
C. Database subscription services (e.g., EBSCO, Gale, Lexis-Nexis)
D. Information needed for list of works cited
  1. URL of specific document
  2. URL of search page
  3. No URL
VII. Other library resources and services   *[cf. 1.4.7]*
A. Microforms (microfilm, microfiche, microcard)
B. Media center (audio recordings, video recordings, multimedia materials)
C. Electronic and other resources (e.g., photocopying, computers, Internet access, software applications, printers)
D. Interlibrary loans
VIII. Internet sources   *[cf. 1.4.8]*
A. Range of sources
  1. Types of useful sites
  2. Resources available (information sources, full texts, audio-visual materials)
B. Using professionally recommended sites
C. Gateway sites (e.g., *Voice of the Shuttle, Social Science Information Gateway, Women's Studies Database*)
D. Peer-reviewed sites (*Abzu, Byzantium*, etc.)
E. Searching the Internet
  1. Search tools (e.g., *Google, Yahoo!*)
  2. Specific searches
  3. Current issues and current events (newspapers, magazines, television and radio)

4. Bookmarking and recording the URL
5. Recording the date of access
6. Internet sources among other sources

IX. Summing up   *[cf. 1.4.9]*

Creating Computer Files for Major Topics

If you have stored your notes in your computer, a helpful intermediate activity between outlining and writing is to incorporate your notes into your outline. Using this strategy, you should create a separate file for each major topic of your outline and shift relevant material, in appropriate order, from note files into the various topic files. Then, as you write, you can call up the topic files one by one and blend material from them into the text of the paper. Be sure to save and to back up your outline files.

1.8.4. SUMMING UP

- **A working outline** is a useful intermediary document between research and writing. It helps you gain an overview of the paper and keep track of all important aspects of the subject.
- **A thesis statement** is a single sentence that formulates both your topic and your point of view. It is an answer to the central question or problem you have raised. When preparing the thesis statement, keep in mind your purpose in writing and the audience you are writing for.
- **The final outline** helps you organize your ideas and research into a coherent paper. Organizing principles include chronology, cause and effect, and deductive and inductive logic. The most common forms of outlining are the topic outline and the sentence outline. If you create a separate computer file for each major topic, you can write the paper by calling up each file in turn, following the progression of the outline.

1.9. WRITING DRAFTS

1.9.1. The First Draft

Do not expect your first draft to be the finished product. The success-ful research paper is usually the culmination of a series of drafts. Habits, capacities, and practices of writers differ widely. Some indi-viduals write more slowly and come close to a final draft the first time through. Others prefer to work in stages and expect to under-take several drafts. In any case, review and rewriting are always nec-essary. Plan ahead and leave plenty of time for revision.

You might start off by trying to set down all your ideas in the order in which you want them to appear. Do not be concerned if the writ-ing in the first draft is hasty and fairly rough. Attempt to stay focused by following your outline closely. Revise the outline, of course, whenever new ideas occur to you and it no longer works. After you complete a rough draft, read it over and try to refine it.

1.9.2. Subsequent Drafts

In revising, you may add, eliminate, and rearrange material. If a sec-tion in the first draft seems unclear or sketchy, you may have to expand it by writing another sentence or two or even a new para-graph. Similarly, to improve the fluency and coherence of the paper, you may need to add transitions between sentences and paragraphs or to define connections or contrasts. Delete any material that is irrel-evant, unimportant, repetitive, or dull and dispensable. If the presen-tation of ideas seems illogical or confusing, you may find that you can clarify by rearranging phrases, clauses, sentences, or paragraphs.

In later drafts you should concern yourself with the more mechan-ical kinds of revision. For example, strive for more precise and eco-nomical wording. Try, in addition, to vary your sentence patterns as well as your choice of words. Finally, correct all technical errors, using a standard writing guide to check punctuation, grammar, and usage and consulting a standard dictionary for the spelling and meaning of words. Your last draft, carefully proofread and corrected, is the text of your research paper.

1.9.3. Writing with a Word Processor

a. Advantages

If you do not own a computer, see whether your school has personal computers available for student use. With a word processor, you can store a first draft—or just a portion of one—and later retrieve and revise it. If you create a different file for each draft, you can return to a preceding draft whenever you wish.

Word processing makes it easy to insert words into, or delete words from, your text and to shift a word or a block of words from one part of the text to another. Moreover, you can produce a printed version of a revision without having to retype the whole new draft. Word processing can also help you center titles, format pages, and perform other such mechanical tasks. For example, the global revision feature of word processing permits you to search for and automatically change text. Thus, if you realize you misspelled the same word several times in your draft, you can correct all the misspellings with a single command.

Word processing similarly allows for more efficient transitions between the various activities related to the research paper. After developing an outline, for instance, you can copy it into a new file, where the outline can serve as the basis for your writing of the text. Or if you created a file of notes for each major topic in your outline (see 1.8.3), you can copy into the text file each topic file in sequence as you write. If your paper will be short and you have taken few notes, you may choose to copy the entire note file into the text file. Using this approach, you can scroll up and down the file and transfer what you want into the text of the paper. If your paper will be longer and you have created a separate file for each of numerous sources, you can readily transfer material (e.g., an effective quotation) from a note file to the text file. You might find it easier to print out all your notes before writing the paper and to decide in advance which ones you want to use in the text. In this way, when you retrieve note files, you will know exactly what parts you are seeking.

Another way to proceed is to use split screens or multiple windows to read note files as you write the paper. When you have completed your final draft, you can simply add the file containing the works-cited list to the end of the paper. With practice and planning, then, as you write your paper you can use a word processor strategically to draw on outline, note, and bibliography files that you created earlier in the project.

b. Limitations

Word processing has certain limitations. Since no more than a fixed number of lines of text are visible on a computer screen, you may find it difficult to get a sense of your whole project. Some writers like to print out text regularly to see better how the writing is developing from paragraph to paragraph and from page to page. Use spelling and usage checkers cautiously, for they are only as effective as the dictionaries they contain. On the one hand, a spelling checker will call your attention to words that are correctly spelled if they are not in its dictionary. On the other, it will not point out misspellings that match words in the dictionary—for example, *their* used for *there* or *its* for *it's*.

Finally, in working on a computer file, you run the risk of losing it, through a technical mistake, equipment failure, or a power outage. Be sure to save your work frequently (after writing a page or so), not just when you finish with it or leave the computer. It is also a good idea to keep a paper copy of text you write and to create a backup disk in case something happens to the disk you are using to prepare the paper. Most important of all, leave yourself ample time to cope with any technical problems that may arise.

1.9.4. The Final Draft and the Research Project Portfolio

All instructors require submission of the final draft of the research paper. Some instructors ask students to prepare and submit a research project portfolio, which documents the evolution of the paper. The portfolio might contain such items as the approved thesis statement, the final outline, an early draft, and the final draft.

1.9.5. SUMMING UP

Research papers are normally composed through a series of drafts. The first draft is usually rough, and subsequent drafts are increasingly refined revisions of the original version. A word processor is

useful for writing research papers, although it has some limitations as well. The assignment concludes with the submission of
the final draft or of a research project portfolio.

1.10. LANGUAGE AND STYLE

Effective writing depends as much on clarity and readability as on
content. The organization and development of your ideas, the unity
and coherence of your presentation, and your command of sentence
structure, grammar, and diction are all important considerations, as
are the mechanics of writing—capitalization, spelling, punctuation,
and so on. The key to successful communication is using the right
language for the audience you are addressing. In all writing, the
challenge is to find the words, phrases, clauses, sentences, and paragraphs that express your thoughts and ideas precisely and that make
them interesting to others.

Because good scholarship requires objectivity, careful writers of
research papers avoid language that implies unsubstantiated or irrel-
evant generalizations about such personal qualities as age, economic
class, ethnicity, sexual orientation, political or religious beliefs, race,
or sex. Discussions about this subject have generally focused on
wording that could be labeled sexist. For example, many writers no
longer use *he*, *him*, or *his* to express a meaning that includes women
or girls: "If a young artist is not confident, he can quickly become
discouraged." The use of *she*, *her*, and *hers* to refer to a person who
may be of either sex can also be distracting and momentarily confusing. Both usages can often be avoided through a revision that recasts
the sentence into the plural or that eliminates the pronoun: "If young
artists are not confident, they can quickly become discouraged" or
"A young artist who is not confident can quickly become discouraged." Another technique is to make the discussion refer to a person
who is identified, so that there is a reason to use a specific singular
pronoun. *They*, *them*, *their*, and *theirs* cannot logically be applied to
a single person, and *he or she* and *her or him* are cumbersome alternatives to be used sparingly. Many authors now also avoid terms that
unnecessarily integrate a person's sex with a job or role. For
instance, *anchorman*, *policeman*, *stewardess*, and *poetess* are commonly replaced with *anchor*, *police officer*, *flight attendant*, and

poet. For advice on current practices, consult your instructor or one of the guides to bias-free language listed in 1.11.

1.11. GUIDES TO WRITING

A good dictionary is an essential tool for all writers. Your instructor will probably recommend a standard American dictionary such as *The American Heritage College Dictionary, Merriam-Webster's Collegiate Dictionary,* or *Random House Webster's College Dictionary.* Because dictionaries vary in matters like word division and spelling preference, you should, to maintain consistency, use the same one throughout your paper.

You should also keep on hand at least one reliable guide to writing. A selected list of writing guides appears below, classified under three headings: dictionaries of usage, guides to bias-free language, and books on style. Your instructor can help you choose among these titles.

Dictionaries of Usage

Bernstein, Theodore M. *The Careful Writer: A Modern Guide to English Usage.* New York: Atheneum, 1965.

Bryant, Margaret M. *Current American Usage: How Americans Say It and Write It.* New York: Funk, 1962.

Copperud, Roy H. *American Usage and Style: The Consensus.* New York: Van Nostrand, 1980.

Evans, Bergen, and Cornelia Evans. *A Dictionary of Contemporary American Usage.* New York: Random, 1957.

Follett, Wilson. *Modern American Usage: A Guide.* Ed. Jacques Barzun. New York: Hill, 1966.

———. *Modern American Usage: A Guide.* Rev. Erik Wensberg. Rev. ed. New York: Hill-Farrar, 1998.

Fowler, H[enry] W. *A Dictionary of Modern English Usage.* Ed. Ernest Gowers. 2nd ed. New York: Oxford UP, 1965.

———. *The New Fowler's Modern English Usage.* Ed. R. W. Burchfield. Rev. 3rd ed. New York: Oxford UP, 1998.

Garner, Bryan A. *A Dictionary of Modern American Usage.* New York: Oxford UP, 1998.

——. *The Oxford Dictionary of American Usage and Style.* New York: Oxford UP, 2000.

Lovinger, Paul W. *The Penguin Dictionary of American English Usage and Style.* New York: Penguin, 2002.

Mager, Nathan H., and Sylvia K. Mager. *Prentice Hall Encyclopedic Dictionary of English Usage.* 2nd ed. Englewood Cliffs: Prentice, 1992.

Morris, William, and Mary Morris. *Harper Dictionary of Contemporary Usage.* 2nd ed. New York: Harper, 1985.

Nicholson, Margaret. *A Dictionary of American-English Usage Based on Fowler's* Modern English Usage. New York: Oxford UP, 1957.

Waite, Maurice, Edmund S. Weiner, and Andrew Delahunty. *The Oxford Dictionary and Usage Guide to the English Language.* New York: Oxford UP, 1995.

Weiner, Edmund S., and Andrew Delahunty. *The Oxford Guide to English Usage.* 2nd ed. New York: Oxford UP, 1994.

Wilson, Kenneth G. *The Columbia Guide to Standard American English.* New York: Columbia UP, 1993.

Guides to Bias-Free Language

American Psychological Association. "Guidelines to Reduce Bias in Language." *Publication Manual of the American Psychological Association.* 5th ed. Washington: Amer. Psychological Assn., 2001. 61–76.

Frank, Francine Wattman, and Paula A. Treichler, with others. *Language, Gender, and Professional Writing: Theoretical Approaches and Guidelines for Nonsexist Usage.* New York: MLA, 1989.

International Association of Business Communication. *Without Bias: A Guidebook for Nondiscriminatory Communication.* Ed. Judy E. Pickens, Patricia W. Rao, and Linda C. Roberts. 2nd ed. New York: Wiley, 1982.

Maggio, Rosalie. *The Bias-Free Word Finder: A Dictionary of Nondiscriminatory Language.* Boston: Beacon, 1992.

——. *The Dictionary of Bias-Free Usage: A Guide to Nondiscriminatory Language.* Phoenix: Oryx, 1991.

——. *The Nonsexist Word Finder: A Dictionary of Gender-Free Usage.* Phoenix: Oryx, 1987.

——. *Talking about People: A Guide to Fair and Accurate Language.* Phoenix: Oryx, 1997.

Miller, Casey, and Kate Swift. *The Handbook of Nonsexist Writing.* 2nd ed. New York: Harper, 1988.

————. *Words and Women*. Rev. ed. New York: Harper, 1991.

Schwartz, Marilyn, and the Task Force of the Association of American University Presses. *Guidelines for Bias-Free Writing*. Bloomington: Indiana UP, 1995.

Sorrels, Bobbye D. *The Nonsexist Communicator: Solving the Problems of Gender and Awkwardness in Modern English*. Englewood Cliffs: Prentice, 1983.

Warren, Virginia L. "Guidelines for the Nonsexist Use of Language." *American Philosophical Association Proceedings* 59 (1986): 471–84.

Books on Style

Barzun, Jacques. *Simple and Direct: A Rhetoric for Writers*. 4th ed. New York: Harper, 2001.

Beardsley, Monroe C. *Thinking Straight: Principles of Reasoning for Readers and Writers*. 4th ed. Englewood Cliffs: Prentice, 1975.

Cook, Claire Kehrwald. *Line by Line: How to Edit Your Own Writing*. Boston: Houghton, 1985.

Eastman, Richard M. *Style: Writing and Reading as the Discovery of Outlook*. 3rd ed. New York: Oxford UP, 1984.

Elbow, Peter. *Writing without Teachers*. 2nd ed. New York: Oxford UP, 1998.

————. *Writing with Power: Techniques for Mastering the Writing Process*. 2nd ed. New York: Oxford UP, 1998.

Gibson, Walker. *Tough, Sweet, and Stuffy: An Essay on Modern American Prose Styles*. Bloomington: Indiana UP, 1966.

Gowers, Ernest. *The Complete Plain Words*. Ed. Sidney Greenbaum and Janet Whitcut. Rev. ed. Boston: Godine, 1990.

Lanham, Richard A. *Style: An Anti-textbook*. New Haven: Yale UP, 1974.

Smith, Charles K. *Styles and Structures: Alternative Approaches to College Writing*. New York: Norton, 1974.

Strunk, William, Jr., and E. B. White. *The Elements of Style*. 4th ed. New York: Longman-Allyn, 2000.

Williams, Joseph M. *Style: Ten Lessons in Clarity and Grace*. 7th ed. New York: Longman-Allyn, 2002.

————. *Style: Toward Clarity and Grace*. Chicago: U of Chicago P, 1990.

2 Plagiarism

You have probably read or heard about charges of plagiarism in disputes in the publishing and recording industries. You may also have had classroom discussions about student plagiarism in particular and academic dishonesty in general. Many schools have developed guidelines or procedures regarding plagiarism. Honor codes and other means to promote academic integrity are also common.

2.1. DEFINITION OF PLAGIARISM

Derived from the Latin word *plagiarius* ("kidnapper"), *plagiarism* refers to a form of cheating that has been defined as "the false assumption of authorship: the wrongful act of taking the product of another person's mind, and presenting it as one's own" (Alexander Lindey, *Plagiarism and Originality* [New York: Harper, 1952] 2). Plagiarism involves two kinds of wrongs. Using another person's ideas, information, or expressions without acknowledging that person's work constitutes intellectual theft. Passing off another person's ideas, information, or expressions as your own to get a better grade or gain some other advantage constitutes fraud. Plagiarism is sometimes a moral and ethical offense rather than a legal one since some instances of plagiarism fall outside the scope of copyright infringement, a legal offense (see 2.7.3).

2.2. CONSEQUENCES OF PLAGIARISM

Plagiarism is almost always seen as a shameful act, and plagiarists are usually regarded with pity and scorn. They are pitied because they have demonstrated their inability to develop and express their own thoughts. They are scorned because of their dishonesty and their willingness to deceive others for personal gain. As Verlyn Klinkenborg points out, "Plagiarism is an ugly word and an all-encompassing one. We make more distinction among degrees of murder than we do among kinds of plagiarism" ("From the Pulpit, a Borrowed Word," *New York Times* 16 Mar. 2002, late ed.: A14).We not only distinguish degrees of murder; we also recognize degrees of theft. These distinctions allow us to urge leniency for a starving person who steals a loaf of bread and to approve a substantial prison term for a wealthy CEO who steals from employees' pension funds. We are less likely to consider extenuating circumstances when someone takes credit for another person's work, because fraud is involved. Plagiarism is plagiarism whether the theft is committed by a student or an experienced journalist. Moreover, although many of us would agree that a starving person who steals a loaf of bread can be rehabilitated, plagiarists rarely recover the trust of those they try to deceive.

The charge of plagiarism is a serious one for all writers. Students exposed as plagiarists suffer severe penalties, ranging from failure in the assignment or in the course to expulsion from school. They must also live with the distrust that follows an attempt to deceive others for personal gain. When professional writers, like journalists, are exposed as plagiarists, they are likely to lose their jobs, and they are certain to suffer public embarrassment and loss of prestige. For example, a well-known historian charged with plagiarism was asked to resign from prominent public positions even though she admitted responsibility for the theft, compensated the author whose work she took, and announced her intention to issue a corrected edition of her book. Almost always, the course of a professional writer's career is permanently affected by a single act of plagiarism.

The serious consequences of plagiarism reflect the value the public places on trustworthy information. A complex society that depends on well-informed citizens maintains high standards of quality and reliability for documents that are publicly circulated and used in government, business, industry, the professions, higher education, and the media. Because research has the power to affect opinions and actions, responsible writers compose their work with great care. They specify when they refer to another author's ideas, facts, and words, whether they want to agree with, object to, or analyze the source. This kind of documentation not only recognizes the work writers do; it also tends to discourage the circulation of error, by inviting readers to determine for themselves whether a reference to another text presents a reasonable account of what that text says. Plagiarists undermine these important public values.

Student plagiarism does considerable harm. For one thing, it damages teachers' relationships with students, turning teachers into detectives instead of mentors and fostering suspicion instead of trust. By undermining institutional standards for assigning grades and awarding degrees, student plagiarism also becomes a matter of significance to the public. When graduates' skills and knowledge fail to match their grades, an institution's reputation is damaged. For example, no one would choose to be treated by a physician who obtained a medical degree by fraud. Finally, students who plagiarize harm themselves. They waste their tuition and lose an important opportunity to learn how to write a research paper. Knowing how to collect and analyze information and reshape it in essay form is essential to academic success. This knowledge is also required in a wide range of careers in law, journalism, engineering, public policy, teaching, business, government, and not-for-profit organizations.

Plagiarism betrays the personal element in writing as well. Discussing the history of copyright, Mark Rose notes the tie between our writing and our sense of self—a tie that, he believes, influenced the idea that a piece of writing could belong to the person who wrote it. Rose says that our sense of ownership of the words we write "is deeply rooted in our conception of ourselves as individuals with at least a modest grade of singularity, some degree of personality" (*Authors and Owners: The Invention of Copyright* [Cambridge: Harvard UP, 1993] 142). Gaining skill as a writer opens the door to learning more about yourself and to developing a personal voice and approach in your writing.

2.3. INFORMATION SHARING TODAY

Innumerable documents on a host of subjects are posted on the Web apparently for the purpose of being shared. The availability of research materials and the ease of transmitting, modifying, and using them have influenced the culture of the Internet, where the free exchange of information is an ideal. In this sea of materials, some students may question the need to acknowledge the authorship of individual documents. Professional writers, however, have no doubt about the matter. They recognize the importance of avoiding plagiarism whether they base their research on print or electronic publications. And so they continue to cite their sources and to mark the passages they quote.

In the culture of the academy, too, the free exchange of information is a long-standing ideal. Under certain circumstances, this ideal is described as academic freedom. But nothing about academic freedom or the free exchange of information implies ignoring authorship. Academic standards require student and experienced writers to acknowledge the authors whose work they use when preparing papers and other kinds of studies and reports.

New technologies have made information easier to locate and obtain, but research projects only begin with identifying and collecting source material. The essential intellectual tasks of a research project have not changed. These tasks call for a student to understand the published facts, ideas, and insights about a subject and to integrate them with the student's own views on the topic. To achieve this goal, student writers must rigorously distinguish between what they borrow and what they create.

As information sharing has become easier, so has plagiarism. For instance, on the Internet it is possible to buy and download completed research papers. Some students are misinformed about buying research papers, on the Internet or on campus. They believe that if they buy a paper, it belongs to them, and therefore they can use the ideas, facts, sentences, and paragraphs in it, free from any worry about plagiarism. Buying a paper, however, is the same as buying a book or a magazine. You own the physical copy of the book or magazine, which you may keep in your bookcase, give to a friend, or sell. And you may use whatever you learn from reading it in your own writing. But you are never free from the obligation to let your readers know the source of the ideas, facts, words, or sentences you borrow. Whether in print or electronic formats, publications are a special kind of property. You can own them physically, but the publisher or author retains rights to the content. You should also know that purchased papers are readily recognizable, and teachers can often trace downloaded materials through an Internet search.

2.4. UNINTENTIONAL PLAGIARISM

The purpose of a research paper is to synthesize previous research and scholarship with your ideas on the subject. Therefore, you should feel free to use other persons' words, facts, and thoughts in your research paper, but the material you borrow must not be presented as if it were your own creation. When you write your research paper, remember that you must document everything that you borrow—not only direct quotations and paraphrases but also information and ideas.

Often plagiarism in student writing is unintentional, as when an elementary school pupil, assigned to do a report on a certain topic, goes home and copies down, word for word, everything on the subject in an encyclopedia. Unfortunately, some students continue to use such "research methods" in high school and even in college, not realizing that these practices constitute plagiarism. To guard against the possibility of unintentional plagiarism during research and writing, keep careful notes that always distinguish among three types of material: your ideas, your summaries and paraphrases of others' ideas and facts, and exact wording you copy from sources. Plagiarism sometimes happens because researchers do not keep precise records of their reading, and by the time they return to their notes, they have forgotten whether their summaries and paraphrases contain quoted material that is poorly marked or unmarked. Presenting an author's exact wording without marking it as a quotation is plagiarism, even if you cite the source. For this reason, recording only quotations is the most reliable method of note-taking in substantial research projects, especially for beginning students. It is the surest way, when you work with notes, to avoid unintentional plagiarism. Similar problems can occur in notes kept electronically. When you copy and paste passages, make sure that you add quotation marks around them. (See 1.7 for more on note-taking.)

Another kind of unintentional plagiarism happens when students write research papers in a second language. In an effort to avoid grammatical errors, they may copy the structure of an author's sentences. When replicating grammatical patterns, they sometimes inadvertently plagiarize the author's ideas, information, words, and expressions.

If you realize after handing a paper in that you accidentally plagiarized an author's work, you should report the problem to your instructor as soon as possible. In this way you eliminate the element of fraud. You may receive a lower grade than you had hoped for, but getting a lower grade is better than failing a course or being expelled. It is also better than experiencing the shame of plagiarism.

2.5. FORMS OF PLAGIARISM

The most blatant form of plagiarism is to obtain and submit as your own a paper written by someone else (see 2.3). Other, less conspicuous forms of plagiarism include the failure to give appropriate acknowledgment when repeating or paraphrasing another's wording, when taking a particularly apt phrase, and when paraphrasing another's argument or presenting another's line of thinking.

Repeating or Paraphrasing Wording

Suppose, for example, that you want to use the material in the following passage, which appears on page 625 of an essay by Wendy Martin in the book *Columbia Literary History of the United States.*

ORIGINAL SOURCE

Some of Dickinson's most powerful poems express her firmly held conviction that life cannot be fully comprehended without an understanding of death.

If you write the following sentence without documentation, you have plagiarized because you borrowed another's wording without acknowledgment, even though you changed its form:

PLAGIARISM

Emily Dickinson firmly believed that we cannot fully comprehend life unless we also understand death.

But you may present the material if you cite your source:

As Wendy Martin has suggested, Emily Dickinson firmly believed that we cannot fully comprehend life unless we also understand death (625).

The source is indicated, in accordance with MLA style, by the name of the author ("Wendy Martin") and by a page reference in parentheses, preferably at the end of the sentence. The name refers the reader to the corresponding entry in the works-cited list, which appears at the end of the paper.

Martin, Wendy. "Emily Dickinson." Columbia Literary History of the United States. Emory Elliott, gen. ed. New York: Columbia UP, 1988. 609-26.

Taking a Particularly Apt Phrase

ORIGINAL SOURCE

Everyone uses the word *language* and everybody these days talks about *culture.* . . . "Languaculture" is a reminder, I hope, of the *necessary* connection between its two parts. . . . (Michael Agar, *Language Shock: Understanding the Culture of Conversation* [New York: Morrow, 1994] 60)

If you write the following sentence without documentation, you have committed plagiarism because you borrowed without acknowledgment a term ("languaculture") invented by another writer:

PLAGIARISM

At the intersection of language and culture lies a concept that we might call "languaculture."

But you may present the material if you cite your source:

At the intersection of language and culture lies a concept that Michael Agar has called "languaculture" (60).

In this revision, the author's name refers the reader to the full description of the work in the works-cited list at the end of the paper, and the parenthetical documentation identifies the location of the borrowed material in the work.

Agar, Michael. Language Shock: Understanding the Culture of Conversation. New York: Morrow, 1994.

Paraphrasing an Argument or Presenting a Line of Thinking

ORIGINAL SOURCE

Humanity faces a quantum leap forward. It faces the deepest social upheaval and creative restructuring of all time. Without clearly recognizing it, we are engaged in building a remarkable civilization from the ground up. This is the meaning of the Third Wave.

Until now the human race has undergone two great waves of change, each one largely obliterating earlier cultures or civilizations and replacing them with the ways of life inconceivable to those who came before. The First Wave of change—the agricultural revolution—took thousands of years to play itself out. The Second Wave—the rise of industrial civilization—took a mere hundred years. Today history is even more accelerative, and it is likely that the Third Wave will sweep across history and complete itself in a few decades. (Alvin Toffler, *The Third Wave* [1980; New York: Bantam, 1981] 10)

If you write the following sentence without documentation, you have committed plagiarism because you borrowed another writer's line of thinking without acknowledgment:

PLAGIARISM

There have been two revolutionary periods of change in history: the agricultural revolution and the industrial revolution. The agricultural revolution determined the course of history for thousands of years; the industrial civilization lasted about a century. We are now on the threshold of a new period of revolutionary change, but this one may last for only a few decades.

But you may present the material if you cite your source:

According to Alvin Toffler, there have been two revolutionary periods of change in history: the agricultural revolution and the industrial revolution. The agricultural revolution determined the course of history for thousands of years; the industrial civilization lasted about a century. We are now on the threshold of a new period of revolutionary change, but this one may last for only a few decades (10).

In this revision, the author's name refers the reader to the full description of the work in the works-cited list at the end of the paper, and the parenthetical documentation identifies the location of the borrowed material in the work.

Toffler, Alvin. The Third Wave. 1980. New York: Bantam, 1981.

2.6. WHEN DOCUMENTATION IS NOT NEEDED

Common sense as well as ethics should determine your documentation. For example, you rarely need to give sources for familiar proverbs ("You can't judge a book by its cover"), well-known quotations ("We shall overcome"), or common knowledge ("George Washington was the first president of the United States"; "At a red light, drivers come to a full stop"). But you must indicate the source of any information or material that you took from someone else. If you have any doubt about whether you are committing plagiarism, cite your source or sources.

2.7. OTHER ISSUES

Other issues related to plagiarism include reusing a research paper, collaborative work, and copyright infringement.

2.7.1. Reusing a Research Paper

If you must complete a research project to earn a grade in a course, handing in a paper you already earned credit for in another course is deceitful. Moreover, you lose the opportunity to improve your knowledge and skills. If you want to rework a paper that you prepared for another course, ask your current instructor for permission to do so.

2.7.2. Collaborative Work

An example of collaborative work is a group project you carry out with other students. Joint participation in research and writing is common and, in fact, encouraged in many courses and in many professions. It does not constitute plagiarism provided that credit is given for all contributions. One way to give credit, if roles were clearly demarcated or were unequal, is to state exactly who did what. Another way, especially if roles and contributions were merged and shared, is to acknowledge all concerned equally. Ask your instructor for advice if you are not certain how to acknowledge collaboration.

2.7.3. Copyright Infringement

Whereas summaries, paraphrases, and brief quotations in research papers are normally permissible with appropriate acknowledgment, reproducing and distributing an entire copyrighted document or significant portions of it without obtaining permission to do so from the author or publisher is an infringement of copyright law and a legal offense, even if the violator acknowledges the source. This is true for documents published on the Internet or in print. For a detailed discussion of copyright and other legal issues related to publishing, see chapter 2 of the *MLA Style Manual and Guide to Scholarly Publishing* (2nd ed. [New York: MLA, 1998]).

2.8. SUMMING UP

You have plagiarized if

- you took notes that did not distinguish summary and paraphrase from quotation and then you presented wording from the notes as if it were all your own.
- while browsing the Web, you copied text and pasted it into your paper without quotation marks or without citing the source.
- you presented facts without saying where you found them.
- you repeated or paraphrased someone's wording without acknowledgment.
- you took someone's unique or particularly apt phrase without acknowledgment.
- you paraphrased someone's argument or presented someone's line of thought without acknowledgment.
- you bought or otherwise acquired a research paper and handed in part or all of it as your own.

You can avoid plagiarism by

- making a list of the writers and viewpoints you discovered in your research and using this list to double-check the presentation of material in your paper.
- keeping the following three categories distinct in your notes: your ideas, your summaries of others' material, and exact wording you copy.
- identifying the sources of all material you borrow—exact wording, paraphrases, ideas, arguments, and facts.
- checking with your instructor when you are uncertain about your use of sources.

3 The Mechanics of Writing

Although the scope of this book precludes a detailed discussion of grammar, usage, style, and related aspects of writing, this chapter addresses mechanical questions that you will likely encounter in writing research papers.

1. Spelling
2. Punctuation
3. Italics (underlining)
4. Names of persons
5. Numbers
6. Titles of works in the research paper
7. Quotations
8. Capitalization and personal names in languages other than English

3.1. SPELLING

3.1.1. Consistency

Spelling, including hyphenation, should be consistent throughout the research paper—except in quotations, which must retain the spelling of the original, whether correct or incorrect. You can best ensure consistency by always adopting the spelling that your dictionary gives first in any entry with variant spellings. (See 1.11 for titles of standard dictionaries.)

3.1.2. Word Division

To save time and avoid possible errors, do not divide words at the ends of lines. If a word you are about to type on a typewriter will not fit on the line, you may leave the line short and begin the word on the next line. The "word-wrap" feature of word-processing programs performs this operation automatically. If you choose to divide a word, consult your dictionary about where the break should occur.

3.1.3. Plurals

The plurals of English words are generally formed by adding the suffix *-s* or *-es* (*laws, taxes*), with several exceptions (e.g., *children, halves, mice, sons-in-law, bison*). The tendency in American English is to form the plurals of words naturalized from other languages in the standard manner. The plurals *librettos* and *formulas* are therefore now more common in American English than *libretti* and *formulae*. But some adopted words, like *alumnus* and *phenomenon*, retain their original plurals (*alumni, phenomena*). Consult a dictionary for guidance. If the dictionary gives more than one plural form for a word (*appendixes, appendices*), use the first listed. (See 3.2.7 for plurals of letters and for possessive forms of plurals.)

3.1.4. Foreign Words

If you quote material in a foreign language, you must reproduce all accents and other marks exactly as they appear in the original (*école, pietà, tête, leçon, Fähre, año*). If you need marks that are not available on your word processor or typewriter, write them in by hand. On the use of foreign words in an English text, see 3.3.2; on capitalization and personal names in languages other than English, see 3.8.

3.2. PUNCTUATION

3.2.1. The Purpose of Punctuation

The primary purpose of punctuation is to ensure the clarity and readability of writing. Punctuation clarifies sentence structure, separating some words and grouping others. It adds meaning to written words and guides the understanding of readers as they move through sentences. The rules set forth here cover many of the situations you will encounter in writing research papers. For the punctuation of quotations in your text, see 3.7. For the punctuation of parenthetical references and bibliographies, see chapters 5 and 6. See also the individual listings in the index for specific punctuation marks.

3.2.2. Commas

a. Use a comma before a coordinating conjunction (*and, but, for, nor, or, yet,* or *so*) joining independent clauses in a sentence.

Congress passed the bill, and the president signed it into law.

The poem is ironic, for the poet's meaning contrasts with her words.

Take along a tape recorder, or you risk misquoting your interviewee.

Other wars were longer, but few were as costly in human lives.

b. Use commas to separate words, phrases, and clauses in a series.

WORDS

Boccaccio's tales have inspired plays, films, operas, and paintings.

PHRASES

Alfred the Great established a system of fortified towns, reorganized the military forces, and built a fleet of warships.

CLAUSES

In the Great Depression, millions lost their jobs, businesses failed, and charitable institutions closed their doors.

But use semicolons when items in a series have internal commas.

Pollsters focused their efforts on Columbus, Ohio; Des Moines, Iowa; and Saint Louis, Missouri.

c. Use a comma between coordinate adjectives—that is, adjectives that separately modify the same noun.

Critics praise the novel's unaffected, unadorned style.   (The adjectives *unaffected* and *unadorned* each modify *style.*)

The new regime imposed harsh, repressive laws.   (The adjectives *harsh* and *repressive* each modify *laws.*)

But note:

Most of the characters are average city dwellers.   (The adjective *average* modifies *city dwellers.*)

A famous photo shows Marianne Moore in a black tricornered hat.   (The adjective *black* modifies *tricornered hat.*)

d. Use commas to set off a parenthetical comment, or an aside, if it is brief and closely related to the rest of the sentence. (For punctuation of longer, more intrusive, or more complex parenthetical elements, see 3.2.5.)

The Tudors, for example, ruled for over a century.

The vernacular, after all, was the language of everyday life.

Tonight's performance, I'm sorry to say, has been canceled.

e. Use commas to set off a nonrestrictive modifier—that is, a modifier that is not essential to the meaning of the sentence. A nonrestrictive modifier, unlike a restrictive one, could be dropped without changing the main sense of the sentence. Modifiers in the following three categories are either nonrestrictive or restrictive. (For the use of parentheses and dashes around complex nonrestrictive modifiers, see 3.2.5b.)

Words in apposition

NONRESTRICTIVE

The color of the costume, blue, acquires symbolic meaning in the story.

The theme song of the campaign, "Happy Days Are Here Again," is indelibly associated with the Great Depression.

Isabel Allende, the Chilean novelist, will appear at the arts forum tonight.

RESTRICTIVE

The color blue acquires symbolic meaning in the story.

The campaign song "Happy Days Are Here Again" is indelibly associated with the Great Depression.

The Chilean novelist Isabel Allende will appear at the arts forum tonight.

Clauses that begin with *who, whom, whose, which,* and *that*

NONRESTRICTIVE

Scientists, who must observe standards of objectivity in their work, can contribute usefully to public-policy debates.

The Italian sonnet, which is exemplified in Petrarch's Canzoniere, developed into the English sonnet.

RESTRICTIVE

Scientists who receive the Nobel Prize sometimes contribute usefully to public-policy debates.

The sonnet that is exemplified in Petrarch's Canzoniere developed into the English sonnet.

Note that some writers prefer to use *which* to introduce nonrestrictive clauses and *that* to introduce restrictive clauses.

Adverbial phrases and clauses

NONRESTRICTIVE

The novel takes place in China, where many languages are spoken.

The ending is sad, as the narrator hinted it would be.

RESTRICTIVE

The novel takes place in a land where many languages are spoken.

The ending is as the narrator hinted it would be.

f. Use a comma after a long introductory phrase or clause.

PHRASE

After years of anxiety over the family's finances, Linda Loman looks forward to the day the mortgage will be paid off.

CLAUSE

Although she was virtually unknown in her day, scholars have come to recognize the originality of her work.

g. Use commas to set off alternative or contrasting phrases.

The king remains a tragic figure, despite his appalling actions.

A determined, even obsessed, taxi driver tells of his ambitions.

It is Julio, not his mother, who sets the plot in motion.

But note:

Several cooperative but autonomous republics were formed.   (The conjunction *but* links *cooperative* and *autonomous*, making a comma inappropriate.)

h. Do not use a comma between subject and verb.

Many of the characters who dominate the early chapters and then disappear [no comma] are portraits of the author's friends.

i. Do not use a comma between verb and object.

The agent reported to the headquarters staff [no comma] that the documents had been traced to an underground garage.

j. Do not use a comma between the parts of a compound subject, compound object, or compound verb.

COMPOUND SUBJECT

A dozen wooden chairs [no comma] and a window that admits a shaft of light complete the stage setting.

COMPOUND OBJECT

Ptolemy devised a system of astronomy accepted until the sixteenth century [no comma] and a scientific approach to the study of geography.

COMPOUND VERB

He composed several successful symphonies [no comma] but won the most fame for his witticisms.

k. Do not use a comma between two parallel subordinate elements.

Nona thought of the crew members, who worked from dawn to dusk [no comma] but whose lives seemed free and joyful.

She broadens her analysis by exploring the tragic elements of the play [no comma] and by integrating the hunting motif with the themes of death and resurrection.

The farmhouse stood on top of a hill [no comma] and just beyond the Silver Creek bridge.

l. Use a comma in a date whose order is month, day, and year. If such a date comes in the middle of a sentence, include a comma after the year.

Martin Luther King, Jr., was born on January 15, 1929, and died on April 4, 1968.

But commas are not used with dates whose order is day, month, and year.

Martin Luther King, Jr., was born on 15 January 1929 and died on 4 April 1968.

m. Do not use a comma between a month and a year or between a season and a year.

The events of July 1789 are as familiar to the French as those of July 1776 are to Americans.

I passed my oral exams in spring 1999.

See 3.7.7 for commas with quotations.

3.2.3. Semicolons

a. Use a semicolon between independent clauses not linked by a conjunction.

The coat is tattered beyond repair; still, Akaky hopes the tailor can mend it.

b. Use semicolons between items in a series when the items contain commas.

Present at the symposium were Henri Guillaume, the art critic; Sam Brown, the Daily Tribune reporter; and Maria Rosa, the conceptual artist.

3.2.4. Colons

The colon is used between two parts of a sentence when the first part creates a sense of anticipation about what follows in the second. Leave only one space after a colon, not two.

a. Use a colon to introduce a list, an elaboration of what was just said, or the formal expression of a rule or principle.

LIST

The reading list includes three Latin American novels: The Death of Artemio Cruz, One Hundred Years of Solitude, and The Green House.

ELABORATION

The plot is founded on deception: the three main characters have secret identities.

RULE OR PRINCIPLE

Many books would be briefer if their authors followed the logical principle known as Occam's razor: Explanations should not be multiplied unnecessarily.   (A rule or principle after a colon should begin with a capital letter.)

But do not use a colon before a list if the list is grammatically essential to the introductory wording.

The novels on the reading list include The Death of Artemio Cruz, One Hundred Years of Solitude, and The Green House.   (The list is the object of the verb *include*.)

The reading list includes such novels as The Death of Artemio Cruz, One Hundred Years of Solitude, and The Green House.   (The list continues the expression *such . . . as*.)

b. Use a colon to introduce a quotation that is independent from the structure of the main sentence.

In The Awakening, Mme Ratignolle exhorts Robert Lebrun to stop flirting with Edna: "She is not one of us; she is not like us."

A quotation that is integral to the sentence structure is generally preceded by no punctuation or, if a verb of saying (*says, exclaims, notes, writes*) introduces the quotation, by a comma. A colon is used after a verb of saying, however, if the verb introduces certain kinds of formal literary quotations, such as long quotations set off from the main text (see 3.7.2–4, 3.7.7).

3.2.5. Dashes and Parentheses

Dashes make a sharper break in the continuity of the sentence than commas do, and parentheses make a still sharper one. To indicate a dash in typing, use two hyphens, with no space before, between, or after. (Some word processors have a dash, and you may use it instead of hyphens.) Your writing will be smoother and more readable if you use dashes and parentheses sparingly. Limit the number of dashes in a sentence to two paired dashes or one unpaired dash.

a. Use dashes or parentheses to enclose a sentence element that interrupts the train of thought.

Soaring in a balloon--inventors first performed this feat in 1783--is a way to recapture the wonder that early aviators must have felt.

The "hero" of the play (the townspeople see him as heroic, but he is the focus of the author's satire) introduces himself as a veteran of the war.

b. Use dashes or parentheses to set off a parenthetical element that contains a comma and that might be misread if set off with commas.

The colors of the costume--blue, scarlet, and yellow--acquire symbolic meaning in the story.

The Italian sonnet (which is exemplified in Petrarch's Canzoniere, along with other kinds of poems) developed into the English sonnet.

c. Use a dash to introduce words that summarize a preceding series.

Ruthlessness and acute sensitivity, greed and compassion--the main character's contradictory qualities prevent any simple interpretation of the film.

A dash may also be used instead of a colon to introduce a list or an elaboration of what was just said (see 3.2.4a).

3.2.6. Hyphens

Compound words of all types—nouns, verbs, adjectives, and so on—are written as separate words (*hard drive, hard labor*), with hyphens (*hard-and-fast, hard-boiled*), and as single words (*hardcover, hardheaded*). The dictionary shows how to write many compounds. A compound not in the dictionary should usually be written as separate words unless a hyphen is needed to prevent readers from misunderstanding the relation between the words. Following are some rules to help you decide whether you need a hyphen in compounds and other terms that may not appear in the dictionary.

a. Use a hyphen in a compound adjective beginning with an adverb such as *better, best, ill, lower, little,* or *well* when the adjective precedes a noun.

> better-prepared ambassador
>
> best-known work
>
> ill-informed reporter
>
> lower-priced tickets
>
> well-dressed announcer

But do not use a hyphen when the compound adjective comes after the noun it modifies.

> The ambassador was better prepared than the other delegates.

b. Do not use a hyphen in a compound adjective beginning with an adverb ending in *-ly* or with *too, very,* or *much.*

> thoughtfully presented thesis
>
> very contrived plot
>
> too hasty judgment
>
> much maligned performer

c. Use a hyphen in a compound adjective ending with the present participle (e.g., *loving*) or the past participle (e.g., *inspired*) of a verb when the adjective precedes a noun.

> sports-loving throng
>
> fear-inspired loyalty
>
> hate-filled speech

d. Use a hyphen in a compound adjective formed by a number and a noun when the adjective precedes a noun.

twelfth-floor apartment

second-semester courses

early-thirteenth-century architecture

e. Use hyphens in other compound adjectives before nouns to prevent misreading.

continuing-education program   (The hyphen indicates that the term refers
   to a program of continuing education and not to an education program
   that is continuing.)

Portuguese-language student   (The hyphen makes it clear that the term
   refers to a student who is studying Portuguese and not to a language
   student who is Portuguese.)

f. Do not use hyphens in familiar unhyphenated compound terms, such as *social security*, *high school*, *liberal arts*, and *show business*, when they appear before nouns as modifiers.

social security tax

high school reunion

liberal arts curriculum

show business debut

g. Use hyphens to join coequal nouns.

writer-critic

scholar-athlete

author-chef

But do not use a hyphen in a pair of nouns in which the first noun modifies the second.

father figure

opera lover

h. In general, do not use hyphens after prefixes (e.g., *anti-*, *co-*, *multi-*, *non-*, *over-*, *post-*, *pre-*, *re-*, *semi-*, *sub-*, *un-*, *under-*).

antiwar	overpay	semiretired
coworker	postwar	subsatellite
multinational	prescheduled	unambiguous
nonjudgmental	reinvigorate	underrepresented

But sometimes a hyphen is called for after a prefix:

post-Victorian   (Use a hyphen before a capital letter.)

re-cover   (The hyphen distinguishes this verb, meaning "cover again," from *recover*, meaning "get back" or "recuperate.")

anti-icing   (Without the hyphen, the doubled vowel would make the term hard to recognize.)

3.2.7. Apostrophes

A principal function of apostrophes is to indicate possession. They are also used to form contractions (*can't, wouldn't*), which are rarely acceptable in research papers, and the plurals of the letters of the alphabet (*p's and q's, three A's*).

a. To form the possessive of a singular noun, add an apostrophe and an *s*.

the zebra's stripes

a poem's meter

the dean's list

b. To form the possessive of a plural noun ending in *s*, add only an apostrophe.

photographers' props

firefighters' trucks

tourists' luggage

c. To form the possessive of an irregular plural noun not ending in *s*, add an apostrophe and an *s*.

children's entertainment

the media's role

women's studies

d. To form the possessive of nouns in a series, add a single apostrophe and an *s* if the ownership is shared.

Palmer and Colton's book on European history

Fred, Lucinda, and Nan's house

But if the ownership is separate, place an apostrophe and an *s* after each noun.

Fred's, Lucinda's, and Nan's coats

e. To form the possessive of any singular proper noun, add an apostrophe and an *s*.

Venus's beauty

Dickens's reputation

Descartes's philosophy

Marx's precepts

f. To form the possessive of a plural proper noun, add only an apostrophe.

the Vanderbilts' estate

the Dickenses' economic woes

g. Do not use an apostrophe to form the plural of an abbreviation or a number.

PhDs	1990s
MAs	fours
VCRs	SAT score in the 1400s
IRAs	

On using apostrophes to abbreviate dates, see 3.5.5.

3.2.8. Quotation Marks

a. Place quotation marks around a word or phrase given in a special sense or purposefully misused.

A silver dome concealed the robot's "brain."

Their "friend" brought about their downfall.

If introduced unnecessarily, this device can make writing heavy-handed. Quotation marks are not needed after *so-called*.

Their so-called friend brought about their downfall.

b. Use quotation marks for a translation of a foreign word or phrase.

Et ux., a legal abbreviation for the Latin et uxor, means "and wife."

The first idiomatic Spanish expression I learned was irse todo en humo ("to go up in smoke").

You may use single quotation marks for a translation that follows the original directly, without intervening words or punctuation.

The word text derives from the Latin verb texere 'to weave.'

On quotation marks with titles, see 3.6.3–4. On quotation marks with quotations and with translations of quotations, see 3.7.7 and 3.7.8, respectively.

3.2.9. Square Brackets

Use square brackets around a parenthesis within a parenthesis, so that the levels of subordination can be easily distinguished. Insert square brackets by hand if they are not available on your word processor or typewriter.

The sect known as the Jansenists (after Cornelius Jansen [1585-1638]) faced opposition from both the king and the pope.

The labors of Heracles (Hercules) included the slaying of the Nemean lion (so called because Hera [Juno] sent it to destroy the Nemean plain).

For square brackets around an ellipsis or an interpolation in a quotation, see 3.7.5 and 3.7.6, respectively. For square brackets around missing, unverified, or interpolated data in documentation, see 5.6.1, 5.6.23, and 5.6.25.

3.2.10. Slashes

The slash, or diagonal, is rarely necessary in formal prose. Other than in quotations of poetry (see 3.7.3), the slash has a place mainly between two terms paired as opposites or alternatives and used together as a noun.

The writer discussed how fundamental oppositions like good/evil,

East/West, and aged/young affect the way cultures view historical events.

But use a hyphen when such a compound precedes and modifies a noun.

nature-nurture conflict

either-or situation

East-West relations

3.2.11. Periods, Question Marks, and Exclamation Points

A sentence can end with a period, a question mark, or an exclamation point. Periods end declarative sentences. (For the use of periods with ellipsis points, see 3.7.5.) Question marks follow interrogative sentences. Except in direct quotation, avoid exclamation points in research writing.

Place a question mark inside a closing quotation mark if the quoted passage is a question. Place a question mark outside if the quotation ends a sentence that is a question. If a question mark occurs where a comma or period would normally be required, omit the comma or period. Note the use of the question mark and other punctuation marks in the following sentences:

Whitman asks, "Have you felt so proud to get at the meaning of poems?"

Where does Whitman speak of "the meaning of poems"?

"Have you felt so proud to get at the meaning of poems?" Whitman asks.

3.2.12. Spacing after Concluding Punctuation Marks

Publications in the United States today usually have the same spacing after a period, a question mark, or an exclamation point as between words on the same line. Since word processors make available the same fonts used by typesetters for printed works, many writers, influenced by the look of typeset publications, now leave only one space after a concluding punctuation mark. In addition, most publishers' guidelines for preparing a manuscript on disk ask professional authors to type only the spaces that are to appear in print.

Because it is increasingly common for papers and manuscripts to be prepared with a single space after all concluding punctuation marks, this spacing is shown in the examples in this handbook. As a practical matter, however, there is nothing wrong with using two spaces after concluding punctuation marks unless an instructor requests that you do otherwise. Whichever spacing you choose, be sure to use it consistently in all parts of your paper—the works-cited list as well as the main text. By contrast, internal punctuation marks, such as a colon, a comma, and a semicolon, should always be followed by one space.

3.3. ITALICS (UNDERLINING)

Italic is a style of type in which the characters slant to the right (*Casablanca*). In research papers and manuscripts submitted for publication, words that would be italicized in print are best underlined.

Casablanca

Most word-processing programs and computer printers permit the reproduction of italic type. In material that will be graded, edited, or typeset, however, the type style of every letter and punctuation mark must be easily recognizable. Italic type is sometimes not distinctive enough for this purpose, and you can avoid ambiguity by using underlining when you intend italics. If you wish to use italics rather than underlining, check your instructor's preferences. When preparing a manuscript for electronic publication, consult your editor or instructor on how to represent italicization.

In electronic environments that do not permit underlining, it is common to place one underline before and after each word or group of words that would be italicized in print.

Casablanca

Life Is a Dream

The rest of this section discusses using italics for words and letters referred to as words and letters (3.3.1), foreign words in an English text (3.3.2), and emphasis (3.3.3). (See 3.6.2 for italicizing of titles.)

3.3.1. Words and Letters Referred to as Words and Letters

Underline words and letters that are referred to as words and letters.

Shaw spelled Shakespeare without the final e.

The word albatross probably derives from the Spanish and Portuguese word alcatraz.

3.3.2. Foreign Words in an English Text

In general, underline foreign words used in an English text.

The Renaissance courtier was expected to display sprezzatura, or nonchalance, in the face of adversity.

The numerous exceptions to this rule include quotations entirely in another language ("Julius Caesar said, 'Veni, vidi, vici'"); non-English titles of short works (poems, short stories, essays, articles), which are placed in quotation marks and not underlined ("El sueño," the title of a poem by Quevedo); proper names (Marguerite de Navarre); and foreign words anglicized through frequent use. Since American English rapidly naturalizes words, use a dictionary to decide whether a foreign expression requires italics. Following are some adopted foreign words, abbreviations, and phrases commonly not underlined:

ad hoc	et al.	laissez-faire
cliché	etc.	lieder
concerto	genre	raison d'être
e.g.	hubris	versus

3.3.3. Emphasis

Italics for emphasis ("Booth *does* concede, however . . .") is a device that rapidly becomes ineffective. It is rarely appropriate in research writing.

3.4. NAMES OF PERSONS

3.4.1. First and Subsequent Uses of Names

In general, the first time you use a person's name in the text of your research paper, state it fully and accurately, exactly as it appears in your source.

Arthur George Rust, Jr.

Victoria M. Sackville-West

Do not change Arthur George Rust, Jr., to Arthur George Rust, for example, or drop the hyphen in Victoria M. Sackville-West. In subsequent references to the person, you may give the last name only (Rust, Sackville-West)—unless, of course, you refer to two or more persons with the same last name—or you may give the most common form of the name (e.g., Garcilaso for Garcilaso de la Vega). In casual references to the very famous—say, Mozart, Shakespeare, or Michelangelo—it is not necessary to give the full name initially.

In some languages (e.g., Chinese, Hungarian, Japanese, Korean, and Vietnamese), surnames precede given names; consult the *MLA Style Manual and Guide to Scholarly Publishing* (2nd ed. [New York: MLA, 1998], 3.6.7, 3.6.12) and other relevant reference works for guidance on these names. For rules concerning names of persons in other languages, see 3.8.

3.4.2. Titles of Persons

In general, do not use formal titles (Mr., Mrs., Miss, Ms., Dr., Professor, Reverend) in referring to men or women, living or dead (Churchill, not Mr. Churchill; Einstein, not Professor Einstein; Hess, not Dame Myra; Montagu, not Lady Montagu). A few women in history are traditionally known by their titles as married women (e.g., Mrs. Humphry Ward, Mme de Staël). Treat other women's names the same as men's.

FIRST USE	SUBSEQUENT USES
Emily Dickinson	Dickinson (not Miss Dickinson)
Harriet Beecher Stowe	Stowe (not Mrs. Stowe)
Margaret Mead	Mead (not Ms. Mead)

The appropriate way to refer to persons with titles of nobility can vary. For example, the full name and title of Henry Howard, earl of Surrey, should be given at first mention, and thereafter Surrey alone may be used. In contrast, for Benjamin Disraeli, first earl of Beaconsfield, it is sufficient to give Benjamin Disraeli initially and Disraeli subsequently. Follow the example of your sources in citing titles of nobility.

3.4.3. Names of Authors and Fictional Characters

It is common and acceptable to use simplified names of famous authors (Vergil for Publius Vergilius Maro, Dante for Dante Alighieri). Also acceptable are pseudonyms of authors.

Molière   (Jean-Baptiste Poquelin)

Voltaire   (François-Marie Arouet)

George Sand   (Amandine-Aurore-Lucie Dupin)

George Eliot   (Mary Ann Evans)

Mark Twain   (Samuel Clemens)

Stendhal   (Marie-Henri Beyle)

Novalis   (Friedrich von Hardenberg)

Refer to fictional characters in the same way that the work of fiction does. You need not always use their full names, and you may retain titles (Dr. Jekyll, Mme Defarge).

3.5. NUMBERS

3.5.1. Arabic Numerals

Although there are still a few well-established uses for roman numerals (see 3.5.7), virtually all numbers not spelled out are commonly represented today by arabic numerals. If your keyboard does not have the number *1*, use a small letter el (*l*), not capital *I*, for the arabic numeral. If your keyboard has the number *1*, do not substitute the small el.

3.5.2. Use of Words or Numerals

If you are writing about literature or another subject that involves infrequent use of numbers, you may spell out numbers written in one or two words and represent other numbers by numerals (*one, thirty-six, ninety-nine, one hundred, fifteen hundred, two thousand, three million,* but *2½, 101, 137, 1,275*). To form the plural of a spelled-out number, treat the word like an ordinary noun (*sixes, sevens*).

If your project is one that calls for frequent use of numbers—say, a paper on a scientific subject or a study of statistical findings—use numerals for all numbers that precede technical units of measurement (*16 amperes, 5 milliliters*). In such a project, also use numerals for numbers that are presented together and that refer to similar things, such as in comparisons or reports of experimental data. Spell out other numbers if they can be written in one or two words. In the following example of statistical writing, neither "ten years" nor "six-state region" is presented with related figures, so the numbers are spelled out, unlike the other numbers in the sentence.

> In the ten years covered by the study, the number of participating institutions in the United States doubled, reaching 90, and membership in the six-state region rose from 4 to 15.

But do not begin a sentence with a numeral.

> Nineteen ninety-two began with several good omens.

Except at the beginning of a sentence, always use numerals in the following instances:

WITH ABBREVIATIONS OR SYMBOLS

6 lbs.	4:20 p.m.	3%
8 KB	$9	2"

IN ADDRESSES

4401 13th Avenue

IN DATES

1 April 2001

April 1, 2001

IN DECIMAL FRACTIONS

8.3

IN PAGE REFERENCES

page 7

For large numbers, you may use a combination of numerals and words.

4.5 million

Express related numbers in the same style.

only 5 of the 250 delegates
exactly 3 automobiles and 129 trucks
from 1 billion to 1.2 billion

3.5.3. Commas in Numbers

Commas are usually placed between the third and fourth digits from the right, the sixth and seventh, and so on.

1,000
20,000
7,654,321

Following are some of the exceptions to this practice:

PAGE AND LINE NUMBERS

on page 1014

ADDRESSES

at 4132 Broadway

FOUR-DIGIT YEAR NUMBERS

in 1999

But commas are added in year numbers of five or more figures.

in 20,000 BC

3.5.4. Percentages and Amounts of Money

Treat percentages and amounts of money like other numbers: use numerals with the appropriate symbols.

1%	$5.35	68¢
45%	$35	
100%	$2,000	

In discussions involving infrequent use of numbers, you may spell out a percentage or an amount of money if you can do so in three words or fewer (*five dollars, forty-five percent, two thousand dollars, sixty-eight cents*). Do not combine spelled forms of numbers with symbols.

3.5.5. Dates and Times of the Day

Be consistent in writing dates: use either the day-month-year style (*22 July 1999*) or the month-day-year style (*July 22, 1999*) but not both. (If you begin with the month, be sure to add a comma after the day and also after the year, unless another punctuation mark goes there, such as a period or a question mark.) Do not use a comma between month and year (*August 1998*).

Spell out centuries in lowercase letters.

the twentieth century

Hyphenate centuries when they are used as adjectives before nouns.

eighteenth-century thought

nineteenth- and twentieth-century literature

Decades are usually written out without capitalization (*the nineties*), but it is acceptable to express them in figures (*the 1990s, the '60s*). Whichever form you use, be consistent.

The abbreviation *BC* follows the year, but *AD* precedes it.

19 BC

AD 565

Instead of *BC* and *AD,* some writers prefer to use *BCE,* "before the common era," and *CE,* "common era," both of which follow the year.

Numerals are used to indicate most times of the day (*2:00 p.m.*, *the 6:20 flight*). Exceptions include time expressed in quarter and half hours and in hours followed by *o'clock*.

a quarter to twelve

half past ten

five o'clock

3.5.6. Inclusive Numbers

In a range of numbers, give the second number in full for numbers through ninety-nine.

2-3	21-48
10-12	89-99

For larger numbers, give only the last two digits of the second number, unless more are necessary.

96-101	923-1,003
103-04	1,003-05
395-401	1,608-774

In a range of years beginning in AD 1000 or later, omit the first two digits of the second year if they are the same as the first two digits of the first year. Otherwise, write both years in full.

2000-03

1898-1901

In a range of years beginning from AD 1 through 999, follow the rules for inclusive numbers in general.

73-76

600-62

Do not abbreviate ranges of years that begin before AD 1.

748-742 BC

143 BC-AD 149

3.5.7. Roman Numerals

Use capital roman numerals for the primary divisions of an outline (see 1.8) and after the names of individuals in a series.

Elizabeth II

John D. Rockefeller IV

John Paul II

Use lowercase roman numerals for citing pages of a book that are so numbered (e.g., the pages in a preface). Write out inclusive roman numerals in full: *xxv–xxvi, xlvi–xlix*. Your instructor may prefer that you use roman numerals to designate acts and scenes of plays (see 6.4.8, on citing literary works).

3.6. TITLES OF WORKS IN THE RESEARCH PAPER

3.6.1. Capitalization and Punctuation

Whenever you cite the title of a published work in your research paper, take the title from the title page, not from the cover or from a running head at the top of a page. Do not reproduce any unusual typographic characteristics, such as special capitalization or lower-casing of all letters. A title page may present a title designed like one of the following examples:

MODERNISM & NEGRITUDE

BERNARD BERENSON
The Making of a Connoisseur

Turner's early sketchbooks

These titles should appear in a research paper as follows:

Modernism and Negritude

Bernard Berenson: The Making of a Connoisseur

Turner's Early Sketchbooks

The rules for capitalizing titles are strict. In a title or a sub-title, capitalize the first word, the last word, and all principal words, including those that follow hyphens in compound terms. Therefore, capitalize the following parts of speech:

- Nouns (e.g., *flowers* and *Europe*, as in *The Flowers of Europe*)
- Pronouns (e.g., *our*, as in *Save Our Children*; *that*, as in *The Mouse That Roared*)
- Verbs (e.g., *watches*, as in *America Watches Television*; *is*, as in *What Is Literature?*)
- Adjectives (e.g., *ugly*, as in *The Ugly Duckling*; *that*, as in *Who Said That Phrase?*)
- Adverbs (e.g., *slightly*, as in *Only Slightly Corrupt*; *down*, as in *Go Down, Moses*)
- Subordinating conjunctions (e.g., *after, although, as if, as soon as, because, before, if, that, unless, until, when, where, while*, as in *One If by Land* and *Anywhere That Chance Leads*)

Do not capitalize the following parts of speech when they fall in the middle of a title:

- Articles (*a, an, the*, as in *Under the Bamboo Tree*)
- Prepositions (e.g., *against, between, in, of, to*, as in *The Merchant of Venice* and "A Dialogue between the Soul and Body")
- Coordinating conjunctions (*and, but, for, nor, or, so, yet*, as in *Romeo and Juliet*)
- The *to* in infinitives (as in *How to Play Chess*)

Use a colon and a space to separate a title from a subtitle, unless the title ends in a question mark, an exclamation point, or a dash. Include other punctuation only if it is part of the title.

The following examples illustrate how to capitalize and punctuate a variety of titles. For a discussion of which titles to underline and which to place in quotation marks, see 3.6.2–3.

Death of a Salesman

The Teaching of Spanish in English-Speaking Countries

Storytelling and Mythmaking: Images from Film and Literature

Life As I Find It
The Artist as Critic
What Are You Doing in My Universe?
Whose Music? A Sociology of Musical Language
Where Did You Go? Out. What Did You Do? Nothing.
"Ode to a Nightingale"
"Italian Literature before Dante"
"What Americans Stand For"
"Why Fortinbras?"

When the first line of a poem serves as the title of the poem, reproduce the line exactly as it appears in the text.

Dickinson's poem "I heard a Fly buzz--when I died--" contrasts the everyday
and the momentous.

For rules concerning capitalization of titles in languages other
than English, see 3.8. See 3.6.4 for titles and quotations within titles.

3.6.2. Underlined Titles

In general, underline the titles of works published independently
(for works published within larger works, see 3.6.3). Titles to be underlined include the names of books, plays, long poems published as
books, pamphlets, periodicals (newspapers, magazines, and journals), films, radio and television programs, compact discs, audiocas-
settes, record albums, ballets, operas and other long musical
compositions (except those identified simply by form, number, and
key; see 3.6.5), paintings, works of sculpture, ships, aircraft, and
spacecraft. In the following examples, note that the underlining is
not broken between words. While there is no need to underline the
spaces between words, a continuous line is often the default in
word-processing programs, and it guards against the error of failing
to underline the punctuation within a title.

The Awakening   (book)
The Importance of Being Earnest   (play)
The Waste Land   (long poem published as a book)
New Jersey Driver Manual   (pamphlet)

Wall Street Journal   (newspaper)

Time   (magazine)

It's a Wonderful Life   (film)

Star Trek   (television program)

Sgt. Pepper's Lonely Hearts Club Band   (compact disc, audiocassette, record album)

The Nutcracker   (ballet)

Rigoletto   (opera)

Berlioz's Symphonie fantastique   (long musical composition identified by name)

Chagall's I and My Village   (painting)

French's The Minute Man   (sculpture)

USS Arizona   (ship)

Spirit of St. Louis   (aircraft)

Challenger   (spacecraft)

3.6.3. Titles in Quotation Marks

Use quotation marks for the titles of works published within larger works. Such titles include the names of articles, essays, short stories, short poems, chapters of books, individual episodes of television and radio programs, and short musical compositions (e.g., songs). Also use quotation marks for unpublished works, such as lectures and speeches.

"Rise in Aid to Education Is Proposed"   (newspaper article)

"Sources of Energy in the Next Decade"   (magazine article)

"Etruscan"   (encyclopedia article)

"The Fiction of Langston Hughes"   (essay in a book)

"The Lottery"   (short story)

"Kubla Khan"   (poem)

"The American Economy before the Civil War"   (chapter in a book)

"The Trouble with Tribbles"   (episode of the television program *Star Trek*)

"Mood Indigo"   (song)

"Preparing for a Successful Interview"   (lecture)

3.6.4. Titles and Quotations within Titles

Underline a title normally indicated by underlining when it appears within a title enclosed in quotation marks.

> "Romeo and Juliet and Renaissance Politics"   (an article about a play)
>
> "Language and Childbirth in The Awakening"   (an article about a novel)

Enclose in single quotation marks a title normally indicated by quotation marks when it appears within another title requiring quotation marks.

> "Lines after Reading 'Sailing to Byzantium'"   (a poem about a poem)
>
> "The Uncanny Theology of 'A Good Man Is Hard to Find'"   (an article about a short story)

Also place single quotation marks around a quotation that appears within a title requiring quotation marks.

> "Emerson's Strategies against 'Foolish Consistency'"   (an article with a quotation in its title)

Use quotation marks around a title normally indicated by quotation marks when it appears within an underlined title.

> "The Lottery" and Other Stories   (a book of short stories)
>
> New Perspectives on "The Eve of St. Agnes"   (a book about a poem)

If a period is required after an underlined title that ends with a quotation mark, place the period before the quotation mark.

> The study appears in New Perspectives on "The Eve of St. Agnes."

There are two common methods for identifying a normally underlined title when it appears within an underlined title. In one practice, the title within is neither underlined nor enclosed in quotation marks. This method is preferred in publications of the Modern Language Association.

> Approaches to Teaching Murasaki Shikibu's The Tale of Genji   (a book about a novel)
>
> From The Lodger to The Lady Vanishes: Hitchcock's Classic British Thrillers   (a book about films)

In the other method, all titles within underlined titles are placed in quotation marks and underlined.

Approaches to Teaching Murasaki Shikibu's "The Tale of Genji"

From "The Lodger" to "The Lady Vanishes": Hitchcock's Classic British

Thrillers

Each approach has advantages and disadvantages. In the first method, the titles of works published independently and the material containing them are always given opposite treatments. This practice has the advantage of consistency, but it can lead to ambiguity: it is sometimes hard to tell where a title like *Approaches to Teaching Murasaki Shikibu's* The Tale of Genji ends and where the adjacent text begins.

The second method prevents confusion between titles and the adjacent text. However, it treats titles of works published independently two ways: they receive quotation marks in underlined titles but nowhere else. In addition, within underlined titles this method abandons the distinction between works that are published independently and those that are not.

Whichever practice you choose or your instructor requires, follow it consistently throughout your paper.

3.6.5. Exceptions

The convention of using underlining and quotation marks to indicate titles does not apply to the names of sacred writings (including all books and versions of the Bible); of laws, acts, and similar political documents; of instrumental musical compositions identified by form, number, and key; of series, societies, buildings, and monuments; and of conferences, seminars, workshops, and courses. These terms all appear without underlining or quotation marks.

SACRED WRITINGS

Bible	Gospels
King James Version	Talmud
Old Testament	Koran
Genesis	Upanishads

But underline titles of individual published editions of sacred writings (*The Interlinear Bible, The Talmud of the Land of Israel: A Preliminary Translation and Explanation, The Upanishads: A Selection for the Modern Reader*) and treat the editions in the works-cited list like any other published book.

LAWS, ACTS, AND SIMILAR POLITICAL DOCUMENTS

Magna Carta

Declaration of Independence

Bill of Rights

Treaty of Trianon

INSTRUMENTAL MUSICAL COMPOSITIONS IDENTIFIED BY FORM, NUMBER, AND KEY

Beethoven's Symphony no. 7 in A, op. 92

Vivaldi's Concerto for Two Trumpets and Strings in C, RV539

SERIES

Bollingen Series

University of North Carolina Studies in Comparative Literature

Masterpiece Theatre

SOCIETIES

American Medical Association

Renaissance Society of America

BUILDINGS AND MONUMENTS

Moscone Center

Sears Tower

Arch of Constantine

CONFERENCES, SEMINARS, WORKSHOPS, AND COURSES

Strengthening the Cooperative Effort in Biomedical Research: A National
    Conference for Universities and Industry

Geographic Information Analysis Workshop

MLA Annual Convention

Introduction to Calculus

Anthropology 102

Words designating the divisions of a work are also not underlined or put within quotation marks, nor are they capitalized when used in the text ("The author says in her preface . . . ," "In canto 32 Ariosto writes . . .").

preface	appendix	scene 7
introduction	index	stanza 20
list of works cited	chapter 2	canto 32
bibliography	act 4	

3.6.6. Shortened Titles

If you cite a title often in the text of your paper, you may, after stating the title in full at least once, use a shortened form, preferably a familiar or obvious one (e.g., "Nightingale" for "Ode to a Nightingale"), or an abbreviation (for standard abbreviated titles of literary and religious works, see 7.7).

3.7. QUOTATIONS

3.7.1. Use and Accuracy of Quotations

Quotations are effective in research papers when used selectively. Quote only words, phrases, lines, and passages that are particularly interesting, vivid, unusual, or apt, and keep all quotations as brief as possible. Overquotation can bore your readers and might lead them to conclude that you are neither an original thinker nor a skillful writer.

The accuracy of quotations in research writing is extremely important. They must reproduce the original sources exactly. Unless indicated in brackets or parentheses (see 3.7.6), changes must not be made in the spelling, capitalization, or interior punctuation of the source. You must construct a clear, grammatically correct sentence that allows you to introduce or incorporate a quotation with complete accuracy. Alternatively, you may paraphrase the original and quote only fragments, which may be easier to integrate into the text. If you change a quotation in any way, make the alteration clear to the reader, following the rules and recommendations below.

3.7.2. Prose

If a prose quotation runs no more than four lines and requires no special emphasis, put it in quotation marks and incorporate it into the text.

> "It was the best of times, it was the worst of times," wrote Charles Dickens of the eighteenth century.

You need not always reproduce complete sentences. Sometimes you may want to quote just a word or phrase as part of your sentence.

> For Charles Dickens the eighteenth century was both "the best of times" and "the worst of times."

You may put a quotation at the beginning, middle, or end of your sentence or, for the sake of variety or better style, divide it by your own words.

> Joseph Conrad writes of the company manager in Heart of Darkness, "He was obeyed, yet he inspired neither love nor fear, nor even respect."

or

> "He was obeyed," writes Joseph Conrad of the company manager in Heart of Darkness, "yet he inspired neither love nor fear, nor even respect."

If a quotation ending a sentence requires a parenthetical reference, place the sentence period after the reference. (For more information on punctuating quotations, see 3.7.7.)

> For Charles Dickens the eighteenth century was both "the best of times" and "the worst of times" (35).

> "He was obeyed," writes Joseph Conrad of the company manager in Heart of Darkness, "yet he inspired neither love nor fear, nor even respect" (87).

If a quotation runs to more than four lines in your paper, set it off from your text by beginning a new line, indenting one inch (or ten spaces if you are using a typewriter) from the left margin, and typing it double-spaced, without adding quotation marks. A colon generally introduces a quotation displayed in this way, though sometimes the context may require a different mark of punctuation or none at all. If you quote only a single paragraph or part of one, do not indent the first line more than the rest. A parenthetical reference to a prose quotation set off from the text follows the last line of the quotation.

> At the conclusion of <u>Lord of the Flies</u>, Ralph and the other boys realize the
> horror of their actions:
>
>> The tears began to flow and sobs shook him. He gave himself up
>> to them now for the first time on the island; great, shuddering
>> spasms of grief that seemed to wrench his whole body. His voice
>> rose under the black smoke before the burning wreckage of the
>> island; and infected by that emotion, the other little boys began to
>> shake and sob too. (186)

If you need to quote two or more paragraphs, indent the first line of each paragraph an additional quarter inch (or three spaces on a typewriter). If the first sentence quoted does not begin a paragraph in the source, however, do not indent it the additional amount. Indent only the first lines of the successive paragraphs.

> In <u>Moll Flanders</u> Defoe maintains the pseudoautobiographical narration
> typical of the picaresque tradition:
>
>> My true name is so well known in the records, or registers, at
>> Newgate and in the Old Bailey, and there are some things of such
>> consequence still depending there relating to my particular
>> conduct, that it is not to be expected I should set my name or the
>> account of my family to this work. . . .
>>> It is enough to tell you, that . . . some of my worst comrades,
>> who are out of the way of doing me harm . . . know me by the
>> name of Moll Flanders. . . . (1)

On omitting words within quotations, see 3.7.5. For translations of quotations, see 3.7.8.

3.7.3. Poetry

If you quote part or all of a single line of verse that does not require special emphasis, put it in quotation marks within your text. You may also incorporate two or three lines in this way, using a slash with a space on each side (/) to separate them.

Bradstreet frames the poem with a sense of mortality: "All things within this
fading world hath end" (1).

Reflecting on the "incident" in Baltimore, Cullen concludes, "Of all the
things that happened there / That's all that I remember" (11-12).

Verse quotations of more than three lines should begin on a new
line. Unless the quotation involves unusual spacing, indent each
line one inch (or ten spaces on a typewriter) from the left margin
and double-space between lines, adding no quotation marks that do
not appear in the original. A parenthetical reference for a verse quotation set off from the text follows the last line of the quotation (as
in quotations of prose); a parenthetical reference that will not fit on
the line should appear on a new line, flush with the right margin of
the page.

Elizabeth Bishop's "In the Waiting Room" is rich in evocative detail:

It was winter. It got dark

early. The waiting room

was full of grown-up people,

arctics and overcoats,

lamps and magazines. (6-10)

A line that is too long to fit within the right margin should be continued on the next line and the continuation indented an additional
quarter inch (or three spaces). You may reduce the indentation of the
quotation to less than one inch (or ten spaces) from the left margin
if doing so will eliminate the need for such continuations. If the
spatial arrangement of the original lines, including indentation and
spacing within and between them, is unusual, reproduce it as accurately as possible.

E. E. Cummings concludes the poem with this vivid description of a carefree
scene, reinforced by the carefree form of the lines themselves:

it's

spring

and

    the

        goat-footed

balloonMan   whistles

far

and

wee (16-24)

When a verse quotation begins in the middle of a line, the partial line should be positioned where it is in the original and not shifted to the left margin.

In a poem on Thomas Hardy ("T. H."), Molly Holden recalls her encounter with a "young dog fox" one morning:

>   I remember
> he glanced at me in just that way, independent
> and unabashed, the handsome sidelong look
> that went round and about but never directly
> met my eyes, for that would betray his soul.
> He was not being sly, only careful. (43-48)

For translations of quotations, see 3.7.8.

3.7.4. Drama

If you quote dialogue between two or more characters in a play, set the quotation off from your text. Begin each part of the dialogue with the appropriate character's name indented one inch (or ten spaces if you are using a typewriter) from the left margin and written in all capital letters: HAMLET. Follow the name with a period, and start the quotation. Indent all subsequent lines in that character's speech an additional quarter inch (or three spaces). When the dialogue shifts to another character, start a new line indented one inch (or ten spaces) from the left margin. Maintain this pattern throughout the entire quotation. For the other aspects of formatting, follow the recommendations above for quoting prose and poetry (3.7.2–3).

Marguerite Duras's screenplay for Hiroshima mon amour suggests at the outset the profound difference between observation and experience:

> HE. You saw nothing in Hiroshima. Nothing.
>
> SHE. I saw everything. Everything. . . . The hospital, for instance, I saw it. I'm sure I did. There is a hospital in Hiroshima. How could I help seeing it?
>
> HE. You did not see the hospital in Hiroshima. You saw nothing in Hiroshima. (2505-06)

113

A short time later Lear loses the final symbol of his former power, the
soldiers who make up his train:

> GONERIL.   Hear me, my lord.
> What need you five-and-twenty, ten or five,
> To follow in a house where twice so many
> Have a command to tend you?
> REGAN.   What need one?
> LEAR. O, reason not the need! (2.4.254-58)

3.7.5. Ellipsis

Whenever you wish to omit a word, a phrase, a sentence, or more
from a quoted passage, you should be guided by two principles: fair-
ness to the author quoted and the grammatical integrity of your writing. A quotation should never be presented in a way that could
cause a reader to misunderstand the sentence structure of the original source. If you quote only a word or a phrase, it will be obvious
that you left out some of the original sentence.

> In his inaugural address, John F. Kennedy spoke of a "new frontier."

But if omitting material from the original sentence or sentences
leaves a quotation that appears to be a sentence or a series of sentences, you must use ellipsis points, or spaced periods, to indicate
that your quotation does not completely reproduce the original.
Whenever you omit words from a quotation, the resulting passage—
your prose and the quotation integrated into it—should be grammatically complete and correct.

For an ellipsis within a sentence, use three periods with a space
before each and a space after the last (. . .).

ORIGINAL

Medical thinking, trapped in the theory of astral influences, stressed
air as the communicator of disease, ignoring sanitation or visible
carriers. (Barbara W. Tuchman, *A Distant Mirror: The Calamitous
Fourteenth Century* [1978; New York: Ballantine, 1979] 101–02)

QUOTATION WITH AN ELLIPSIS IN THE MIDDLE

In surveying various responses to plagues in the Middle Ages, Barbara W. Tuchman writes, "Medical thinking . . . stressed air as the communicator of disease, ignoring sanitation or visible carriers."

QUOTATION WITH AN ELLIPSIS IN THE MIDDLE AND A PARENTHETICAL REFERENCE

In surveying various responses to plagues in the Middle Ages, Barbara W. Tuchman writes, "Medical thinking . . . stressed air as the communicator of disease, ignoring sanitation or visible carriers" (101-02).

When the ellipsis coincides with the end of your sentence, use three periods with a space before each following a sentence period—that is, four periods, with no space before the first or after the last.

QUOTATION WITH AN ELLIPSIS AT THE END

In surveying various responses to plagues in the Middle Ages, Barbara W. Tuchman writes, "Medical thinking, trapped in the theory of astral influences, stressed air as the communicator of disease. . . ."

If a parenthetical reference follows the ellipsis at the end of your sentence, however, use three periods with a space before each, and place the sentence period after the final parenthesis.

QUOTATION WITH AN ELLIPSIS AT THE END FOLLOWED BY A PARENTHETICAL REFERENCE

In surveying various responses to plagues in the Middle Ages, Barbara W. Tuchman writes, "Medical thinking, trapped in the theory of astral influences, stressed air as the communicator of disease . . ." (101-02).

In a quotation of more than one sentence, an ellipsis in the middle can indicate the omission of any amount of text.

ORIGINAL

Presidential control reached its zenith under Andrew Jackson, the extent of whose attention to the press even before he became a candidate is suggested by the fact that he subscribed to twenty newspapers. Jackson was never content to have only one organ grinding out his tune. For a time, the *United States Telegraph* and the *Washington Globe* were almost equally favored as party organs, and there were fifty-seven journalists on the government payroll. (William L.

Rivers, *The Mass Media: Reporting, Writing, Editing*, 2nd ed. [New York: Harper, 1975] 7)

QUOTATION OMITTING A SENTENCE

In discussing the historical relation between politics and the press, William L. Rivers notes:

> Presidential control reached its zenith under Andrew Jackson, the extent of whose attention to the press even before he became a candidate is suggested by the fact that he subscribed to twenty newspapers. . . . For a time, the United States Telegraph and the Washington Globe were almost equally favored as party organs, and there were fifty-seven journalists on the government payroll. (7)

QUOTATION WITH AN OMISSION FROM THE MIDDLE OF ONE SENTENCE TO THE END OF ANOTHER

In discussing the historical relation between politics and the press, William L. Rivers notes, "Presidential control reached its zenith under Andrew Jackson. . . . For a time, the United States Telegraph and the Washington Globe were almost equally favored as party organs, and there were fifty-seven journalists on the government payroll" (7).

QUOTATION WITH AN OMISSION FROM THE MIDDLE OF ONE SENTENCE TO THE MIDDLE OF ANOTHER

In discussing the historical relation between politics and the press, William L. Rivers notes that when presidential control "reached its zenith under Andrew Jackson, . . . there were fifty-seven journalists on the government payroll" (7).

The omission of words and phrases from quotations of poetry is also indicated by three or four spaced periods (as in quotations of prose).

ORIGINAL

In Worcester, Massachusetts,
I went with Aunt Consuelo
to keep her dentist's appointment
and sat and waited for her
in the dentist's waiting room.
It was winter. It got dark
early. The waiting room
was full of grown-up people,

arctics and overcoats,
lamps and magazines.
(Elizabeth Bishop, "In the Waiting Room," lines 1–10)

QUOTATION WITH AN ELLIPSIS AT THE END

Elizabeth Bishop's "In the Waiting Room" is rich in evocative detail:

> In Worcester, Massachusetts,
>
> I went with Aunt Consuelo
>
> to keep her dentist's appointment
>
> and sat and waited for her
>
> in the dentist's waiting room.
>
> It was winter. It got dark
>
> early. The waiting room
>
> was full of grown-up people. . . . (1-8)

The omission of a line or more in the middle of a poetry quotation that is set off from the text is indicated by a line of spaced periods approximately the length of a complete line of the quoted poem.

QUOTATION OMITTING A LINE OR MORE IN THE MIDDLE

Elizabeth Bishop's "In the Waiting Room" is rich in evocative detail:

> In Worcester, Massachusetts,
>
> I went with Aunt Consuelo
>
> to keep her dentist's appointment
>
> . . . .
>
> It was winter. It got dark
>
> early. (1-3, 6-7)

Some instructors prefer that square brackets be placed around ellipsis points inserted into quotations, so that all alterations within quotations are indicated by brackets (cf. 3.7.6). Regardless of which practice you follow, if the author you are quoting uses ellipsis points, you should put brackets around your ellipses to distinguish them from those of the author.

ORIGINAL

"We live in California, my husband and I, Los Angeles. . . . This is beautiful country; I have never been here before." (N. Scott Momaday, *House Made of Dawn* [1968; New York: Perennial-Harper, 1977] 29)

QUOTATION WITH AN ADDED ELLIPSIS IN BRACKETS

In N. Scott Momaday's <u>House Made of Dawn</u>, when Mrs. St. John arrives at
the rectory, she tells Father Olguin, "We live in California, my husband and I,
Los Angeles. . . . [. . .] I have never been here before" (29).

3.7.6. Other Alterations of Sources

Occasionally, you may decide that a quotation will be unclear or
confusing to your reader unless you provide supplementary information. For example, you may need to insert material missing from the
original, to add *sic* (from the Latin for "thus" or "so") to assure readers that the quotation is accurate even though the spelling or logic
might make them think otherwise, or to underline words for emphasis. While such contributions to a quotation are permissible, you
should keep them to a minimum and make sure to distinguish them
from the original, usually by explaining them in parentheses after
the quotation or by putting them in square brackets within the
quotation.

A comment or an explanation that immediately follows the closing quotation mark appears in parentheses.

Shaw admitted, "Nothing can extinguish my interest in Shakespear" (sic).

Lincoln specifically advocated a government "<u>for</u> the people" (emphasis
added).

A comment or an explanation that goes inside the quotation must
appear within square brackets, not parentheses.

He claimed he could provide "hundreds of examples [of court decisions] to
illustrate the historical tension between church and state."

Milton's Satan speaks of his "study [pursuit] of revenge."

Similarly, if a pronoun in a quotation seems unclear, you may add an
identification in square brackets.

In the first act he soliloquizes, "Why she would hang on him [Hamlet's
father] / As if increase of appetite had grown / By what it fed on. . . ."

3.7.7. Punctuation with Quotations

Whether set off from the text or run into it, quoted material is usually preceded by a colon if the quotation is formally introduced and
by a comma or no punctuation if the quotation is an integral part of
the sentence structure.

> Shelley held a bold view: "Poets are the unacknowledged legislators of the
> World" (794).

> Shelley thought poets "the unacknowledged legislators of the World" (794).

> "Poets," according to Shelley, "are the unacknowledged legislators of the
> World" (794).

Do not use opening and closing quotation marks to enclose quotations set off from the text, but reproduce any quotation marks that
are in the passage quoted.

> In "Memories of West Street and Lepke," Robert Lowell, a conscientious
> objector (or "C.O."), recounts meeting a Jehovah's Witness in prison:
>> I was so out of things, I'd never heard
>> of the Jehovah's Witnesses.
>> "Are you a C.O.?" I asked a fellow jailbird.
>> "No," he answered, "I'm a J.W." (36-39)

Use double quotation marks around quotations incorporated into
the text, single quotation marks around quotations within those
quotations.

> In "Memories of West Street and Lepke," Robert Lowell, a conscientious
> objector (or "C.O."), recounts meeting a Jehovah's Witness in prison: "'Are
> you a C.O.?' I asked a fellow jailbird. / 'No,' he answered, 'I'm a J.W.'" (38-
> 39).

Except for changing internal double quotation marks to single ones
when you incorporate quotations into your text, you should reproduce internal punctuation exactly as in the original. The closing punctuation, though, depends on where the quoted material appears in
your sentence. Suppose, for example, that you want to quote the following sentence: "You've got to be carefully taught." If you begin

your sentence with this line, you have to replace the closing period with a punctuation mark appropriate to the new context.

> "You've got to be carefully taught," wrote Oscar Hammerstein II about how racial prejudice is perpetuated.

If the quotation ends with a question mark or an exclamation point, however, the original punctuation is retained, and no comma is required.

> "How can I describe my emotions at this catastrophe, or how delineate the wretch whom with such infinite pains and care I had endeavoured to form?" wonders the doctor in Mary Shelley's Frankenstein (42).

> "What a wonderful little almanac you are, Celia!" Dorothea Brooke responds to her sister (7).

By convention, commas and periods that directly follow quotations go inside the closing quotation marks, but a parenthetical reference should intervene between the quotation and the required punctuation. Thus, if a quotation ends with a period, the period appears after the reference.

> N. Scott Momaday's House Made of Dawn begins with an image that also concludes the novel: "Abel was running" (7).

If a quotation ends with both single and double quotation marks, the comma or period precedes both.

> "Read 'Kubla Khan,'" he told me.

All other punctuation marks—such as semicolons, colons, question marks, and exclamation points—go outside a closing quotation mark, except when they are part of the quoted material.

ORIGINAL

I believe taxation without representation is tyranny!

QUOTATIONS

He attacked "taxation without representation" (32).

Did he attack "taxation without representation"?

What dramatic events followed his attack on "taxation without representation"!

but

> He declared, "I believe taxation without representation is tyranny!"

If a quotation ending with a question mark or an exclamation point concludes your sentence and requires a parenthetical reference, retain the original punctuation within the quotation mark and follow with the reference and the sentence period outside the quotation mark.

> In Mary Shelley's Frankenstein, the doctor wonders, "How can I describe my emotions at this catastrophe, or how delineate the wretch whom with such infinite pains and care I had endeavoured to form?" (42).

> Dorothea Brooke responds to her sister, "What a wonderful little almanac you are, Celia!" (7).

3.7.8. Translations of Quotations

If you believe that a significant portion of your audience will not be familiar with the language of a quotation you present, you should add a translation. If the translation is not yours, give its source in addition to the source of the quotation. In general, the translation should immediately follow the quotation whether they are run into or set off from the text, although their order may be reversed if most readers will not likely be able to read the original. If the quotation is run into the text, use double quotation marks around a translation placed in parentheses following the quotation but single quotation marks around a translation that immediately follows without intervening punctuation.

> Chaucer's setting is April, the time of "shoures soote" ("sweet showers"; GP 1).
> Chaucer's setting is April, the time of "shoures soote" 'sweet showers' (GP 1).

Do not use quotation marks around quotations and translations set off from the text.

> Dante's Inferno begins literally in the middle of things:
>> Nel mezzo del cammin di nostra vita
>> mi ritrovai per una selva oscura,
>> ché la diritta via era smarrita.

Ahi quanto a dir qual era è cosa dura

esta selva selvaggia e aspra e forte

che nel pensier rinova la paura! (1.1-6)

Midway in our life's journey, I went astray

from the straight road and woke to find myself

alone in a dark wood. How shall I say

what wood that was! I never saw so drear,

so rank, so arduous a wilderness!

Its very memory gives a shape to fear. (Ciardi 28)

See also 3.2.8b for guidelines on translating a foreign word or phrase within a sentence.

3.8. CAPITALIZATION AND PERSONAL NAMES IN LANGUAGES OTHER THAN ENGLISH

The following section contains recommendations for writing personal names and for capitalizing in French, German, Italian, Spanish, and Latin. If you need such rules for other languages or if you need information on transliterating from languages that do not use the Latin alphabet, such as Russian or Chinese, consult the *MLA Style Manual and Guide to Scholarly Publishing*.

3.8.1. French

Personal Names

With some exceptions, especially in English-language contexts, French *de* following a first name or a title such as *Mme* or *duc* is not used with the last name alone.

La Boétie   (Etienne de La Boétie)

La Bruyère   (Jean de La Bruyère)

Maupassant   (Guy de Maupassant)

Nemours   (Louis-Charles d'Orléans, duc de Nemours)

Ronsard   (Pierre de Ronsard)

Scudéry   (Madeleine de Scudéry)

but

De Quincey (Thomas De Quincey)

When the last name has only one syllable, however, *de* is usually retained.

de Gaulle (Charles de Gaulle)

The preposition also remains, in the form *d'*, when it elides with a last name beginning with a vowel.

d'Arcy (Pierre d'Arcy)

d'Arsonval (Arsène d'Arsonval)

The forms *du* and *des*—combinations of *de* with *le* and *les*—are always used with last names and are capitalized.

Des Périers (Bonaventure Des Périers)

Du Bos (Charles Du Bos)

A hyphen is frequently used between French given names, as well as between their initials (Marie-Joseph Chénier, M.-J. Chénier). Note that *M.* and *P.* before names may be abbreviations for the titles *Monsieur* 'Mr.' and *Père* 'Father' (M. René Char, P. J. Reynard).

Capitalization

In prose and verse, French capitalization is the same as English except that the following terms are not capitalized in French unless they begin sentences or, sometimes, lines of verse: (1) the subject pronoun *je* 'I,' (2) the names of months and days of the week, (3) the names of languages, (4) adjectives derived from proper nouns, (5) titles preceding personal names, and (6) the words meaning "street," "square," "lake," "mountain," and so on, in most place-names.

Un Français m'a parlé anglais près de la place de la Concorde.

Hier j'ai vu le docteur Maurois qui conduisait une voiture Ford.

Le capitaine Boutillier m'a dit qu'il partait pour Rouen le premier jeudi d'avril avec quelques amis normands.

There are two widely accepted methods of capitalizing French titles and subtitles of works. One method is to capitalize the first word in titles and subtitles and all proper nouns in them. This method is normally followed in publications of the Modern Language Association.

L'ami du peuple

La chambre claire: Note sur la photographie

Du côté de chez Swann

Le grand Meaulnes

La guerre de Troie n'aura pas lieu

Nouvelle revue d'onomastique

In the other method, when a title or subtitle begins with an article, the first noun and any preceding adjectives are also capitalized.

L'Ami du peuple

La Chambre claire: Note sur la photographie

Du côté de chez Swann

Le Grand Meaulnes

La Guerre de Troie n'aura pas lieu

In this system, all major words in titles of series and periodicals are sometimes capitalized.

Nouvelle Revue d'Onomastique

Whichever practice you choose or your instructor requires, follow it consistently throughout your paper.

3.8.2. German

Personal Names

German *von* is generally not used with the last name alone, but there are some exceptions, especially in English-language contexts, where the *von* is firmly established by convention.

Droste-Hülshoff   (Annette von Droste-Hülshoff)

Kleist   (Heinrich von Kleist)

but

Von Braun   (Wernher Von Braun)

Von Trapp   (Maria Von Trapp)

In alphabetizing a German name with an umlaut (the mark over the vowel in *ä*, *ö*, *ü*), Germanists treat the umlauted vowel as if it were followed by an *e*; thus *Götz* would be alphabetized as *Goetz* and would precede *Gott* in an alphabetical listing. Nonspecialists, however, and many libraries in English-speaking countries alphabetize such names without regard to the umlaut; in this practice, *Götz* would be alphabetized as *Gotz* and would therefore follow *Gott* in an alphabetical listing.

Capitalization

In prose and verse, German capitalization differs considerably from English. Always capitalized in German are all nouns—including adjectives, infinitives, pronouns, prepositions, and other parts of speech used as nouns—as well as the pronoun *Sie* 'you' and its possessive, *Ihr* 'your,' and their inflected forms. Not capitalized unless they begin sentences or, usually, lines of verse are (1) the subject pronoun *ich* 'I,' (2) the names of languages and of days of the week used as adjectives, adverbs, or complements of prepositions, and (3) adjectives and adverbs formed from proper nouns, except when the proper nouns are names of persons and the adjectives and adverbs refer to the persons' works or deeds.

Ich glaube an das Gute in der Welt.

Er schreibt, nur um dem Auf und Ab der Buch-Nachfrage zu entsprechen.

Fahren Sie mit Ihrer Frau zurück?

Ein französischer Schriftsteller, den ich gut kenne, arbeitet sonntags immer an seinem neuen Buch über die platonische Liebe.

Der Staat ist eine der bekanntesten Platonischen Schriften.

In letters and ceremonial writings, the pronouns *du* and *ihr* 'you' and their derivatives are capitalized.

In a title or a subtitle, capitalize the first word and all words normally capitalized.

Thomas Mann und die Grenzen des Ich

Ein treuer Diener seines Herrn

Zeitschrift für vergleichende Sprachforschung

3.8.3. Italian

Personal Names

The names of many Italians who lived before or during the Renaissance are alphabetized by first name.

Dante Alighieri

Giotto di Bondone

Leonardo da Vinci

Michelangelo Buonarroti

Piero della Francesca

But other names of the period follow the standard practice.

Boccaccio, Giovanni

Cellini, Benvenuto

Stampa, Gaspara

The names of members of historic families are also usually alphabetized by last name.

Este, Beatrice d'

Medici, Lorenzo de'

In modern times, Italian *da, de, del, della, di,* and *d'* are used with the last name. They are usually capitalized and are treated as an integral part of the name, even though a space may separate the prepositional from the nominal part of the name.

D'Annunzio   (Gabriele D'Annunzio)

Da Ponte   (Lorenzo Da Ponte)

Del Buono   (Oreste Del Buono)

Della Robbia   (Andrea Della Robbia)

De Sica   (Vittorio De Sica)

Di Costanzo   (Angelo Di Costanzo)

Capitalization

In prose and verse, Italian capitalization is the same as English except that in Italian, centuries and other large divisions of time are capitalized (*il Seicento*) and the following terms are not capitalized unless they begin sentences or, usually, lines of verse: (1) the subject pronoun *io* 'I,' (2) the names of months and days of the week, (3) the names of languages and nationalities, (4) nouns, adjectives, and adverbs derived from proper nouns, (5) titles preceding personal names, and (6) the words meaning "street," "square," and so on, in most place-names.

Un italiano parlava francese con uno svizzero in piazza di Spagna.

Il dottor Bruno ritornerà dall'Italia giovedì otto agosto e io partirò il nove.

In a title or a subtitle, capitalize only the first word and all words normally capitalized.

L'arte tipografica in Urbino

Bibliografia della critica pirandelliana

Collezione di classici italiani

Dizionario letterario Bompiani

Studi petrarcheschi

3.8.4. Spanish

Personal Names

Spanish *de* is not used before the last name alone.

Las Casas (Bartolomé de Las Casas)

Madariaga (Salvador de Madariaga)

Rueda (Lope de Rueda)

Timoneda (Juan de Timoneda)

Spanish *del*, formed from the fusion of the preposition *de* and the definite article *el*, is capitalized and used with the last name alone.

Del Río (Angel Del Río)

A Spanish surname may include both the paternal name and the maternal name, with or without the conjunction *y*. The surname of a married woman usually includes her paternal surname and her husband's paternal surname, connected by *de*. Alphabetize Spanish names by the full surnames (consult your sources or a biographical dictionary for guidance in distinguishing surnames and given names).

Carreño de Miranda, Juan

Cervantes Saavedra, Miguel de

Díaz del Castillo, Bernal

García Márquez, Gabriel

Larra y Sánchez de Castro, Mariano José

López de Ayala, Pero

Matute, Ana María

Ortega y Gasset, José

Quevedo y Villegas, Francisco Gómez de

Sinues de Marco, María del Pilar

Zayas y Sotomayor, María de

Even persons commonly known by the maternal portions of their surnames, such as Galdós and Lorca, should be indexed under their full surnames.

García Lorca, Federico

Pérez Galdós, Benito

Capitalization

In prose and verse, Spanish capitalization is the same as English except that the following terms are not capitalized in Spanish unless they begin sentences or, sometimes, lines of verse: (1) the subject pronoun *yo* 'I,' (2) the names of months and days of the week, (3) the names of languages and nationalities, (4) nouns and adjectives derived from proper nouns, (5) titles preceding personal names, and (6) the words meaning "street," "square," and so on, in most place-names.

El francés hablaba inglés en la plaza Colón.

Ayer yo vi al doctor García en un coche Ford.

Me dijo don Jorge que iba a salir para Sevilla el primer martes de abril con unos amigos neoyorkinos.

In a title or a subtitle, capitalize only the first word and words normally capitalized.

Breve historia del ensayo hispanoamericano

Extremos de América

La gloria de don Ramiro

Historia verdadera de la conquista de la Nueva España

Revista de filología española

Trasmundo de Goya

Some instructors follow other rules. In titles of series and periodicals, they capitalize all major words: *Revista de Filología Española*.

3.8.5. Latin

Personal Names

Roman male citizens generally had three names: a praenomen (given name), a nomen (clan name), and a cognomen (family or familiar name). Men in this category are usually referred to by nomen, cognomen, or both; your source or a standard reference book such as *The Oxford Classical Dictionary* will provide guidance.

Brutus   (Marcus Iunius Brutus)

Calpurnius Siculus   (Titus Calpurnius Siculus)

Cicero   (Marcus Tullius Cicero)

Lucretius   (Titus Lucretius Carus)

Plautus   (Titus Maccius Plautus)

Roman women usually had two names—a nomen (the clan name in the feminine form) and a cognomen (often derived from the father's cognomen): Livia Drusilla (daughter of Marcus Livius Drusus). Sometimes a woman's cognomen indicates her chronological order among the daughters of the family: Antonia Minor (younger daughter of Marcus Antonius). Most Roman women are referred to by nomen: Calpurnia, Clodia, Octavia, Sulpicia. Some, however, are better known by cognomen: Agrippina (Vipsania Agrippina).

When citing Roman names, use the forms most common in English.

Horace (Quintus Horatius Flaccus)

Julius Caesar (Gaius Iulius Caesar)

Juvenal (Decimus Iunius Iuvenalis)

Livy (Titus Livius)

Ovid (Publius Ovidius Naso)

Quintilian (Marcus Fabius Quintilianus)

Terence (Publius Terentius Afer)

Vergil (Publius Vergilius Maro)

Finally, some medieval and Renaissance figures are best known by their adopted or assigned Latin names.

Albertus Magnus (Albert von Bollstädt)

Comenius (Jan Amos Komenský)

Copernicus (Niklas Koppernigk)

Paracelsus (Theophrastus Bombast von Hohenheim)

Capitalization

Although practice varies, Latin most commonly follows the English rules for capitalization, except that *ego* 'I' is not capitalized.

Semper ego auditor tantum? Numquamne reponam / Vexatus totiens rauci Theseide Cordi?

Quidquid id est, timeo Danaos et dona ferentes.

Nil desperandum.

Quo usque tandem abutere, Catilina, patientia nostra?

In a title or a subtitle, however, capitalize only the first word and all words normally capitalized.

De senectute

Liber de senectute

Medievalia et humanistica

4 The Format of the Research Paper

If your instructor has specific requirements for the format of a research paper, check them before preparing your final draft. The recommendations presented in this chapter are the most common.

4.1. PRINTING OR TYPING

If you composed your paper on a computer, keep the following guidelines in mind:

- Choose a standard, easily readable typeface (e.g., Times Roman) and type size (e.g., 12 point).
- Do not justify the lines of your paper at the right margin.
- Turn off your word processor's automatic hyphenation feature.
- Use a high-quality printer.
- Print on one side of the paper only.
- Keep a backup copy on disk.

If you are using a typewriter, make certain the ribbon produces dark, clear type, and type on one side of the paper. Instructors who accept handwritten work similarly require neatness, legibility, dark blue or black ink, and the use of only one side of the paper. Always be sure to keep a copy of the paper.

4.2. PAPER

Use only white, 8½-by-11-inch paper of good quality. Do not submit work typed on erasable paper, which smudges easily. If you find erasable paper convenient to use for your final draft, submit a high-quality photocopy to your instructor.

4.3. MARGINS

Except for page numbers, leave margins of one inch at the top and bottom and on both sides of the text. (For placement of page numbers, see 4.6.) Indent the first word of a paragraph one-half inch (or five spaces) from the left margin. Indent set-off quotations one inch (or ten spaces) from the left margin. (For examples, see 3.7 and the sample first page of a research paper at the end of this book.)

4.4. SPACING

A research paper must be double-spaced throughout, including quotations, notes, and the list of works cited. In a handwritten paper, skip every other ruled line. Leave one space after a period or other concluding punctuation mark, unless your instructor prefers two spaces. (See the sample pages of a research paper at the end of this book.)

4.5. HEADING AND TITLE

A research paper does not need a title page. Instead, beginning one inch from the top of the first page and flush with the left margin, type your name, your instructor's name, the course number, and the date on separate lines, double-spacing between the lines. Double-space again and center the title. Double-space also between the lines of the title, and double-space between the title and the first line of the text (see fig. 9). Do not underline your title or put it in quotation marks or type it in all capital letters. Follow the rules for capitalization in 3.6.1, and underline only the words that you would underline in the text (see 3.3 and 3.6.2).

Local Television Coverage of International News Events

The Attitude toward Violence in <u>A Clockwork Orange</u>

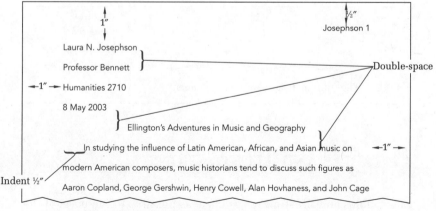

Fig. 9. The top of the first page of a research paper.

The Use of the Words <u>Fair</u> and <u>Foul</u> in Shakespeare's <u>Macbeth</u>

Romanticism in England and the <u>Scapigliatura</u> in Italy

Do not use a period after your title or after any heading in the paper (e.g., *Works Cited*).

If your teacher requires a title page, format it according to the instructions you are given.

4.6. PAGE NUMBERS

Number all pages consecutively throughout the research paper in the upper right-hand corner, one-half inch from the top and flush with the right margin. Type your last name before the page number, as a precaution in case of misplaced pages. Word processors with automatic page numbering will save you the time and effort of numbering every page. A word processor allows you to create a running head that consists of your last name followed by a space and the page number. Do not use the abbreviation *p.* before a page number or add a period, a hyphen, or any other mark or symbol. Beginning with page 2, position the first line of text one inch from the top of the page (see fig. 10). The word processor may automatically insert your running head on every page of your paper if you do not specify otherwise. Some teachers, however, prefer that no number appear on the first page. Follow your teacher's preference.

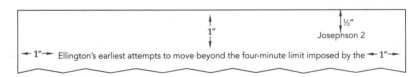

Fig. 10. The running head of a research paper.

4.7. TABLES AND ILLUSTRATIONS

Place tables and illustrations as close as possible to the parts of the text to which they relate. A table is usually labeled *Table*, given an arabic numeral, and captioned. Type both label and caption flush left on separate lines above the table, and capitalize them as you would a title (do not use all capital letters). Give the source of the table and any notes immediately below the table. To avoid confusion between notes to the text and notes to the table, designate notes to the table with lowercase letters rather than with numerals. Double-space throughout; use dividing lines as needed (see fig. 11).

Table 1

Earned Degrees in Modern Foreign Languages Conferred by Institutions of
  Higher Education in the United States[a]

Year	Bachelor's Degrees	Master's Degrees	Doctor's Degrees
1987-88	9,790	1,795	380
1988-89	10,498	1,821	389
1989-90	11,092	1,931	475
1990-91	11,724	1,973	477
1991-92	12,367	2,119	537
1992-93	12,819	2,353	535
1993-94	12,785	2,343	578
1994-95	12,309	2,306	626
1995-96	13,020	2,443	636
1996-97	12,256	2,229	622
1997-98	12,769	2,064	628

Source: United States, Dept. of Educ., Office of Educ. Research and
  Improvement, Natl. Center for Educ. Statistics, Digest of Education
  Statistics, 2000 (Washington: GPO, 2000) table 288.
  [a] These figures include degrees conferred in a single modern foreign
language or a combination of modern foreign languages and exclude degrees
in linguistics, Latin, classical Greek, and some not commonly taught modern
languages.

Fig. 11. A table in a research paper.

135

Any other type of illustrative visual material—for example, a photograph, map, line drawing, graph, or chart—should be labeled *Figure* (usually abbreviated *Fig.*), assigned an arabic numeral, and given a title or caption: "Fig. 1. Mary Cassatt, *Mother and Child*, Wichita Art Museum." A label and title or caption ordinarily appear directly below the illustration and have the same one-inch margins as the text of the paper (see fig. 12).

Fig. 1. Manticore, woodcut from Edward Topsell, The History of Four-Footed Beasts and Serpents . . . (London, 1658) 344; rpt. in Konrad Gesner, Curious Woodcuts of Fanciful and Real Beasts (New York: Dover, 1971) 8.

Fig. 12. A figure in a research paper.

If your research papers have many illustrations, you will probably want to become familiar with the various kinds of software for the creation of tables, graphs, drawings, and so forth, on a computer. These programs automatically number tables and illustrations, set them appropriately into the text, and generate a listing of all tables and illustrations created for the paper.

Musical illustrations are labeled *Example* (usually abbreviated *Ex.*), assigned an arabic numeral, and given a title or caption: "Ex. 1.

Ex. 1. Ludwig van Beethoven, Symphony no. 3 in E flat, op. 55 (Eroica), first movement, opening.

Fig. 13. A musical example in a research paper.

Pyotr Ilich Tchaikovsky, Symphony no. 6 in B, op. 74 (*Pathétique*), finale." A label and title or caption ordinarily appear directly below the example and have the same one-inch margins as the text of the paper (see fig. 13).

4.8. CORRECTIONS AND INSERTIONS

Proofread and correct your research paper carefully before submitting it. If you find a mistake in the final copy and you are using a word processor, recall the file, make the appropriate revisions, and reprint the corrected page or pages. Be sure to save the changed file. Some writers find such software as spelling checkers and usage checkers helpful when used with caution (see 1.9.3). If you are not using a computer and if your instructor permits brief corrections, write them neatly and legibly in ink directly above the lines involved, using carets (∧) to indicate where they go. Do not use the margins or write a change below the line it affects. If corrections on any page are numerous or substantial, retype the page.

4.9. BINDING

Pages of your research paper may get misplaced or lost if they are left unattached or merely folded down at a corner. Although a plastic folder or some other kind of binder may seem an attractive finishing touch, most instructors find such devices a nuisance in reading and commenting on students' work. Many prefer that a paper be secured with a simple paper clip, which can be easily removed and restored.

4.10. ELECTRONIC SUBMISSION

There are at present no commonly accepted standards for the electronic submission of research papers. If you are asked to submit your paper electronically, obtain from your teacher guidelines for formatting, mode of submission (e.g., on disk, by e-mail, on a Web site), and so forth, and follow them closely.

To facilitate discussion of your work, you should incorporate in the paper reference markers that can be cited the way page numbers in a printed paper are. Numbering paragraphs is becoming common in electronic publications. If you use this system, place the appropriate number, in brackets—"[12]"—and followed by a space, at the beginning of each paragraph.

⑤ Documentation: Preparing the List of Works Cited

5.1. DOCUMENTING SOURCES

Nearly all research builds on previous research. Researchers commonly begin a project by studying past work in the area and deriving relevant information and ideas from their predecessors. This process is largely responsible for the continual expansion of human knowledge. In presenting their work, researchers generously acknowledge their debts to predecessors by carefully documenting each source, so that earlier contributions receive appropriate credit.

As you prepare your paper, you should similarly seek to build on the work of previous writers and researchers. And whenever you draw on another's work, you must also document your source by indicating what you borrowed—whether facts, opinions, or quotations—and where you borrowed it from. If you have not already done so, read carefully the earlier section on plagiarism (ch. 2) to learn what you must document in your paper.

5.2. MLA STYLE

In MLA documentation style, you acknowledge your sources by keying brief parenthetical citations in your text to an alphabetical list of works that appears at the end of the paper. The parenthetical citation that concludes the following sentence is typical of MLA style.

Ancient writers attributed the invention of the monochord to Pythagoras, who lived in the sixth century BC (Marcuse 197).

The citation "(Marcuse 197)" tells readers that the information in the sentence was derived from page 197 of a work by an author named Marcuse. If readers want more information about this source, they can turn to the works-cited list, where, under the name Marcuse, they would find the following information.

Marcuse, Sibyl. A Survey of Musical Instruments. New York: Harper, 1975.

This entry states that the work's author is Sibyl Marcuse and its title is *A Survey of Musical Instruments*. The remaining information relates, in shortened form, that the work was published in New York City by Harper and Row in 1975.

A citation in MLA style contains only enough information to

enable readers to find the source in the works-cited list. If the author's name is mentioned in the text, only the page number appears in the citation: "(197)." If more than one work by the author is in the list of works cited, a shortened version of the title is given: "(Marcuse, *Survey* 197)." (See ch. 6 for a fuller discussion of parenthetical citations in MLA style.)

MLA style is not the only way to document sources. Many disciplines have their own documentation systems. MLA style is widely used in the humanities. Although generally simpler and more economical than other documentation styles, it shares with most others its central feature: parenthetical citations keyed to a works-cited list. If you learn MLA documentation style at an early stage in your school career, you will probably have little difficulty in adapting to other styles.

Documentation styles differ according to discipline because they are shaped by the kind of research and scholarship undertaken. For example, in the sciences, where timeliness of research is crucial, the date of publication is usually given prominence. Thus, in the style recommended by the American Psychological Association (APA), a typical citation includes the date of publication (as well as the abbreviation *p.* before the page number). Compare APA and MLA parenthetical citations for the same source.

APA

(Marcuse, 1975, p. 197)

MLA

(Marcuse 197)

In the humanities, where most important scholarship remains relevant for a substantial period, publication dates receive less attention: though always stated in the works-cited list, they are omitted in parenthetical references. An important reason for this omission is that many humanities scholars like to keep their texts as readable and as free of disruptions as possible.

In an entry for a book in an APA-style works-cited list, the date (in parentheses) immediately follows the name of the author (whose first name is written only as an initial), just the first word of the title is capitalized, and the publisher's full name is generally provided. In APA style, the titles of books and journals are italicized. (See also B.2.)

APA

Marcuse, S. (1975). *A survey of musical instruments*. New York: Harper &
Row.

By contrast, in an MLA-style entry, the author's name appears as
given in the work (normally in full), every important word of the
title is capitalized, the publisher's name is shortened, and the publication date is placed at the end. A book title is underlined (on
underlining vs. italics, see 3.3). In both styles, the first line of the
entry is flush with the left margin, and second and subsequent lines
are indented.

MLA

Marcuse, Sibyl. A Survey of Musical Instruments. New York: Harper,
1975.

Chapters 5 and 6 offer an authoritative and comprehensive presentation of MLA style. For descriptions of other systems of documentation, including one using endnotes and footnotes, see appendix B.

5.3. THE LIST OF WORKS CITED AND OTHER SOURCE LISTS

Although the list of works cited appears at the end of your paper,
you need to draft the section in advance, so that you will know what
information to give in parenthetical references as you write. For
example, you have to include shortened titles if you cite two or more
works by the same author, and you have to add initials or first names
if two of the cited authors have the same last name: "(K. Roemer
123–24)," "(M. Roemer 67)." This chapter therefore explains how to
prepare a list of works cited, and the next chapter demonstrates how
to document sources where you use them in your text.

As the heading *Works Cited* indicates, this list contains all the
works that you will cite in your text. The list simplifies documentation by permitting you to make only brief references to these works
in the text. For example, when you have the following entry in your
list of works cited, a citation such as "(Thompson 32–35)" fully
identifies your source to readers (provided that you cite no other
work by an author with the same last name).

Thompson, Stith. The Folktale. New York: Dryden, 1946.

Other names for such a listing are *Bibliography* (literally, "description of books") and *Literature Cited.* Usually, however, the broader title *Works Cited* is most appropriate, since research papers often draw not only on books and articles but also on films, recordings, television programs, and other nonprint sources.

Titles used for other kinds of source lists include *Annotated Bibliography, Works Consulted,* and *Selected Bibliography.* An annotated bibliography, also called *Annotated List of Works Cited,* contains descriptive or evaluative comments on the sources. (For more information on such listings, see James L. Harner, *On Compiling an Annotated Bibliography,* 2nd ed. [New York: MLA, 2000].)

Thompson, Stith. The Folktale. New York: Dryden, 1946. A comprehensive survey of the most popular folktales, including their histories and their uses in literary works.

The title *Works Consulted* indicates that the list is not confined to works cited in the paper. The heading *Selected Bibliography,* or *Selected List of Works Consulted,* is appropriate for lists suggesting readings in the field.

5.4. FORMAT OF THE LIST OF WORKS CITED

The list of works cited appears at the end of the paper. Begin the list on a new page and number each page, continuing the page numbers of the text. For example, if the text of your research paper ends on page 10, the works-cited list begins on page 11. The page number appears in the upper right-hand corner, half an inch from the top and flush with the right margin (see fig. 14, on the next page). Center the title, *Works Cited,* an inch from the top of the page. Double-space between the title and the first entry. Begin each entry flush with the left margin; if an entry runs more than one line, indent the subsequent line or lines one-half inch (or five spaces if you are using a typewriter) from the left margin. This format is sometimes called *hanging indention,* and you can set your word processor to create it automatically for a group of paragraphs. Hanging indention makes alphabetical lists easier to use. Double-space the entire list, both between and within entries. Continue the list on as many pages as necessary.

145

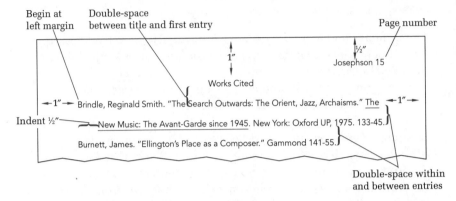

Fig. 14. The top of the first page of a works-cited list.

5.5. ARRANGEMENT OF ENTRIES

In general, alphabetize entries in the list of works cited by the author's last name, using the letter-by-letter system. In this system, the alphabetical order of names is determined by the letters before the commas that separate last names and first names. Spaces and other punctuation marks are ignored. The letters after the commas are considered only when two or more last names are identical. The following examples are alphabetized letter by letter. (For more information on alphabetizing foreign names, see 3.8.)

Descartes, René
De Sica, Vittorio

MacDonald, George
McCullers, Carson

Morris, Robert
Morris, William
Morrison, Toni

Saint-Exupéry, Antoine de
St. Denis, Ruth

If two or more entries citing coauthors begin with the same name, alphabetize by the last names of the second authors listed.

Scholes, Robert, and Robert Kellogg

Scholes, Robert, Carl H. Klaus, and Michael Silverman

Scholes, Robert, and Eric S. Rabkin

If the author's name is unknown, alphabetize by the title, ignoring any initial *A*, *An*, or *The*. For example, the title *An Encyclopedia of the Latin-American Novel* would be alphabetized under *e* rather than *a*. An alphabetical listing makes it easy for the reader to find the entry corresponding to a citation in the text.

Other kinds of bibliographies may be arranged differently. An annotated list, a list of works consulted, or a list of selected readings for a historical study, for example, may be organized chronologically by publication date. Some bibliographies are divided into sections and the items alphabetized in each section. A list may be broken down into primary and secondary sources or into different research media (books, articles, recordings). Alternatively, it may be arranged by subject matter (literature and law, law in literature, law as literature), by period (classical utopia, Renaissance utopia), or by area (Egyptian mythology, Greek mythology, Norse mythology).

5.6. CITING BOOKS AND OTHER NONPERIODICAL PUBLICATIONS

5.6.1. The Basic Entry: A Book by a Single Author

One of the most common items in students' works-cited lists is the entry for a book by a single author. Such an entry characteristically has three main divisions:

Author's name. Title of the book. Publication information.

Here is an example:

Fukuyama, Francis. Our Posthuman Future: Consequences of the Biotechnology Revolution. New York: Farrar, 2002.

Author's Name

Reverse the author's name for alphabetizing, adding a comma after the last name (Porter, Katherine Anne). Put a period after the complete name (see fig. 15).

Fukuyama, Francis.

Apart from reversing the order, give the author's name as it appears on the title page. Never abbreviate a name given in full. If, for example, the title page lists the author as "Carleton Brown," do not enter the name as "Brown, C." But use initials if the title page does.

Eliot, T. S.

McLuhan, H. Marshall.

You may spell out a name abbreviated on the title page if you think the additional information would be helpful to readers. Put square brackets around the material you add.

Rowling, J[oanne] K[athleen].

Tolkien, J[ohn] R[onald] R[euel].

Similarly, you may give the real name of an author listed under a pseudonym, enclosing the added name in square brackets.

Le Carré, John [David Cornwell].

In general, omit titles, affiliations, and degrees that precede or follow names.

ON TITLE PAGE	IN WORKS-CITED LIST
Anthony T. Boyle, PhD	Boyle, Anthony T.
Sister Jean Daniel	Daniel, Jean.
Gerard Manley Hopkins, SJ	Hopkins, Gerard Manley.
Lady Mary Wortley Montagu	Montagu, Mary Wortley.
Sir Philip Sidney	Sidney, Philip.
Saint Teresa de Jesús	Teresa de Jesús.

A suffix that is an essential part of the name—like *Jr.* or a roman numeral—appears after the given name, preceded by a comma.

Rockefeller, John D., IV.

Rust, Arthur George, Jr.

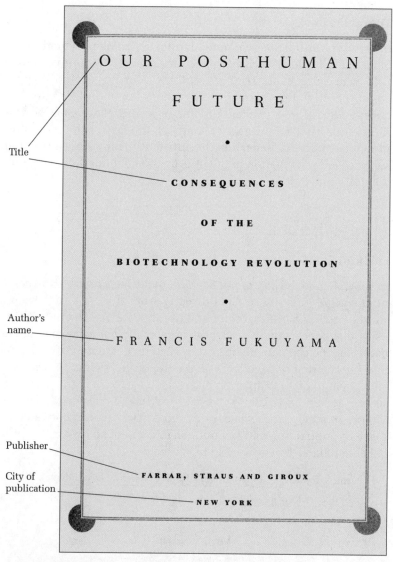

Fig. 15. The title page of a book, with full title, author's name, publisher, and city of publication. Give the author's name as on the title page. Reverse the name for alphabetizing: "Fukuyama, Francis." Place a colon between a main title and a subtitle (unless the main title ends in a question mark, an exclamation point, or a dash). Follow the capitalization rules in 3.6.1 regardless of how the title is printed on the title page: *Our Posthuman Future: Consequences of the Biotechnology Revolution.* Shorten the publisher's name, following the guidelines in 7.5: "New York: Farrar." (See fig. 16, on the next page, for the publication date of this book.)

Title of the Book

In general, follow the recommendations for titles provided in 3.6. State the full title of the book, including any subtitle, as given on the title page of the book (see fig. 15). If the book has a subtitle, put a colon directly after the main title, unless the main title ends in a question mark, an exclamation point, or a dash. Place a period after the entire title (including any subtitle), unless it ends in another punctuation mark. Underline the entire title, including any colon, subtitle, and punctuation in the title, but do not underline the period that follows the title.

> Fukuyama, Francis. Our Posthuman Future: Consequences of the
> Biotechnology Revolution.

Publication Information

In general, give the *city of publication*, *publisher's name*, and *year of publication*. Take these facts directly from the book, not from a source such as a bibliography or a library catalog. The publisher's name that appears on the title page is generally the name to cite. The name may be accompanied there by the city and date. Any publication information not available on the title page (see fig. 15) can usually be found on the copyright page (i.e., the reverse of the title page; see fig. 16) or, particularly in books published outside the United States, on a page at the back of the book. Use a colon between the place of publication and the publisher, a comma between the publisher and the date, and a period after the date.

> Fukuyama, Francis. Our Posthuman Future: Consequences of the
> Biotechnology Revolution. New York: Farrar, 2002.

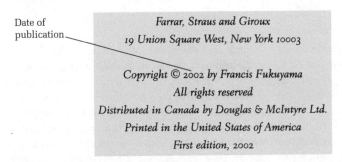

Date of
publication

Farrar, Straus and Giroux
19 Union Square West, New York 10003

Copyright © 2002 by Francis Fukuyama
All rights reserved
Distributed in Canada by Douglas & McIntyre Ltd.
Printed in the United States of America
First edition, 2002

Fig. 16. The year of publication. If no year appears on the title page, look on the copyright page. Usually the latest copyright date should be cited.

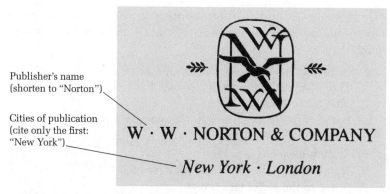

Publisher's name
(shorten to "Norton")

Cities of publication
(cite only the first:
"New York")

W · W · NORTON & COMPANY

New York · London

Fig. 17. More than one city of publication. If several cities are listed, give only the first: "New York: Norton."

If several cities are listed in the book, give only the first (see fig. 17). For cities outside the United States, add an abbreviation of the country (or of the province for cities in Canada) if the name of the city may be ambiguous or unfamiliar to your reader (see 7.3 for abbreviations of geographic names).

Manchester, Eng.

Sherbrooke, QC

Shorten the publisher's name, following the guidelines in 7.5. If the year of publication is not recorded on the title page, use the latest copyright date.

Here are some additional examples of the basic book entry:

Berlage, Gai Ingham. Women in Baseball: The Forgotten History. Westport: Greenwood, 1994.

Freedman, Richard R. What Do Unions Do? New York: Basic, 1984.

Kurlansky, Mark. Salt: A World History. New York: Walker, 2002.

Le Carré, John [David Cornwell]. The Constant Gardener. New York: Scribner's, 2001.

Rowling, J[oanne] K[athleen]. Harry Potter and the Goblet of Fire. New York: Levine-Scholastic, 2000.

Silver, Lee M. Remaking Eden: Cloning and Beyond in a Brave New World. New York: Avon, 1997.

Tatar, Maria. Off with Their Heads! Fairy Tales and the Culture of Childhood. Princeton: Princeton UP, 1992.

Sometimes additional information is required. This list shows most of the possible components of a book entry and the order in which they are normally arranged:

1. Author's name
2. Title of a part of the book (see esp. 5.6.7–9)
3. Title of the book
4. Name of the editor, translator, or compiler (see esp. 5.6.7 and 5.6.12–13)
5. Edition used (see 5.6.14)
6. Number(s) of the volume(s) used (see 5.6.15)
7. Name of the series (see 5.6.16)
8. Place of publication, name of the publisher, and date of publication
9. Page numbers (see esp. 5.6.7)
10. Supplementary bibliographic information and annotation (see esp. 5.6.13 and 5.6.15)

The rest of 5.6 explains how to cite these items. To cite an online book, see 5.9.3.

5.6.2. An Anthology or a Compilation

To cite an anthology or a compilation (e.g., a bibliography) that was edited or compiled by someone whose name appears on the title page, begin your entry with the name of the editor or compiler, followed by a comma and the abbreviation *ed.* or *comp.* If the person named performed more than one function—serving, say, as editor and translator—give both roles in the order in which they appear on the title page (see fig. 18).

Lopate, Phillip, ed. The Art of the Personal Essay: An Anthology from the Classical Era to the Present. New York: Anchor-Doubleday, 1994.

Sevillano, Mando, comp. The Hopi Way: Tales from a Vanishing Culture. Flagstaff: Northland, 1986.

Spafford, Peter, comp. and ed. Interference: The Story of Czechoslovakia in the Words of Its Writers. Cheltenham: New Clarion, 1992.

Weisser, Susan Ostrov, ed. Women and Romance: A Reader. New York: New York UP, 2001.

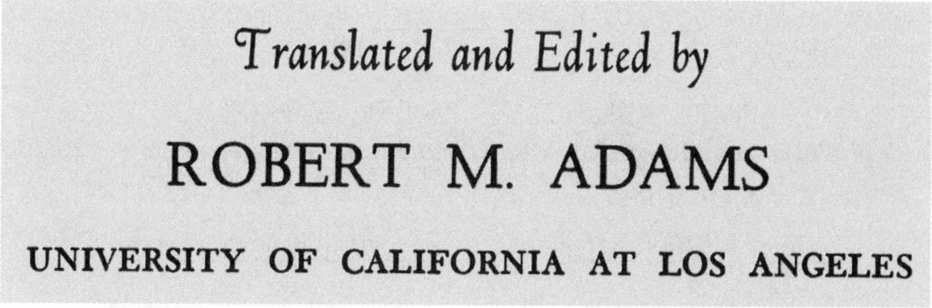

Translated and Edited by

ROBERT M. ADAMS

UNIVERSITY OF CALIFORNIA AT LOS ANGELES

Fig. 18. More than one role. If someone is credited with more than one role
on the title page, cite the roles in the order in which they are listed: "Adams,
Robert M., trans. and ed." (or "Trans. and ed. Robert M. Adams" [see 5.6.7]).

See also the sections on works in an anthology (5.6.7); introductions,
prefaces, and similar parts of books (5.6.9); editions (5.6.12); and
translations (5.6.13).

5.6.3. Two or More Books by the Same Author

To cite two or more books by the same author, give the name in the
first entry only. Thereafter, in place of the name, type three hyphens,
followed by a period and the title. The three hyphens stand for
exactly the same name as in the preceding entry. If the person named
edited, translated, or compiled the book, place a comma (not a
period) after the three hyphens, and write the appropriate abbreviation (*ed., trans.,* or *comp.*) before giving the title. If the same person
served as, say, the editor of two or more works listed consecutively,
the abbreviation *ed.* must be repeated with each entry. This sort of
label does not affect the order in which entries appear; works listed
under the same name are alphabetized by title.

Borroff, Marie. Language and the Past: Verbal Artistry in Frost, Stevens, and
     Moore. Chicago: U of Chicago P, 1979.

---, trans. Sir Gawain and the Green Knight. New York: Norton, 1967.

---, ed. Wallace Stevens: A Collection of Critical Essays. Englewood Cliffs:
     Prentice, 1963.

Frye, Northrop. Anatomy of Criticism: Four Essays. Princeton: Princeton
UP, 1957.

---, ed. Design for Learning: Reports Submitted to the Joint Committee of
the Toronto Board of Education and the University of Toronto. Toronto:
U of Toronto P, 1962.

---. The Double Vision: Language and Meaning in Religion. Toronto: U of
Toronto P, 1991.

---, ed. Sound and Poetry. New York: Columbia UP, 1957.

5.6.4. A Book by Two or More Authors

To cite a book by two or three authors, give their names in the same
order as on the title page—not necessarily in alphabetical order.
Reverse only the name of the first author, add a comma, and give the
other name or names in normal form (Wellek, René, and Austin Warren). Place a period after the last name. Even if the authors have the
same last name, state each name in full (Durant, Will, and Ariel
Durant). If the persons listed on the title page are editors, translators,
or compilers, place a comma (not a period) after the final name and
add the appropriate abbreviation (*eds., trans.,* or *comps.,* for "editors," "translators," or "compilers").

Eggins, Suzanne, and Diana Slade. Analysing Casual Conversation. London:
Cassell, 1997.

Hutcheon, Linda, and Michael Hutcheon. Bodily Charm: Living Opera.
Lincoln: U of Nebraska P, 2000.

Marquart, James W., Sheldon Ekland Olson, and Jonathan R. Sorensen. The
Rope, the Chair, and the Needle: Capital Punishment in Texas, 1923-
1990. Austin: U of Texas P, 1994.

Rabkin, Eric S., Martin H. Greenberg, and Joseph D. Olander, eds. No Place
Else: Explorations in Utopian and Dystopian Fiction. Carbondale:
Southern Illinois UP, 1983.

If there are more than three authors, you may name only the first and
add *et al.* ("and others"), or you may give all names in full in the
order in which they appear on the title page (see fig. 19).

Gilman, Sander, et al. Hysteria beyond Freud. Berkeley: U of California
P, 1993.

A
COMPREHENSIVE
GRAMMAR
OF THE
ENGLISH
LANGUAGE

Randolph Quirk
Sidney Greenbaum
Geoffrey Leech
Jan Svartvik

Fig. 19. More than three authors. Give either the first name only, followed by *et al.* ("and others")—"Quirk, Randolph, et al."—or all names in full in the order in which they appear on the title page: "Quirk, Randolph, Sidney Greenbaum, Geoffrey Leech, and Jan Svartvik."

Quirk, Randolph, et al. A Comprehensive Grammar of the English Language. London: Longman, 1985.

or

Gilman, Sander, Helen King, Roy Porter, George Rousseau, and Elaine Showalter. Hysteria beyond Freud. Berkeley: U of California P, 1993.

Quirk, Randolph, Sidney Greenbaum, Geoffrey Leech, and Jan Svartvik. A Comprehensive Grammar of the English Language. London: Longman, 1985.

If a single author cited in an entry is also the first of multiple authors in the following entry, repeat the name in full; do not substitute three hyphens. Repeat the name in full whenever you cite the same person as part of a different authorship. The three hyphens are never used in combination with persons' names.

Scholes, Robert. The Crafty Reader. New Haven: Yale UP, 2001.

---. Textual Power: Literary Theory and the Teaching of English. New Haven: Yale UP, 1985.

Scholes, Robert, and Robert Kellogg. The Nature of Narrative. New York: Oxford UP, 1966.

Scholes, Robert, and Eric S. Rabkin. Science Fiction: History, Science, Vision. New York: Oxford UP, 1977.

Tannen, Deborah, ed. Gender and Conversational Interaction. New York: Oxford UP, 1993.

---. You Just Don't Understand: Women and Men in Conversation. New York: Morrow, 1990.

Tannen, Deborah, and James E. Alatis, eds. Languages and Linguistics: The Interdependence of Theory, Data, and Application. Washington: Georgetown UP, 1986.

Tannen, Deborah, and Muriel Saville-Troike, eds. Perspectives on Silence. Norwood: Ablex, 1985.

5.6.5. Two or More Books by the Same Authors

To cite two or more books by the same authors, give the names in the first entry only. Thereafter, in place of the names, type three hyphens, followed by a period and the title. The three hyphens stand for exactly the same names as in the preceding entry.

Durant, Will, and Ariel Durant. The Age of Voltaire. New York: Simon, 1965.

---. A Dual Autobiography. New York: Simon, 1977.

Gilbert, Sandra M. Ghost Volcano: Poems. New York: Norton, 1995.

---, ed. Inventions of Farewell: A Book of Elegies. New York: Norton, 2001.

Gilbert, Sandra M., and Susan Gubar. The Madwoman in the Attic: The Woman Writer and the Nineteenth-Century Literary Imagination. New Haven: Yale UP, 1979.

---, eds. The Norton Anthology of Literature by Women: The Tradition in
     English. 2nd ed. New York: Norton, 1996.

5.6.6. A Book by a Corporate Author

A corporate author may be a commission, an association, a committee, or any other group whose individual members are not identified
on the title page. Omit any initial article (*A, An, The*) in the name of
the corporate author (see fig. 20). Cite the book by the corporate
author, even if the corporate author is the publisher. (On citing government publications, see 5.6.21.)

American Medical Association. The American Medical Association
     Encyclopedia of Medicine. Ed. Charles B. Clayman. New York:
     Random, 1989.
National Research Council. Beyond Six Billion: Forecasting the World's
     Population. Washington: Natl. Acad., 2000.
Public Agenda Foundation. The Health Care Crisis: Containing Costs,
     Expanding Coverage. New York: McGraw, 1992.

Fig. 20. A corporate author. In citing a book by a corporate author, omit any
initial *A, An,* or *The* in the name of the group. The entry for this publication
would begin "American Philosophical Association."

5.6.7. A Work in an Anthology

If you are citing an essay, a short story, a poem, or another work that appears within an anthology or some other book collection, you need to add the following information to the basic book entry (5.6.1).

Author, title, and (if relevant) translator of the part of the book being cited. Begin the entry with the author and title of the piece, normally enclosing the title in quotation marks.

> Allende, Isabel. "Toad's Mouth."

But if the work was originally published independently (as, e.g., autobiographies, plays, and novels generally are), underline its title instead (see the sample entries below for Douglass and Hansberry). Follow the title of the part of the book with a period. If the anthology contains the work of more than one translator, give the translator's name next, preceded by the abbreviation *Trans.* ("Translated by").

> Allende, Isabel. "Toad's Mouth." Trans. Margaret Sayers Peden.

Then state the title of the anthology (underlined).

> Allende, Isabel. "Toad's Mouth." Trans. Margaret Sayers Peden. A Hammock
> beneath the Mangoes: Stories from Latin America.

Name of the editor, translator, or compiler of the book being cited. If all the works in the collection have the same translator or if the book has an editor or compiler, write *Trans., Ed.,* or *Comp.* ("Translated by," "Edited by," or "Compiled by"), as appropriate, after the book title and give that person's name.

> Allende, Isabel. "Toad's Mouth." Trans. Margaret Sayers Peden. A Hammock
> beneath the Mangoes: Stories from Latin America. Ed. Thomas Colchie.

If someone served in more than one role—say, as editor and translator—state the roles in the order in which they appear on the title page (e.g., "Ed. and trans."; see the entry below for Hanzlík). Similarly, if more than one person served in different roles, give the names in the order in which they appear on the title page: "Trans. Jessie Coulson. Ed. George Gibian."

Page numbers of the cited piece. Give the inclusive page numbers of the piece you are citing. Be sure to provide the page numbers for the entire piece, not just for the material you used. Inclusive page numbers, usually without any identifying abbreviation, follow the publication date and a period. (If the book has no page numbers, see 5.6.25.)

Allende, Isabel. "Toad's Mouth." Trans. Margaret Sayers Peden. A Hammock beneath the Mangoes: Stories from Latin America. Ed. Thomas Colchie. New York: Plume, 1992. 83-88.

Here are some additional sample entries for works in anthologies:

Franco, Veronica. "To the Painter Jacopo Tintoretto." Poems and Selected Letters. Ed. and trans. Ann Rosalind Jones and Margaret F. Rosenthal. Chicago: U of Chicago P, 1998. 35-37.

Hansberry, Lorraine. A Raisin in the Sun. Black Theater: A Twentieth-Century Collection of the Work of Its Best Playwrights. Ed. Lindsay Patterson. New York: Dodd, 1971. 221-76.

Hanzlík, Josef. "Vengeance." Trans. Ewald Osers. Interference: The Story of Czechoslovakia in the Words of Its Writers. Comp. and ed. Peter Spafford. Cheltenham: New Clarion, 1992. 54.

More, Hannah. "The Black Slave Trade: A Poem." British Women Poets of the Romantic Era. Ed. Paula R. Feldman. Baltimore: Johns Hopkins UP, 1997. 472-82.

"A Witchcraft Story." The Hopi Way: Tales from a Vanishing Culture. Comp. Mando Sevillano. Flagstaff: Northland, 1986. 33-42.

Often the works in anthologies have been published before. If you wish to inform your reader of the date when a previously published piece other than a scholarly article first appeared, you may follow the title of the piece with the year of original publication and a period.

Douglass, Frederick. Narrative of the Life of Frederick Douglass, an American Slave, Written by Himself. 1845. Slave Narratives. Ed. William L. Andrews and Henry Louis Gates, Jr. New York: Lib. of Amer., 2000. 267-368.

Franklin, Benjamin. "Emigration to America." 1782. The Faber Book of America. Ed. Christopher Ricks and William L. Vance. Boston: Faber, 1992. 24-26.

To cite a previously published scholarly article in a collection, give the complete data for the earlier publication and then add *Rpt. in* ("Reprinted in"), the title of the collection, and the new publication facts. (On citing articles in periodicals, see 5.7.)

> Frye, Northrop. "Literary and Linguistic Scholarship in a Postliterate Age." PMLA 99 (1984): 990-95. Rpt. in Myth and Metaphor: Selected Essays, 1974-88. Ed. Robert D. Denham. Charlottesville: UP of Virginia, 1990. 18-27.
>
> Holladay, Hillary. "Narrative Space in Ann Petry's Country Place." Xavier Review 16 (1996): 21-35. Rpt. in Twentieth-Century Literary Criticism. Ed. Linda Pavlovski and Scott Darga. Vol. 112. Detroit: Gale, 2002. 356-62.

If the article was originally published under a different title, first state the new title and publication facts, followed by *Rpt. of* ("Reprint of"), the original title, and the original publication facts.

> Lewis, C. S. "Viewpoints: C. S. Lewis." Twentieth-Century Interpretations of Sir Gawain and the Green Knight. Ed. Denton Fox. Englewood Cliffs: Prentice, 1968. 100-01. Rpt. of "The Anthropological Approach." English and Medieval Studies Presented to J. R. R. Tolkien on the Occasion of His Seventieth Birthday. Ed. Norman Davis and C. L. Wrenn. London: Allen, 1962. 219-23.

If you refer to more than one piece from the same collection, you may wish to cross-reference each citation to a single entry for the book (see 5.6.10). On citing articles in reference books, see 5.6.8. On citing introductions, prefaces, and the like, see 5.6.9. On citing a piece in a multivolume anthology, see 5.6.15.

5.6.8. An Article in a Reference Book

Treat an encyclopedia article or a dictionary entry as you would a piece in a collection (5.6.7), but do not cite the editor of the reference work. If the article is signed, give the author first (often articles in reference books are signed with initials identified elsewhere in the work); if it is unsigned, give the title first. If the encyclopedia or dictionary arranges articles alphabetically, you may omit volume and page numbers.

When citing familiar reference books, especially those that frequently appear in new editions, do not give full publication information. For such works, list only the edition (if stated) and the year of publication.

"Azimuthal Equidistant Projection." Merriam-Webster's Collegiate
Dictionary. 10th ed. 1993.

"Ginsburg, Ruth Bader." Who's Who in America. 56th ed. 2002.

"Mandarin." The Encyclopedia Americana. 1994 ed.

Mohanty, Jitendra M. "Indian Philosophy." The New Encyclopaedia
Britannica: Macropaedia. 15th ed. 1987.

"Noon." The Oxford English Dictionary. 2nd ed. 1989.

If you are citing a specific definition, among several, add the abbreviation *Def.* ("Definition") and the appropriate designation (e.g., number, letter).

"Noon." Def. 4b. The Oxford English Dictionary. 2nd ed. 1989.

When citing less familiar reference books, however, especially those that have appeared in only one edition, give full publication information.

Allen, Anita L. "Privacy in Health Care." Encyclopedia of Bioethics. Ed.
Warren T. Reich. Rev. ed. 5 vols. New York: Macmillan-Simon, 1995.

Le Patourel, John. "Normans and Normandy." Dictionary of the Middle
Ages. Ed. Joseph R. Strayer. 13 vols. New York: Scribner's, 1987.

5.6.9. An Introduction, a Preface, a Foreword, or an Afterword

To cite an introduction, a preface, a foreword, or an afterword, begin with the name of its author and then give the name of the part being cited, capitalized but neither underlined nor enclosed in quotation marks (*Introduction, Preface, Foreword, Afterword*). If the writer of the piece is different from the author of the complete work, cite the author of the work after its title, giving the full name, in normal order, preceded by the word *By.* If the writer of the piece is also the author of the complete work, use only the last name after *By.* Continue with full publication information and, finally, the inclusive page numbers.

Borges, Jorge Luis. Foreword. Selected Poems, 1923-1967. By Borges. Ed.
Norman Thomas Di Giovanni. New York: Delta-Dell, 1973. xv-xvi.

Coetzee, J. M. Introduction. The Confusions of Young Törless. By Robert
Musil. Trans. Shaun Whiteside. New York: Penguin, 2001. v-xiii.

Drabble, Margaret. Introduction. Middlemarch. By George Eliot. New York:
Bantam, 1985. vii-xvii.

Hamill, Pete. Introduction. The Brooklyn Reader: Thirty Writers Celebrate
America's Favorite Borough. Ed. Andrea Wyatt Sexton and Alice
Leccese Powers. New York: Harmony, 1994. xi-xiv.

Marsalis, Wynton. Foreword. Beyond Category: The Life and Genius of Duke
Ellington. By John Edward Hasse. New York: Simon, 1993. 13-14.

Sears, Barry. Afterword. The Jungle. By Upton Sinclair. New York: Signet,
2001. 343-47.

If the introduction, preface, foreword, or afterword has a title, give
the title, enclosed in quotation marks, immediately before the name
of the part.

Brodsky, Joseph. "Poetry as a Form of Resistance to Reality." Foreword.
Winter Dialogue. By Tomas Venclova. Trans. Diana Senechal. Evanston:
Hydra-Northwestern UP, 1997. vii-xviii.

Doody, Margaret Anne. "In Search of the Ancient Novel." Introduction. The
True Story of the Novel. New Brunswick: Rutgers UP, 1996. 1-11.

5.6.10. Cross-References

To avoid unnecessary repetition in citing two or more works from
the same collection, you may create a complete entry for the collection and cross-reference individual pieces to the entry. In a cross-
reference, state the author and the title of the piece, the last name of
the editor of the collection, and the inclusive page numbers. If the
piece is a translation, add the name of the translator after the title,
unless one person translated the entire volume.

Agee, James. "Knoxville: Summer of 1915." Oates and Atwan 171-75.

Atwan, Robert. Foreword. Oates and Atwan x-xvi.

Kingston, Maxine Hong. "No Name Woman." Oates and Atwan 383-94.

Oates, Joyce Carol, and Robert Atwan, eds. The Best American Essays of
the Century. Boston: Houghton, 2000.

Rodriguez, Richard. "Aria: A Memoir of a Bilingual Childhood." Oates and
Atwan 447-66.

Walker, Alice. "Looking for Zora." Oates and Atwan 395-411.

If you list two or more works under the editor's name, however, add
the title (or a shortened version of it) to the cross-reference.

Angelou, Maya. "Pickin Em Up and Layin Em Down." Baker, Norton 276-78.

Baker, Russell, ed. The Norton Book of Light Verse. New York: Norton, 1986.

---, ed. Russell Baker's Book of American Humor. New York: Norton, 1993.

Hurston, Zora Neale. "Squinch Owl Story." Baker, Russell Baker's Book 458-
59.

Lebowitz, Fran. "Manners." Baker, Russell Baker's Book 556-59.

Lennon, John. "The Fat Budgie." Baker, Norton 357-58.

5.6.11. An Anonymous Book

If a book has no author's or editor's name on the title page, begin the
entry with the title. Do not use either *Anonymous* or *Anon.* Alphabetize the entry by the title, ignoring any initial *A*, *An*, or *The*. (Note
in the sample entries that *The Holy Bible: New International Version*
is alphabetized under *h*.)

Encyclopedia of Virginia. New York: Somerset, 1993.

The Holy Bible: New International Version. Grand Rapids: Zondervan, 1984.

New York Public Library American History Desk Reference. New York:
Macmillan, 1997.

5.6.12. An Edition

Every published book is, in at least one sense, an edition; for example, a book may be a first edition, a second edition, and so forth (see
5.6.14). Researchers also use the term *edition*, however, to denote a
work that was prepared for publication by someone other than the
author—by an editor. For example, a 2003 printing of Shakespeare's
Hamlet was obviously not prepared for publication by Shakespeare.

An editor selected a version of *Hamlet* from the various versions available, decided on any changes in spelling or punctuation, and perhaps added explanatory notes or wrote an introduction. This 2003 version of *Hamlet* would be called an "edition," and the editor's name would most likely appear on the title page along with Shakespeare's.

To cite an edition, begin with the author (or the title, for an anonymous work) if you refer primarily to the text itself; give the editor's name, preceded by the abbreviation *Ed.* ("Edited by"), after the title. If for clarity you wish to indicate the original date of publication, place the year directly after the title (see the entry for Crane and fig. 21).

Austen, Jane. Sense and Sensibility. Ed. Claudia Johnson. New York: Norton, 2001.

Crane, Stephen. The Red Badge of Courage: An Episode of the American Civil War. 1895. Ed. Fredson Bowers. Charlottesville: UP of Virginia, 1975.

Edgeworth, Maria. Castle Rackrent and Ennui. Ed. Marilyn Butler. London: Penguin, 1992.

Octovian. Ed. Frances McSparran. Early English Text Soc. 289. London: Oxford UP, 1986.

Fig. 21. An edition. Unless you primarily cite the work of the editor, begin with the author's name, and give the editor's name, preceded by *Ed.*, after the title. If you wish to give the original publication date, place the year immediately after the title: "Crane, Stephen. *The Red Badge of Courage: An Episode of the American Civil War.* 1895. Ed. Fredson Bowers."

Shakespeare, William. Hamlet. Ed. Barbara A. Mowat and Paul Werstine.
New York: Washington Square-Pocket, 1992.

Smith, Charlotte. The Collected Letters of Charlotte Smith. Ed. Judith
Stanton. Bloomington: Indiana UP, 2002.

Twain, Mark. Roughing It. Ed. Harriet E. Smith and Edgar M. Branch.
Berkeley: U of California P, 1993.

If your citations are generally to the work of the editor (e.g., the introduction, the notes, or editorial decisions regarding the text), begin the entry with the editor's name, followed by a comma and the abbreviation *ed.* ("editor"), and give the author's name, preceded by the word *By,* after the title.

Bowers, Fredson, ed. The Red Badge of Courage: An Episode of the
American Civil War. By Stephen Crane. 1895. Charlottesville: UP of
Virginia, 1975.

Consult 5.6.15 if you are citing more than one volume of a multivolume work or if the book is a part of a multivolume edition—say, *The Works of Mark Twain*—and you wish to give supplementary information about the entire project.

5.6.13. A Translation

To cite a translation, state the author's name first if you refer primarily to the work itself; give the translator's name, preceded by *Trans.* ("Translated by"), after the title. If the book has an editor as well as a translator, give the names, with appropriate abbreviations, in the order in which they appear on the title page (see the sample entry for *Beowulf*).

Beowulf. Trans. E. Talbot Donaldson. Ed. Nicholas Howe. New York:
Norton, 2001.

Esquivel, Laura. Like Water for Chocolate: A Novel in Monthly Installments,
with Recipes, Romances, and Home Remedies. Trans. Carol Christensen
and Thomas Christensen. New York: Doubleday, 1992.

Hildegard of Bingen. Selected Writings. Trans. Mark Atherton. New York:
Penguin, 2001.

Murasaki Shikibu. The Tale of Genji. Trans. Edward G. Seidensticker. New
York: Knopf, 1976.

If your citations are mostly to the translator's comments or choice of wording, begin the bibliographic entry with the translator's name, followed by a comma and the abbreviation *trans.* ("translator"), and give the author's name, preceded by the word *By*, after the title. (On citing anthologies of translated works by different authors, see 5.6.7.)

> Seidensticker, Edward G., trans. The Tale of Genji. By Murasaki Shikibu. New
> York: Knopf, 1976.

Although not required, some or all of the original publication facts may be added as supplementary information at the end of the entry.

> Esquivel, Laura. Like Water for Chocolate: A Novel in Monthly Installments,
> with Recipes, Romances, and Home Remedies. Trans. Carol
> Christensen and Thomas Christensen. New York: Doubleday, 1992.
> Trans. of Como agua para chocolate: Novelas de entregas mensuales,
> con recetas, amores y remedios caseros. México, DF [Mexico City]:
> Planeta, 1989.
>
> Levi, Primo. Survival in Auschwitz: The Nazi Assault on Humanity. Trans.
> Stuart Woolf. New York: Collier-Macmillan, 1987. Trans. of Se questo è
> un uomo. 1958.

On citing a book in a language other than English, see 5.6.23.

5.6.14. A Book Published in a Second or Subsequent Edition

A book with no edition number or name on its title page is probably a first edition. Unless informed otherwise, readers assume that bibliographic entries refer to first editions. When you use a later edition of a work, identify the edition in your entry by number (*2nd ed.*, *3rd ed.*, *4th ed.*), by name (*Rev. ed.*, for "Revised edition"; *Abr. ed.*, for "Abridged edition"), or by year (*2003 ed.*)—whichever the title page indicates (see fig. 22). The specification of edition comes after the name of the editor, translator, or compiler, if there is one, or otherwise after the title of the book. (On citing encyclopedias, dictionaries, and similar works revised regularly, see 5.6.8.)

> Bondanella, Peter. Italian Cinema: From Neorealism to the Present. 3rd ed.
> New York: Continuum, 2001.

A Reader's Guide to
Contemporary Literary Theory
Third Edition
Raman Selden and Peter Widdowson

Fig. 22. A second or other edition. In the works-cited list, include any label that identifies the edition on the title page. The title of this book would be followed by "3rd ed."

Chaucer, Geoffrey. The Works of Geoffrey Chaucer. Ed. F. N. Robinson. 2nd
    ed. Boston: Houghton, 1957.

Cheyfitz, Eric. The Poetics of Imperialism: Translation and Colonization from
    The Tempest to Tarzan. Expanded ed. Philadelphia: U of Pennsylvania P,
    1997.

Hyde, Margaret O., and Elizabeth Held Forsyth. Suicide: The Hidden
    Epidemic. Rev. ed. New York: Watts, 1986.

Murasaki Shikibu. The Tale of Genji. Trans. Edward G. Seidensticker. Abr. ed.
    New York: Vintage-Random, 1985.

5.6.15. A Multivolume Work

If you are using two or more volumes of a multivolume work, cite the total number of volumes in the work ("5 vols."). This information comes after the title—or after any editor's name or identification of edition—and before the publication information. Specific references to volume and page numbers ("3: 212–13") belong in the text. (See ch. 6 for parenthetical documentation.)

Blanco, Richard L., ed. The American Revolution, 1775-1783: An
    Encyclopedia. 2 vols. Hamden: Garland, 1993.

Doyle, Arthur Conan. The Oxford Sherlock Holmes. Ed. Owen Dudley
    Edwards. 9 vols. New York: Oxford UP, 1993.

Lauter, Paul, et al., eds. The Heath Anthology of American Literature. 4th ed.
    2 vols. Boston: Houghton, 2002.

Rampersad, Arnold. The Life of Langston Hughes. 2nd ed. 2 vols. New York: Oxford UP, 2002.

Sadie, Stanley, ed. The New Grove Dictionary of Music and Musicians. 20 vols. London: Macmillan, 1980.

Schlesinger, Arthur M., Jr., gen. ed. History of U.S. Political Parties. 4 vols. New York: Chelsea, 1973.

If the volumes of the work were published over a period of years, give the inclusive dates at the end of the citation ("1952–70"). If the work is still in progress, write *to date* after the number of volumes ("3 vols. to date") and leave a space after the hyphen that follows the beginning date ("1982– ").

Cassidy, Frederic, ed. Dictionary of American Regional English. 3 vols. to date. Cambridge: Belknap-Harvard UP, 1985- .

Churchill, Winston S. A History of the English-Speaking Peoples. 4 vols. New York: Dodd, 1956-58.

Crane, Stephen. The University of Virginia Edition of the Works of Stephen Crane. Ed. Fredson Bowers. 10 vols. Charlottesville: UP of Virginia, 1969-76.

Lawrence, D. H. The Letters of D. H. Lawrence. Ed. James T. Boulton. 8 vols. New York: Cambridge UP, 1979-2000.

Wellek, René. A History of Modern Criticism, 1750-1950. 8 vols. New Haven: Yale UP, 1955-92.

If you are using only one volume of a multivolume work, state the number of the volume in the bibliographic entry ("Vol. 2") and give publication information for that volume alone; then you need give only page numbers when you refer to that work in the text.

Doyle, Arthur Conan. The Oxford Sherlock Holmes. Ed. Owen Dudley Edwards. Vol. 8. New York: Oxford UP, 1993.

Lawrence, D. H. The Letters of D. H. Lawrence. Ed. James T. Boulton. Vol. 8. New York: Cambridge UP, 2000.

Stowe, Harriet Beecher. "Sojourner Truth, the Libyan Sibyl." 1863. The Heath Anthology of American Literature. Ed. Paul Lauter et al. 4th ed. Vol. 1. Boston: Houghton, 2002. 2530-38.

Although not required, the complete number of volumes may be added as supplementary information at the end of the listing, along with other relevant publication facts, such as inclusive dates of publication if the volumes were published over a period of years (see the sample entry for Wellek).

> Doyle, Arthur Conan. The Oxford Sherlock Holmes. Ed. Owen Dudley
> Edwards. Vol. 8. New York: Oxford UP, 1993. 9 vols.
>
> Stowe, Harriet Beecher. "Sojourner Truth, the Libyan Sibyl." 1863. The
> Heath Anthology of American Literature. Ed. Paul Lauter et al. 4th ed.
> Vol. 1. Boston: Houghton, 2002. 2530-38. 2 vols.
>
> Wellek, René. A History of Modern Criticism, 1750-1950. Vol. 5. New Haven:
> Yale UP, 1986. 8 vols. 1955-92.

If you are using only one volume of a multivolume work and the volume has an individual title, you may cite the book without reference to the other volumes in the work.

> Caro, Robert A. Master of the Senate. New York: Knopf, 2002.
>
> Churchill, Winston S. The Age of Revolution. New York: Dodd, 1957.
>
> Durant, Will, and Ariel Durant. The Age of Voltaire. New York: Simon, 1965.

Although not required, supplementary information about the complete multivolume work may follow the basic citation: the volume number, preceded by *Vol.* and followed by the word *of*; the title of the complete work; the total number of volumes; and, if the work appeared over a period of years, the inclusive publication dates.

> Caro, Robert A. Master of the Senate. New York: Knopf, 2002. Vol. 3 of The
> Years of Lyndon Johnson. 3 vols. to date. 1982- .
>
> Churchill, Winston S. The Age of Revolution. New York: Dodd, 1957. Vol. 3
> of A History of the English-Speaking Peoples. 4 vols. 1956-58.
>
> Durant, Will, and Ariel Durant. The Age of Voltaire. New York: Simon, 1965.
> Vol. 9 of The Story of Civilization. 11 vols. 1935-75.

If the volume you are citing is part of a multivolume scholarly edition (see 5.6.12), you may similarly give supplementary information about the entire edition. Follow the publication information for the volume with the appropriate volume number, preceded by *Vol.* and followed by the word *of*; the title of the complete work; the name of the general editor of the multivolume edition, followed by a comma and *gen. ed.*; the total number of volumes; and the inclusive publication dates for the edition (see the entry for Howells). If the entire edition was edited by one person, state the editor's name after the title of the edition rather than after the title of the volume (see the entry for Crane).

> Crane, Stephen. The Red Badge of Courage: An Episode of the American Civil War. 1895. Charlottesville: UP of Virginia, 1975. Vol. 2 of The University of Virginia Edition of the Works of Stephen Crane. Ed. Fredson Bowers. 10 vols. 1969-76.

> Howells, W. D. Their Wedding Journey. Ed. John K. Reeves. Bloomington: Indiana UP, 1968. Vol. 5 of A Selected Edition of W. D. Howells. Edwin H. Cady, gen. ed. 32 vols. 1968-83.

5.6.16. A Book in a Series

If the title page or the preceding page (the half-title page) indicates that the book you are citing is part of a series (see fig. 23), include the series name, neither underlined nor enclosed in quotation marks,

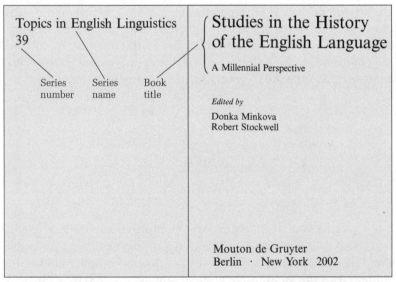

Fig. 23. A book in a series. The title page or a preceding page may indicate that the book is part of a series. This book would be listed as follows (see 7.5 on shortening publishers' names): "Minkova, Donka, and Robert Stockwell, eds. *Studies in the History of the English Language: A Millennial Perspective*. Topics in English Linguistics 39. Berlin: Mouton, 2002."

and the series number, followed by a period, before the publication information. Use common abbreviations for words in the series name (see 7.4), including *Ser.* if *Series* is part of the name.

Mitchell-Boyask, Robin, ed. Approaches to Teaching the Dramas of
Euripides. Approaches to Teaching World Lit. 73. New York: MLA, 2002.

Murck, Alfreda. Poetry and Painting in Song China: The Subtle Art of
Dissent. Harvard-Yenching Inst. Monograph Ser. 50. Cambridge:
Harvard UP, 2000.

Neruda, Pablo. Canto General. Trans. Jack Schmitt. Latin Amer. Lit. and
Culture 7. Berkeley: U of California P, 1991.

Riccoboni, Marie. The Story of Ernestine. Trans. Joan Hinde Stewart and
Philip Stewart. Texts and Trans. 6. New York: MLA, 1998.

5.6.17. A Republished Book

To cite a republished book—for example, a paperback version of a book originally published in a clothbound version—give the original publication date, followed by a period, before the publication information for the book you are citing (see fig. 24).

Atwood, Margaret. The Blind Assassin. 2000. New York: Knopf-Random,
2001.

Doctorow, E. L. Welcome to Hard Times. 1960. New York: Viking-
Penguin, 1996.

HUNGER OF MEMORY: THE EDUCATION OF RICHARD RODRIGUEZ

*A Bantam Book / published by arrangement with
David R. Godine, Publisher, Inc.*

Original
publication
date

PRINTING HISTORY

*David R. Godine edition published February 1982
A Selection of Quality Paperback Book Club, July 1982
Bantam edition / February 1983
6 printings through August 1988*

Date of
republication

Fig. 24. A republished book. Give the original publication date before the publication information for the book you are citing: "1982. New York: Bantam, 1983."

Douglas, Mary. Purity and Danger: An Analysis of the Concepts of Pollution
   and Taboo. 1966. London: Routledge, 1993.

Although not required, supplementary information pertaining to the
original publication may precede the original publication date.

Ishiguro, Kazuo. When We Were Orphans. London: Faber, 2000. New York:
   Vintage-Random, 2001.

New material added to the republication, such as an introduction,
should be cited after the original publication facts.

Dreiser, Theodore. Sister Carrie. 1900. Introd. Richard Lingeman. New York:
   New Amer. Lib.-Penguin, 2000.

To cite a republished book that was originally issued under a different title, first state the new title and publication facts, followed by
Rpt. of ("Reprint of"), the original title, and the original date.

The WPA Guide to 1930s Alabama. Tuscaloosa: U of Alabama P, 2000. Rpt.
   of Alabama: A Guide to the Deep South. 1941.

5.6.18. A Publisher's Imprint

Publishers often group some of their books under imprints, or special names (see fig. 25). Among Doubleday's many imprints, for

Fig. 25. A publisher's imprint. This information on the title page would
appear in the works-cited list as "New York: Perennial-Harper."

example, have been Anchor Books, Crime Club, and Double D Western. If an imprint appears on a title page along with the publisher's name, state the imprint and follow it by a hyphen and the name of the publisher ("Anchor-Doubleday," "Collier-Macmillan," "Vintage-Random").

> Cassidy, Frederic, ed. Dictionary of American Regional English. 3 vols. to
> date. Cambridge: Belknap-Harvard UP, 1985- .
> Lopate, Phillip, ed. The Art of the Personal Essay: An Anthology from the
> Classical Era to the Present. New York: Anchor-Doubleday, 1994.
> Morrison, Toni. Sula. 1973. New York: Plume-Penguin, 2002.

5.6.19. A Book with Multiple Publishers

If the title page lists two or more publishers—not just two or more offices of the same publisher—include all of them, in the order given, as part of the publication information, putting a semicolon after the name of each but the last (see fig. 26).

> Duff, J. Wight. A Literary History of Rome: From the Origins to the Close of
> the Golden Age. Ed. A. M. Duff. 3rd ed. 1953. London: Benn; New
> York: Barnes, 1967.
> Wells, H. G. The Time Machine. 1895. London: Dent; Rutland: Tuttle, 1992.

UNIVERSITY OF TORONTO PRESS
Toronto and Buffalo

ROUTLEDGE
London

Fig. 26. Multiple publishers. These copublishers would be listed as "Toronto: U of Toronto P; London: Routledge."

5.6.20. A Pamphlet

Treat a pamphlet as you would a book.

Washington, DC. New York: Trip Builder, 2000.

Renoir Lithographs. New York: Dover, 1994.

5.6.21. A Government Publication

Government publications emanate from many sources and so present special problems in bibliographic citation. In general, if you do not know the writer of the document, cite as author the government agency that issued it—that is, state the name of the government first, followed by the name of the agency, using an abbreviation if the context makes it clear. (But see below for citing a document whose author is known.)

California. Dept. of Industrial Relations.

United States. Cong. House.

If you are citing two or more works issued by the same government, substitute three hyphens for the name in each entry after the first. If you also cite more than one work by the same government agency, use an additional three hyphens in place of the agency in the second entry and each subsequent one.

United States. Cong. House.

---. ---. Senate.

---. Dept. of Health and Human Services.

The title of the publication, underlined, should follow immediately.
    In citing the *Congressional Record* (abbreviated *Cong. Rec.*), give only the date and page numbers.

Cong. Rec. 7 Feb. 1973: 3831-51.

In citing other congressional documents, include such information as the number and session of Congress, the house (*S* stands for Senate, *H* and *HR* for House of Representatives), and the type and number of the publication. Types of congressional publications include bills (S 33, HR 77), resolutions (S. Res. 20, H. Res. 50), reports (S. Rept. 9, H. Rept. 142), and documents (S. Doc. 333, H. Doc. 222, Misc. Doc. 67).

The usual publication information comes next (i.e., place, publisher, and date). Most federal publications, regardless of the branch of government issuing them, are published by the Government Printing Office (GPO), in Washington, DC; its British counterpart is Her (or His) Majesty's Stationery Office (HMSO), in London. Documents issued by the United Nations and most local governments, however, do not all emanate from a central office; give the publication information that appears on the title page.

Great Britain. Ministry of Agriculture, Fisheries, and Food. Dept. of the
   Environment, Transport, and the Regions. Our Countryside, the Future:
   A Fair Deal for Rural England. London: HMSO, 2000.

New York State. Commission on the Adirondacks in the Twenty-First Century.
   The Adirondack Park in the Twenty-First Century. Albany: State of New
   York, 1990.

---. Committee on State Prisons. Investigation of the New York State Prisons.
   1883. New York: Arno, 1974.

United Nations. Consequences of Rapid Population Growth in Developing
   Countries. New York: Taylor, 1991.

---. Centre on Transnational Corporations. Foreign Direct Investment, the
   Service Sector, and International Banking. New York: United Nations,
   1987.

---. Economic Commission for Africa. Industrial Growth in Africa. New York:
   United Nations, 1963.

United States. Cong. Joint Committee on the Investigation of the Pearl
   Harbor Attack. Hearings. 79th Cong., 1st and 2nd sess. 32 vols.
   Washington: GPO, 1946.

---. ---. Senate. Subcommittee on Constitutional Amendments of the
   Committee on the Judiciary. Hearings on the "Equal Rights"
   Amendment. 91st Cong., 2nd sess. S. Res. 61. Washington: GPO, 1970.

---. Dept. of Labor. Child Care: A Workforce Issue. Washington: GPO, 1988.

---. Dept. of State. The Global 2000 Report to the President: Entering the
   Twenty-First Century. 3 vols. Washington: GPO, 1981.

If known, the name of the document's author may either begin the entry or, if the agency comes first, follow the title and the word *By* or an abbreviation (such as *Ed.* or *Comp.*).

> Poore, Benjamin Perley, comp. A Descriptive Catalogue of the Government Publications of the United States, September 5, 1774-March 4, 1881. US 48th Cong., 2nd sess. Misc. Doc. 67. Washington: GPO, 1885.

or

> United States. Cong. A Descriptive Catalogue of the Government Publications of the United States, September 5, 1774-March 4, 1881. Comp. Benjamin Perley Poore. 48th Cong., 2nd sess. Misc. Doc. 67. Washington: GPO, 1885.

To cite an online government document, see 5.9.3c. To cite a legal source, see 5.8.14.

5.6.22. The Published Proceedings of a Conference

Treat the published proceedings of a conference like a book, but add pertinent information about the conference (unless the book title includes such information).

> Chang, Steve S., Lily Liaw, and Josef Ruppenhofer, eds. Proceedings of the Twenty-Fifth Annual Meeting of the Berkeley Linguistics Society, February 12-15, 1999: General Session and Parasession on Loan Word Phenomena. Berkeley: Berkeley Linguistics Soc., 2000.
>
> Freed, Barbara F., ed. Foreign Language Acquisition Research and the Classroom. Proc. of Consortium for Lang. Teaching and Learning Conf., Oct. 1989, U of Pennsylvania. Lexington: Heath, 1991.

Cite a presentation in the proceedings like a work in a collection of pieces by different authors (see 5.6.7).

> Hualde, José Ignacio. "Patterns of Correspondence in the Adaptation of Spanish Borrowings in Basque." Proceedings of the Twenty-Fifth Annual Meeting of the Berkeley Linguistics Society, February 12-15, 1999: General Session and Parasession on Loan Word Phenomena. Ed. Steve S. Chang, Lily Liaw, and Josef Ruppenhofer. Berkeley: Berkeley Linguistics Soc., 2000. 348-58.

5.6.23. A Book in a Language Other Than English

Cite a book published in a language other than English like any other book. Give the author's name, title, and publication information as they appear in the book. You may need to look in the colophon, at the back of the book, for some or all of the publication information found on the title or copyright page of English-language books. If it seems necessary to clarify the title, provide a translation, in brackets: "*Gengangere* [*Ghosts*]." Similarly, you may use brackets to give the English name of a foreign city—"Wien [Vienna]"—or you may substitute the English name, depending on your reader's knowledge of the language. Shorten the publisher's name appropriately (see 7.5). For capitalization in languages other than English, see 3.8.

Bessière, Jean, ed. Mythologies de l'écriture: Champs critiques. Paris: PUF, 1990.

Dahlhaus, Carl. Musikästhetik. Köln: Gerig, 1967.

Esquivel, Laura. Como agua para chocolate: Novelas de entregas mensuales, con recetas, amores y remedios caseros. México, DF [Mexico City]: Planeta, 1989.

Maraini, Dacia. Amata scrittura: Laboratorio di analisi, letture, proposte, conversazioni. Ed. Viviana Rosi and Maria Pia Simonetti. Milano: Rizzoli, 2000.

Poche, Emanuel. Prazské Palace. Praha [Prague]: Odeon, 1977.

5.6.24. A Book Published before 1900

When citing a book published before 1900, you may omit the name of the publisher and use a comma, instead of a colon, after the place of publication.

Brome, Richard. The Dramatic Works of Richard Brome. 3 vols. London, 1873.

Dewey, John. The School and Society. Chicago, 1899.

Segni, Bernardo. Rettorica et poetica d'Aristotile. Firenze, 1549.

5.6.25. A Book without Stated Publication Information or Pagination

When a book does not indicate the publisher, the place or date of publication, or pagination, supply as much of the missing information as you can, using brackets to show that it did not come from the source.

New York: U of Gotham P, [2003].

If the date can only be approximated, put it after a *c.*, for *circa* 'around': "[c. 1999]." If you are uncertain about the accuracy of the information you supply, add a question mark: "[1993?]." Use the following abbreviations for information you cannot supply.

n.p.	No place of publication given
n.p.	No publisher given
n.d.	No date of publication given
n. pag.	No pagination given

Inserted before the colon, the abbreviation *n.p.* indicates *no place*; after the colon, it indicates *no publisher*. *N. pag.* explains the absence of page references in citations of the work.

NO PLACE

N.p.: U of Gotham P, 2003.

NO PUBLISHER

New York: n.p., 2003.

NO DATE

New York: U of Gotham P, n.d.

NO PAGINATION

New York: U of Gotham P, 2003. N. pag.

The examples above are hypothetical; the following ones are entries for actual books.

Bauer, Johann. Kafka und Prag. [Stuttgart]: Belser, [1971?].

Malachi, Zvi, ed. Proceedings of the International Conference on Literary and Linguistic Computing. [Tel Aviv]: [Fac. of Humanities, Tel Aviv U], n.d.

Michelangelo. The Sistine Chapel. New York: Wings, 1992. N. pag.

Photographic View Album of Cambridge. [Eng.]: n.p., n.d. N. pag.

Sendak, Maurice. Where the Wild Things Are. New York: Harper, 1963.
    N. pag.

5.6.26. An Unpublished Dissertation

Enclose the title of an unpublished dissertation in quotation marks;
do not underline it. Then write the descriptive label *Diss.*, and add
the name of the degree-granting university, followed by a comma
and the year.

Boyle, Anthony T. "The Epistemological Evolution of Renaissance Utopian
    Literature, 1516-1657." Diss. New York U, 1983.

Kelly, Mary. "Factors Predicting Hospital Readmission of Normal Newborns."
    Diss. U of Michigan, 2001.

To cite a master's thesis, substitute the appropriate label (e.g., *MA
thesis, MS thesis*) for *Diss.* For citing a dissertation abstract published in *Dissertation Abstracts* or *Dissertation Abstracts International*, see 5.7.8. For documenting other unpublished writing, see
5.8.12.

5.6.27. A Published Dissertation

Cite a published dissertation like a book, but add pertinent dissertation information before the publication facts. If the work was published by University Microfilms International (UMI), you may add
the order number as supplementary information.

Dietze, Rudolf F. Ralph Ellison: The Genesis of an Artist. Diss. U Erlangen-
    Nürnberg, 1982. Erlanger Beiträge zur Sprach- und Kunstwissenschaft
    70. Nürnberg: Carl, 1982.

Fullerton, Matilda. Women's Leadership in the Public Schools: Towards a
    Feminist Educational Leadership Model. Diss. Washington State U,
    2001. Ann Arbor: UMI, 2001. ATT 3023579.

5.7. CITING ARTICLES AND OTHER PUBLICATIONS IN PERIODICALS

5.7.1. The Basic Entry: An Article in a Scholarly Journal with Continuous Pagination

A periodical is a publication that appears regularly at fixed intervals, such as a newspaper, a magazine, or a scholarly journal. Unlike newspapers and magazines, scholarly journals usually appear only about four times a year, and the issues present learned articles containing original research and original interpretations of data and texts. Such journals are intended not for general readers but for professionals and students. Since the research you do for your papers will inevitably lead you to consult scholarly journals, the entry for an article in a scholarly journal will be among the most common in the works-cited lists you compile.

The entry for an article in a periodical, like that for a book, has three main divisions:

Author's name. "Title of the article." Publication information.

Here is an example:

Trumpener, Katie. "Memories Carved in Granite: Great War Memorials and Everyday Life." PMLA 115 (2000): 1096-103.

Author's Name

In general, follow the recommendations for citing names of authors of books (5.6.1). Take the author's name from the beginning or the end of the article (see fig. 27). Reverse the name for alphabetizing, and put a period after it.

Trumpener, Katie.

Title of the Article

In general, follow the recommendations for titles given in 3.6. State the full title of the article, enclosed in quotation marks (not underlined). Unless the title has its own concluding punctuation (e.g., a question mark), put a period before the closing quotation mark (see fig. 27).

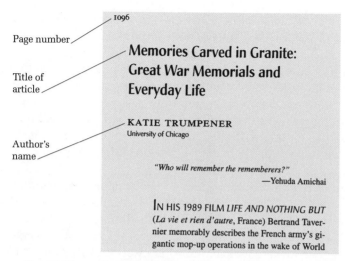

Page number

Title of article

Author's name

Fig. 27. The author, title, and initial page number of a journal article. Take the author's name and the title from the article itself, not from the journal cover or the table of contents.

Trumpener, Katie. "Memories Carved in Granite: Great War Memorials and Everyday Life."

Publication Information

In general, after the title of the article, give the *journal title* (underlined), the *volume number*, the *year of publication* (in parentheses), a colon, the *inclusive page numbers*, and a period.

Trumpener, Katie. "Memories Carved in Granite: Great War Memorials and Everyday Life." <u>PMLA</u> 115 (2000): 1096-103.

Take these facts directly from the journal, not from a source such as a bibliography. Publication information usually appears on the cover or title page of a journal. Omit any introductory article in the title of an English-language journal (*William and Mary Quarterly*, not *The William and Mary Quarterly*; see fig. 28, on the next page). For newspaper titles, see 5.7.5. Do not precede the volume number with the word *volume* or the abbreviation *vol.*

In addition to the volume number, the journal's cover or title page may include an issue number ("Number 3") or a month or season before the year ("January 2003," "Fall 2001"). In general, the issues of a journal published in a single year compose one volume. Volumes are usually numbered in continuous sequence—each new volume is numbered one higher than its predecessor—while the numbering of issues starts over with 1 in each new volume. You may ignore the issue number and the month or season if the journal's pages are numbered continuously throughout each annual volume (see fig. 28). In a journal with such pagination, if the first issue for a year ends on page 130, for instance, the second issue begins on page 131.

Most scholarly journals are paginated continuously throughout each annual volume. Then, at the end of the year, the issues in the volume are bound together and shelved in the library by year number. If you are looking for the print version of the article by Katie Trumpener cited above, for example, which was published in 2000 in an issue of the scholarly journal *PMLA*, you will likely locate it in your library in what appears to be a book with "*PMLA* 2000" printed on the spine. In that volume, you will find all the issues of *PMLA* published during 2000, and the page numbering of the volume will be continuous, from page 1 of the first issue through to the final page of the last issue published in the year. Suppose, then, that you wish to cite the article in your research paper. The title page of the issue

Fig. 28. The publication information for a scholarly journal. Take the information—generally, the journal title, volume number, and year of publication—from the cover or the title page of the journal. Omit any introductory *A*, *An*, or *The* in the journal title. If the journal numbers its pages continuously throughout the annual volume, ignore the issue number and the month or season. The inclusive page numbers for the entire article, preceded by a colon, normally conclude the citation: "*Virginia Quarterly Review* 77 (2001): 247–61."

containing the article includes this publication information: "Volume 115, Number 5, October 2000." But since *PMLA* is paged continuously by volume, you should omit the issue number and the month from your entry, for the reader will be able to find the source by knowing simply the volume number and the page numbers of the article.

Some scholarly journals do not use continuous pagination throughout the annual volume, however, and some use issue numbers alone without volume numbers; on citing articles in such journals, see 5.7.2–3. In addition, entries for newspapers and magazines do not require volume numbers (see 5.7.5–6). Your instructor or a librarian will help you if you are uncertain whether a periodical is a magazine or a scholarly journal. If any doubt remains, include the volume number.

The inclusive page numbers cited should encompass the complete article, not just the portion you used. (Specific page references appear parenthetically at appropriate places in your text; see ch. 6.) Follow the rules for writing inclusive numbers in 3.5.6. Write the page reference for the first page exactly as shown in the source ("198–232," "A32–34," "28/WETA–29," "TV-15–18," "lxii–lxv"). If an article is not printed on consecutive pages—if, for example, after beginning on page 6 it skips to page 10 and then to page 22—write only the first page number and a plus sign, leaving no intervening space: "6+." (See examples in 5.7.5.)

Here are some additional examples of the basic entry for an article in a scholarly journal with continuous pagination:

Hanks, Patrick. "Do Word Meanings Exist?" Computers and the Humanities 34 (2000): 205-15.

Mann, Susan. "Myths of Asian Womanhood." Journal of Asian Studies 59 (2000): 835-62.

McKenna, Bernard. "How Engineers Write: An Empirical Study of Engineering Report Writing." Applied Linguistics 18 (1997): 189-211.

White, Sabina, and Andrew Winzelberg. "Laughter and Stress." Humor 5 (1992): 343-55.

Sometimes additional information is required in an entry. This list shows most of the possible components of an entry for an article in a periodical and the order in which they are normally arranged:

1. Author's name
2. Title of the article
3. Name of the periodical
4. Series number or name (if relevant; see 5.7.4)
5. Volume number (for a scholarly journal)
6. Issue number (if needed; see 5.7.2–3)
7. Date of publication
8. Page numbers
9. Supplementary information (see esp. 5.7.12)

The rest of 5.7 explains how to cite these items. To document an article in an online periodical, see 5.9.4.

5.7.2. An Article in a Scholarly Journal That Pages Each Issue Separately

Some scholarly journals do not number pages continuously throughout an annual volume but begin each issue on page 1. For such journals, you must include the issue number to identify the source. Add a period and the issue number directly after the volume number, without any intervening space: "14.2" signifies volume 14, issue 2; "10.3–4," volume 10, issues 3 and 4 combined.

> Albada, Kelly F. "The Public and Private Dialogue about the American Family on Television." Journal of Communication 50.4 (2000): 79-110.
>
> Barthelme, Frederick. "Architecture." Kansas Quarterly 13.3-4 (1981): 77-80.
>
> Smith, Johanna M. "Constructing the Nation: Eighteenth-Century Geographies for Children." Mosaic 34.2 (2001): 133-48.

5.7.3. An Article in a Scholarly Journal That Uses Only Issue Numbers

Some scholarly journals do not use volume numbers at all, numbering issues only. Treat the issue numbers of such journals as you would volume numbers.

Lajolo, Marisa. "The Female Reader on Trial." Brasil 14 (1995): 61-81.

McNeilly, Kevin. "Home Economics." Canadian Literature 166 (2000): 5-16.

5.7.4. An Article in a Scholarly Journal with More Than One Series

Some scholarly journals have been published in more than one series. In citing a journal with numbered series, write the number (an arabic digit with the appropriate ordinal suffix: *2nd, 3rd, 4th,* etc.) and the abbreviation *ser.* between the journal title and the volume number (see the sample entry for Daniels). For a journal divided into a new series and an original series, indicate the series with *ns* or *os* before the volume number (see the entry for Berman).

Berman, David. "Marketing Poetry." Kenyon Review ns 22.3-4 (2000): 211-22.

Daniels, John. "Indian Population of North America in 1492." William and Mary Quarterly 3rd ser. 49 (1992): 298-320.

5.7.5. An Article in a Newspaper

To cite an English-language newspaper, give the name as it appears on the masthead but omit any introductory article (*New York Times*, not *The New York Times*). If the city of publication is not included in the name of a locally published newspaper, add the city in square brackets, not underlined, after the name: "*Star-Ledger* [Newark]." For nationally published newspapers (e.g., *Wall Street Journal, Chronicle of Higher Education*), you need not add the city of publication. Next give the complete date—day, month, and year. Abbreviate the names of all months except May, June, and July (see 7.2). Do not give the volume and issue numbers even if they are listed. If an edition is named on the masthead, add a comma after the date and specify the edition (e.g., *natl. ed., late ed.*). It is important to state the edition because different editions of the same issue of a newspaper contain different material. Follow the edition—or the date if there is no edition—with a colon and the page number or numbers. Here are examples illustrating how an article appeared in different sections of two editions of the *New York Times* on the same day:

Jeromack, Paul. "This Once, a David of the Art World Does Goliath a Favor." New York Times 13 July 2002, late ed.: B7+.

Jeromack, Paul. "This Once, a David of the Art World Does Goliath a Favor." New York Times 13 July 2002, New England ed.: A13+.

If each section is paginated separately, indicate the appropriate section number or letter. Determining how to indicate a section can be complicated. The *New York Times*, for example, is currently divided in two distinct ways, depending on the day of the week, and each system calls for a different method of indicating section and page. On Monday through Saturday, there are normally several sections, labeled *A*, *B*, *C*, *D*, and so forth, and paginated separately, and the section letter is part of each page number: "A1," "B1," "C5," "D3." Whenever the pagination of a newspaper includes a section designation, give the first page number exactly as it appears.

DAILY *NEW YORK TIMES*

Chang, Kenneth. "The Melting (Freezing) of Antarctica." New York Times 2 Apr. 2002, late ed.: F1+.

The Sunday edition contains numerous individually paged sections (covering the arts and entertainment, business, sports, travel, and so on) designated not by letters but by numbers ("Section 4," "Section 7"), which do not appear as parts of the page numbers. Whenever the section designation of a newspaper is not part of the pagination, put a comma after the date (or after the edition, if any) and add the abbreviation *sec.*, the appropriate letter or number, a colon, and the page number or numbers.

SUNDAY *NEW YORK TIMES*

Hennenberger, Melinda. "The Leonardo Cover-Up." New York Times 21 Apr. 2002, late ed., sec. 6: 42+.

Newspaper articles are often not printed on consecutive pages—for example, an article might begin on page 1, then skip to page 16. For such articles, write only the first page number and a plus sign, leaving no intervening space: "6+," "C3+." The parenthetical reference in the text tells readers the exact page from which material was used.

Here are some additional examples from different newspapers:

Alaton, Salem. "So, Did They Live Happily Ever After?" Globe and Mail [Toronto] 27 Dec. 1997: D1+.

Gopnik, Blake. "Art and Design Bringing Fresh Ideas to the Table." Washington Post 21 Apr. 2002: G1.

Harris, Nicole. "Airports in the Throes of Change." Wall Street Journal 27 Mar. 2002: B1+.

Hirsch, Marianne. "The Day Time Stopped." Chronicle of Higher Education 25 Jan. 2002: B11-14.

5.7.6. An Article in a Magazine

To cite a magazine published every week or every two weeks, give the complete date (beginning with the day and abbreviating the month, except for May, June, and July), followed by a colon and the inclusive page numbers of the article. If the article is not printed on consecutive pages, write only the first page number and a plus sign, leaving no intervening space. Do not give the volume and issue numbers even if they are listed (see fig. 29).

Mehta, Pratap Bhanu. "Exploding Myths." New Republic 6 June 1998: 17-19.

Weintraub, Arlene, and Laura Cohen. "A Thousand-Year Plan for Nuclear Waste." Business Week 6 May 2002: 94-96.

Fig. 29. The publication information for a magazine. When you document works in a magazine, do not cite the volume and issue numbers, even if they are printed in the issue. Give the full date or the month or months and year. The entry for a magazine article ends with a colon and the page-number range of the article: "*American Scientist* Sept.-Oct. 2002: 454–61."

To cite a magazine published every month or every two months, give the month or months and year. If the article is not printed on consecutive pages, write only the first page number and a plus sign, leaving no intervening space. Do not give the volume and issue numbers even if they are listed.

> Amelar, Sarah. "Restoration on 42nd Street." Architecture Mar. 1998: 146-
>   50.
> Fallows, James. "The Early-Decision Racket." Atlantic Monthly Sept.
>   2001: 37-52.
> Kates, Robert W. "Population and Consumption: What We Know, What We
>   Need to Know." Environment Apr. 2000: 10-19.
> Paul, Annie Murphy. "Self-Help: Shattering the Myths." Psychology Today
>   Mar.-Apr. 2001: 60-68.
> Perlstein, Rick. "Abridged Too Far?" Lingua Franca Apr.-May 1997: 23-24.

5.7.7. A Review

To cite a review, give the reviewer's name and the title of the review (if there is one); then write *Rev. of* (neither underlined nor enclosed in quotation marks), the title of the work reviewed, a comma, the word *by*, and the name of the author. If the work of someone other than an author—say, an editor, a translator, or a director—is under review, use the appropriate abbreviation, such as *ed.*, *trans.*, or *dir.*, instead of *by*. For a review of a performance, add pertinent information about the production (see the sample entry for Tommasini). If more than one work is under review, list titles and authors in the order given at the beginning of the review (see the entry for Bordewich). Conclude the entry with the name of the periodical and the rest of the publication information.

If the review is titled but unsigned, begin the entry with the title of the review and alphabetize by that title (see the entry for "The Cooling of an Admiration"). If the review is neither titled nor signed, begin the entry with *Rev. of* and alphabetize under the title of the work reviewed (see the entry for *Anthology of Danish Literature*).

> Rev. of Anthology of Danish Literature, ed. F. J. Billeskov Jansen and P. M.
>   Mitchell. Times Literary Supplement 7 July 1972: 785.

Bordewich, Fergus M. Rev. of <u>Once They Moved like the Wind: Cochise,</u> <u>Geronimo, and the Apache Wars</u>, by David Roberts, and <u>Brave Are My</u> <u>People: Indian Heroes Not Forgotten</u>, by Frank Waters. <u>Smithsonian</u> Mar. 1994: 125-31.

"The Cooling of an Admiration." Rev. of <u>Pound/Joyce: The Letters of Ezra</u> <u>Pound to James Joyce, with Pound's Essays on Joyce</u>, ed. Forrest Read. <u>Times Literary Supplement</u> 6 Mar. 1969: 239-40.

Fassett, Deanna L. Rev. of <u>When Children Don't Learn: Student Failure and</u> <u>the Culture of Teaching</u>, by B. M. Franklin. <u>Communication Education</u> 50 (2001): 83-85.

Kauffmann, Stanley. "Toward the Shadows." Rev. of <u>Iris</u>, dir. Richard Eyre. <u>New Republic</u> 11 Feb. 2002: 26-27.

Tommasini, Anthony. "A Feminist Look at Sophocles." Rev. of <u>Jocasta</u>, by Ruth Schonthal and Hélène Cixous. Voice and Vision Theater Co. Cornelia Connelly Center for Educ., New York. <u>New York Times</u> 11 June 1998, late ed.: E5.

Updike, John. "No Brakes." Rev. of <u>Sinclair Lewis: Rebel from Main Street,</u> by Richard Lingeman. <u>New Yorker</u> 4 Feb. 2002: 77-80.

5.7.8. An Abstract in an Abstracts Journal

An abstracts journal publishes summaries of journal articles and of other literature. If you are citing an abstract, begin the entry with the publication information for the original work. Then add the relevant information for the journal from which you derived the abstract— title (underlined), volume number, year (in parentheses), and either item number or page number, depending on how the journal presents its abstracts. Of the journals cited below, *Current Index to Journals in Education, Psychological Abstracts*, and *Sociological Abstracts* use item numbers; *Dissertation Abstracts* and *Dissertation Abstracts International* use page numbers. Precede an item number with the word *item*. If the title of the journal does not make clear that you are citing an abstract, add the word *Abstract*, neither underlined nor in quotation marks, immediately after the original publication information (see the sample entry for McCabe).

Dissertation Abstracts International (DAI) has a long and complex history that might affect the way you cite an abstract in it. Before volume 30 (1969), *Dissertation Abstracts International* was titled *Dissertation Abstracts (DA)*. From volume 27 to volume 36, *DA* and *DAI* were paginated in two series: *A*, for humanities and social sciences, and *B*, for sciences and engineering. With volume 37, *DAI* added a third separately paginated section: *C*, for abstracts of European dissertations; in 1989, this section expanded its coverage to include institutions throughout the world. (For recommendations on citing dissertations themselves, see 5.6.26–27.)

Apple, Michael W. "Away with All Teachers: The Cultural Politics of Home Schooling." International Studies in Sociology of Education 10 (2000): 61-80. Sociological Abstracts 48 (2000): item 16056.

Ferguson, Tamara J., and Susan L. Crowley. "Gender Differences in the Organization of Guilt and Shame." Sex Roles 37 (1997): 19-44. Psychological Abstracts 85 (1998): item 4265.

Gans, Eric L. "The Discovery of Illusion: Flaubert's Early Works, 1835-1837." Diss. Johns Hopkins U, 1967. DA 27 (1967): 3046A.

Kelly, Mary. "Factors Predicting Hospital Readmission of Normal Newborns." Diss. U of Michigan, 2001. DAI 62 (2001): 2283B.

McCabe, Donald L. "Faculty Responses to Academic Dishonesty: The Influence of Student Honor Codes." Research in Higher Education 34 (1993): 647-58. Abstract. Current Index to Journals in Education 26 (1994): item EJ471017.

5.7.9. An Anonymous Article

If no author's name is given for the article you are citing, begin the entry with the title. Ignore any initial *A, An,* or *The* when you alphabetize the entry.

"Dubious Venture." Time 3 Jan. 1994: 64-65.

"It Barks! It Kicks! It Scores!" Newsweek 30 July 2001: 12.

5.7.10. An Editorial

If you are citing a signed editorial, begin with the author's name, give the title, and then add the descriptive label *Editorial*, neither underlined nor enclosed in quotation marks. Conclude with the appropriate publication information. If the editorial is unsigned, begin with the title and continue in the same way.

"Death of a Writer." Editorial. New York Times 20 Apr. 1994, late ed.: A18.

Gergen, David. "A Question of Values." Editorial. US News and World
Report 11 Feb. 2002: 72.

5.7.11. A Letter to the Editor

To identify a letter to the editor, add the descriptive label *Letter* after the name of the author, but do not underline the word or place it in quotation marks.

Mehlman, Jeffrey. Letter. Partisan Review 69 (2002): 320.

Safer, Morley. Letter. New York Times 31 Oct. 1993, late ed., sec. 2: 4.

Identify a published response to a letter as "Reply to letter of . . . ," adding the name of the writer of the initial letter. Do not underline this phrase or place it in quotation marks.

Gilbert, Sandra M. Reply to letter of Jerry W. Ward, Jr. PMLA 113 (1998):
131.

5.7.12. A Serialized Article

To cite a serialized article or a series of related articles published in more than one issue of a periodical, include all bibliographic information in one entry if each installment has the same author and title.

Garbaccia, Donna R., et al. "Food, Recipes, Cookbooks, and Italian-
American Life." Italian Americana 16 (1998): 5-23, 125-46.

Meserole, Harrison T., and James M. Rambeau. "Articles on American
Literature Appearing in Current Periodicals." American Literature 52
(1981): 688-705; 53 (1981): 164-80, 348-59.

If the installments bear different titles, list each one separately. You may include a brief supplementary description at the end of the entry to indicate that the article is part of a series.

Dugger, Celia W. "Wedding Vows Bind Old World and New." New York
    Times 20 July 1998, late ed.: A1+. Pt. 2 of a series, Here and There:
    Immigration Now, begun 19 July 1998.

Sontag, Deborah. "A Mexican Town That Transcends All Borders." New York
    Times 21 July 1998, late ed.: A1+. Pt. 3 of a series, Here and There:
    Immigration Now, begun 19 July 1998.

Sontag, Deborah, and Celia W. Dugger. "New Immigrant Tide: Shuttle
    between Worlds." New York Times 19 July 1998, late ed.: A1+. Pt. 1 of
    a series, Here and There: Immigration Now.

5.7.13. A Special Issue

To cite an entire special issue of a journal, begin the entry with the
name of the person who edited the issue (if given on the title page),
followed by a comma and the abbreviation *ed.* Next give the title of
the special issue (underlined), followed by "Spec. issue of" and the
name of the journal (underlined). Conclude the entry with the journal's volume number as well as the issue number (separated by a
period: "9.1"), the year of publication (in parentheses), a colon, a
space, and the complete pagination of the issue. If the issue has been
republished in book form, add the relevant information about the
book (city of publication, publisher, and date of publication).

Appiah, Kwame Anthony, and Henry Louis Gates, Jr., eds. Identities. Spec.
    issue of Critical Inquiry 18.4 (1992): 625-884. Chicago: U of Chicago P,
    1995.

Perret, Delphine, and Marie-Denise Shelton, eds. Maryse Condé. Spec. issue
    of Callaloo 18.3 (1995): 535-711.

State Autonomy. Spec. issue of Critical Review 14.2-3 (2000): 139-374.

If you are citing one article from a special issue and wish to indicate
complete publication information about the issue, use the following
form:

Makward, Christiane. "Reading Maryse Condé's Theater." Maryse Condé.
    Ed. Delphine Perret and Marie-Denise Shelton. Spec. issue of Callaloo
    18.3 (1995): 681-89.

Somin, Ilya. "Do Politicians Pander?" State Autonomy. Spec. issue of Critical
    Review 14.2-3 (2000): 147-55.

5.7.14. An Article in a Microform Collection of Articles

If you are citing an article that was provided by a reference source such as NewsBank, which selects periodical articles and makes them available on microfiche, begin the entry with the original publication information. Then add the relevant information concerning the microform from which you derived the article—title of source (underlined), volume number, year (in parentheses), and appropriate identifying numbers ("fiche 42, grids 5–6").

> Chapman, Dan. "Panel Could Help Protect Children." Winston-Salem
> Journal 14 Jan. 1990: 14. NewsBank: Welfare and Social Problems 12
> (1990): fiche 1, grids A8-11.

5.7.15. An Article Reprinted in a Loose-Leaf Collection of Articles

If you are citing a reprinted article that was provided by an information service such as the Social Issues Resources Series (SIRS), which selects articles from periodicals and publishes them in loose-leaf volumes, each dedicated to a specific topic, begin the entry with the original publication information. Then add the relevant information for the loose-leaf volume in which the article is reprinted, treating the volume like a book (see 5.6)—title (underlined), name of editor (if any), volume number (if any), city of publication, publisher, year of publication, and article number (preceded by the abbreviation *Art.*).

> Edmondson, Brad. "AIDS and Aging." American Demographics Mar. 1990:
> 28+. The AIDS Crisis. Ed. Eleanor Goldstein. Vol. 2. Boca Raton: SIRS,
> 1991. Art. 24.

5.8. CITING MISCELLANEOUS PRINT AND NONPRINT SOURCES

5.8.1. A Television or Radio Program

The information in an entry for a television or radio program usually appears in the following order:

1. Title of the episode or segment, if appropriate (in quotation marks)
2. Title of the program (underlined)
3. Title of the series, if any (neither underlined nor in quotation marks)
4. Name of the network
5. Call letters and city of the local station (if any)
6. Broadcast date

For instance, among the examples below, "Frederick Douglass" is an episode of the program *Civil War Journal*; *The Forsyte Saga* is a program in the series Masterpiece Theatre. Use a comma between the call letters and the city ("KETC, St. Louis"). A period follows each of the other items. For the inclusion of other information that may be pertinent (e.g., performers, director, narrator, number of episodes), see the sample entries.

> I Capuleti e i Montecchi. By Vincenzo Bellini. Perf. Andrea Rost and
> Vesselina Kasarova. Lyric Opera of Chicago. Cond. Bruno Campanella.
> Lyric Opera of Chicago Radio Network. WFMT, Chicago. 25 May 2002.
>
> "Death and Society." Narr. Joanne Silberner. Weekend Edition Sunday. Natl.
> Public Radio. WUWM, Milwaukee. 25 Jan. 1998.
>
> The Forsyte Saga. By John Galsworthy. Adapt. Stephen Mallatratt and Jan
> McVerry. Perf. Damian Lewis, Gina McKee, Ioan Gruffudd, Rupert
> Graves, Corin Redgrave, and Amanda Root. 8 episodes. Masterpiece
> Theatre. Introd. Russell Baker. PBS. WGBH, Boston. 6 Oct.-17 Nov.
> 2002.
>
> "Frankenstein: The Making of the Monster." Great Books. Narr. Donald
> Sutherland. Writ. Eugenie Vink. Dir. Jonathan Ward. Learning Channel.
> 8 Sept. 1993.

"Frederick Douglass." Civil War Journal. Narr. Danny Glover. Dir. Craig
  Haffner. Arts and Entertainment Network. 6 Apr. 1993.

Passion. By Stephen Sondheim. Dir. James Lapine. Perf. Donna Murphy, Jere
  Shea, and Marin Mazzie. Amer. Playhouse. PBS. WNET, New York. 7
  Mar. 1996.

"Yes . . . but Is It Art?" Narr. Morley Safer. Sixty Minutes. CBS. WCBS, New
  York. 19 Sept. 1993.

If your reference is primarily to the work of a particular individual,
cite that person's name before the title.

Mallatratt, Stephen, and Jan McVerry, adapts. The Forsyte Saga. By John
  Galsworthy. Perf. Damian Lewis, Gina McKee, Ioan Gruffudd, Rupert
  Graves, Corin Redgrave, and Amanda Root. 8 episodes. Masterpiece
  Theatre. Introd. Russell Baker. PBS. WGBH, Boston. 6 Oct.-17 Nov.
  2002.

Welles, Orson, dir. The War of the Worlds. By H. G. Wells. Adapt. Howard
  Koch. Mercury Theatre on the Air. CBS Radio. WCBS, New York. 30 Oct.
  1938.

If you are citing a transcript of a program, add the description *Transcript* at the end of the entry.

"Death and Society." Narr. Joanne Silberner. Weekend Edition Sunday. Natl.
  Public Radio. WUWM, Milwaukee. 25 Jan. 1998. Transcript.

To cite a music video for a song, begin with the information about
the song that is given before or after the video: performer, title of
song, title of album, name of manufacturer, and date of album. (See
5.8.2 on citing a song on a sound recording.) Follow this information
with the descriptive label *Music video*, the name of the director of
the video (if given), the channel, and the date you viewed the video.

Springsteen, Bruce. "Dancing in the Dark." Born in the USA. Columbia,
  1984. Music video. Dir. Brian De Palma. VH1. 10 May 2002.

See 5.8.7 for interviews on television and radio programs; see also
5.8.2–3 for sound, film, and video recordings, 5.8.4 for performances, and 5.9.9a for television and radio programs online or on
CD-ROM.

5.8.2. A Sound Recording

In an entry for a commercially available recording, which person is cited first (e.g., the composer, conductor, or performer) depends on the desired emphasis. List the title of the recording (or the titles of the works included), the artist or artists, the manufacturer ("Capitol"), and the year of issue (if the year is unknown, write *n.d.*). Place a comma between the manufacturer and the date; periods follow the other items. If you are not using a compact disc, indicate the medium, neither underlined nor enclosed in quotation marks, before the manufacturer's name: *Audiocassette* (see the sample entry for Joplin), *Audiotape* (reel-to-reel tape), or *LP* (long-playing record; see the entry for Ellington).

In general, underline titles of recordings (*Nuevo*), but do not underline or enclose in quotation marks the titles of musical compositions identified only by form, number, and key (see the entry for Norrington). You may wish to indicate, in addition to the year of issue, the date of recording (see, e.g., the entry for Ellington).

Bartoli, Cecilia. Dreams and Fables. London, 2001.

Ellington, Duke, cond. First Carnegie Hall Concert. Duke Ellington Orch. Rec. 23 Jan. 1943. LP. Prestige, 1977.

Gabriel, Peter. Passion: Music for The Last Temptation of Christ, a Film by Martin Scorsese. Rec. 1989. Geffen, 2002.

Holiday, Billie. The Essence of Billie Holiday. Columbia, 1991.

Joplin, Scott. Treemonisha. Perf. Carmen Balthrop, Betty Allen, and Curtis Rayam. Houston Grand Opera Orch. and Chorus. Cond. Gunther Schuller. Audiocassette. Deutsche Grammophon, 1976.

Kronos Quartet. Nuevo. Nonesuch, 2002.

Marsalis, Branford. Creation. Orpheus Chamber Orch. Sony, 2001.

Norrington, Roger, cond. Symphony no. 1 in C, op. 21, and Symphony no. 6 in F, op. 68. By Ludwig van Beethoven. London Classical Players. EMI, 1988.

Sondheim, Stephen. Passion. Orch. Jonathan Tunick. Perf. Donna Murphy, Jere Shea, and Marin Mazzie. Cond. Paul Gemignani. Angel, 1994.

Sting, narr. Peter and the Wolf, op. 67. By Sergei Prokofiev. Chamber Orch. of Europe. Cond. Claudio Abbado. Deutsche Grammophon, 1990.

If you are citing a specific song, place its title in quotation marks.

Bartoli, Cecilia. "Quel chiaro rio." By Christoph W. Gluck. Dreams and
    Fables. London, 2001.

Bono, Brian Eno, the Edge, and Luciano Pavarotti. "Miss Sarajevo." Pavarotti
    and Friends for the Children of Bosnia. London, 1996.

Gabriel, Peter. "A Different Drum." Perf. Gabriel, Shankar, and Youssou
    N'Dour. Passion: Music for The Last Temptation of Christ, a Film by
    Martin Scorsese. Rec. 1989. Geffen, 2002.

Holiday, Billie. "God Bless the Child." Rec. 9 May 1941. The Essence of Billie
    Holiday. Columbia, 1991.

Kronos Quartet and Tambuco. "Sensemaya." By Silvestre Revueltas. Nuevo.
    Nonesuch, 2002.

Treat a spoken-word recording as you would a musical recording.
Begin with the writer, the speaker, or the production director, depending on the desired emphasis. You may add the original publication date of the work immediately after the title.

Burnett, Frances Hodgson. The Secret Garden. 1911. Read by Helena
    Bonham Carter. Audiocassette. Penguin-High Bridge, 1993.

Hermann, Edward, narr. John Adams. By David McCullough. Audiocassette.
    Simon, 2001.

Neruda, Pablo. "Arte Poetica." The Caedmon Poetry Collection: A Century
    of Poets Reading Their Work. Harper, 2000.

Shakespeare, William. Othello. Dir. John Dexter. Perf. Laurence Olivier,
    Maggie Smith, Frank Finley, and Derek Jacobi. LP. RCA Victor, 1964.

Welles, Orson, dir. The War of the Worlds. By H. G. Wells. Adapt. Howard
    Koch. Mercury Theatre on the Air. Rec. 30 Oct. 1938. LP. Evolution, 1969.

Do not underline or enclose in quotation marks the title of a private or archival recording or tape. Include the date recorded (if
known) and the location and identifying number of the recording.

Wilgus, D. K. Southern Folk Tales. Rec. 23-25 Mar. 1965. Audiotape. U of
    California, Los Angeles, Archives of Folklore. B.76.82.

In citing the libretto, the booklet, the liner notes, or other material
accompanying a recording, give the author's name, the title of the

material (if any), and a description of the material (*Libretto*). Then provide the usual bibliographic information for a recording.

> Colette. Libretto. L'enfant et les sortilèges. Music by Maurice Ravel. Orch. National Bordeaux-Aquitaine. Cond. Alain Lombard. Valois, 1993.
>
> Lawrence, Vera Brodsky. "Scott Joplin and Treemonisha." Booklet. Treemonisha. By Scott Joplin. Deutsche Grammophon, 1976.
>
> Lewiston, David. Liner notes. The Balinese Gamelan: Music from the Morning of the World. LP. Nonesuch, n.d.

See 5.9.9b for sound recordings online.

5.8.3. A Film or Video Recording

A film entry usually begins with the title, underlined, and includes the director, the distributor, and the year of release. You may include other data that seem pertinent—such as the names of the writer, performers, and producer—between the title and the distributor.

> It's a Wonderful Life. Dir. Frank Capra. Perf. James Stewart, Donna Reed, Lionel Barrymore, and Thomas Mitchell. RKO, 1946.
>
> Like Water for Chocolate [Como agua para chocolate]. Screenplay by Laura Esquivel. Dir. Alfonso Arau. Perf. Lumi Cavazos, Marco Lombardi, and Regina Torne. Miramax, 1993.

If you are citing the contribution of a particular individual, begin with that person's name.

> Chaplin, Charles, dir. Modern Times. Perf. Chaplin and Paulette Goddard. United Artists, 1936.
>
> Jhabvala, Ruth Prawer, adapt. A Room with a View. By E. M. Forster. Dir. James Ivory. Prod. Ismail Merchant. Perf. Maggie Smith, Denholm Eliot, Helena Bonham Carter, and Daniel Day-Lewis. Cinecom Intl. Films, 1985.
>
> Mifune, Toshiro, perf. Rashomon. Dir. Akira Kurosawa. Daiei, 1950.
>
> Rota, Nino, composer. Juliet of the Spirits [Giulietta degli spiriti]. Dir. Federico Fellini. Perf. Giulietta Masina. Rizzoli, 1965.

Cite a videocassette, DVD (digital videodisc), laser disc, slide program, or filmstrip like a film, but include the original release date (if relevant) and the medium, neither underlined nor enclosed in quotation marks, before the name of the distributor.

Alcohol Use and Its Medical Consequences: A Comprehensive Teaching Program for Biomedical Education. Prod. Project Cork, Dartmouth Medical School. Slide program. Milner-Fenwick, 1982.

Don Giovanni. By Wolfgang Amadeus Mozart. Dir. Joseph Losey. Perf. Ruggero Raimondi and Kiri Te Kanawa. Paris Opera Orch. and Chorus. Cond. Loren Maazel. 1979. DVD. Columbia, 2002.

Hitchcock, Alfred, dir. Suspicion. Perf. Cary Grant and Joan Fontaine. 1941. Laser disc. Turner, 1995.

It's a Wonderful Life. Dir. Frank Capra. Perf. James Stewart, Donna Reed, Lionel Barrymore, and Thomas Mitchell. 1946. DVD. Republic, 2001.

Looking at Our Earth: A Visual Dictionary. Sound filmstrip. Natl. Geographic Educ. Services, 1992.

Mifune, Toshiro, perf. Rashomon. Dir. Akira Kurosawa. 1950. Videocassette. Home Vision, 2001.

Nureyev, Rudolph, chor. Swan Lake. By Pyotr Ilich Tchaikovsky. Perf. Margot Fonteyn and Nureyev. Vienna State Opera Ballet. Vienna Symphony Orch. Cond. John Lanchbery. 1966. DVD. Philips, 1997.

See 5.9.9c for films or film clips online or on CD-ROM.

5.8.4. A Performance

An entry for a performance (play, opera, ballet, concert) usually begins with the title, contains facts similar to those given for a film (see 5.8.3), and concludes with the site of the performance (usually the theater and city, separated by a comma and followed by a period) and the date of the performance.

Gianni Schichi. By Giacomo Puccini. Libretto by Giovacchino Forzano. Dir. Roberto De Simone. Perf. Carlo Guelfi and Daniela Dessì. Cond. Gianluigi Gelmetti. Teatro dell'Opera, Rome. 22 Jan. 2002.

Hamlet. By William Shakespeare. Dir. John Gielgud. Perf. Richard Burton. Shubert Theatre, Boston. 4 Mar. 1964.

Medea. By Euripides. Trans. Alistair Elliot. Dir. Jonathan Kent. Perf. Diana Rigg. Longacre Theatre, New York. 7 Apr. 1994.

The Siege of Paris. Marionettes of the Cooperativa Teatroarte Cuticchio.
Sylvia and Danny Kaye Playhouse, New York. 22 Mar. 1997.

South African Suite. Chor. Arthur Mitchell, Augustus Van Heerder, and
Laveen Naidu. Dance Theatre of Harlem. Cadillac Palace Theatre,
Chicago. 1 June 2002.

If you are citing the contribution of a particular individual or group,
begin with the appropriate name.

Ars Musica Antiqua. In Praise of Women: Music by Women Composers from
the Twelfth through the Eighteenth Centuries. Concert. Scotch Plains
Public Lib., NJ. 5 Apr. 1994.

Domingo, Plácido, tenor. Sly. By Ermanno Wolf-Ferrari. With Cynthia
Lawrence and Juan Pons. Metropolitan Opera. Cond. Marco Armiliato.
Metropolitan Opera House, New York. 4 May 2002.

Joplin, Scott. Treemonisha. Dir. Frank Corsaro. Perf. Carmen Balthrop, Betty
Allen, and Curtis Rayam. Houston Grand Opera Orch. and Chorus.
Cond. Gunther Schuller. Miller Theatre, Houston. 18 May 1975.

Rigg, Diana, perf. Medea. By Euripides. Trans. Alistair Elliot. Dir. Jonathan
Kent. Longacre Theatre, New York. 7 Apr. 1994.

For television and radio broadcasts of performances, see 5.8.1; for
sound recordings of performances, see 5.8.2; for video recordings of
performances, see 5.8.3.

5.8.5. A Musical Composition

To cite a musical composition, begin with the composer's name.
Underline the title of an opera, a ballet, or a piece of instrumental
music identified by name (*Symphonie fantastique*), but do not
underline or enclose in quotation marks the form, number, and key
when used to identify an instrumental composition.

Beethoven, Ludwig van. Symphony no. 7 in A, op. 92.

Berlioz, Hector. Symphonie fantastique, op. 14.

Treat a published score, however, like a book. Give the title, under-lined, as it appears on the title page, and capitalize the abbreviations *no.* and *op.*

> Beethoven, Ludwig van. Symphony No. 7 in A, Op. 92. New York: Dover,
>
> 1998.

If you wish to indicate when a musical composition was written, add the date immediately after the title.

> Beethoven, Ludwig van. Symphony No. 7 in A, Op. 92. 1812. New York:
>
> Dover, 1998.

See 5.8.2 for sound recordings of musical compositions, 5.8.1 for television and radio programs of music, and 5.8.4 for performances of music.

5.8.6. A Painting, Sculpture, or Photograph

To cite a painting or sculpture, state the artist's name first. In general, underline the title. Name the institution that houses the work (e.g., a museum) or, for a work in a private collection, the individual who owns it, and follow the name by a comma and the city.

> Bearden, Romare. The Train. Carole and Alex Rosenberg Collection, New
>
> York.
>
> Bernini, Gianlorenzo. Ecstasy of St. Teresa. Santa Maria della Vittoria, Rome.
>
> Rembrandt van Rijn. Aristotle Contemplating the Bust of Homer.
>
> Metropolitan Museum of Art, New York.

If you use a photograph of a painting or sculpture, indicate not only the institution or private owner and the city but also the complete publication information for the source in which the photograph appears, including the page, slide, figure, or plate number, which-ever is relevant.

> Cassatt, Mary. Mother and Child. Wichita Art Museum. American Painting:
>
> 1560-1913. By John Pearce. New York: McGraw, 1964. Slide 22.
>
> El Greco. Burial of Count Orgaz. San Tomé, Toledo. Renaissance
>
> Perspectives in Literature and the Visual Arts. By Murray Roston.
>
> Princeton: Princeton UP, 1987. 274.

If you wish to indicate when a work of art was created, add the date immediately after the title.

> Bearden, Romare. The Train. 1974. Carole and Alex Rosenberg Collection, New York.
>
> Cassatt, Mary. Mother and Child. 1890. Wichita Art Museum. American Painting: 1560-1913. By John Pearce. New York: McGraw, 1964. Slide 22.

Cite a photograph in a museum or collection as you would a painting or sculpture.

> Evans, Walker. Penny Picture Display. 1936. Museum of Mod. Art, New York.

To cite a personal photograph, begin with a description of its subject, neither underlined nor placed in quotation marks. Indicate the person who took the photograph and the date it was taken.

> Saint Paul's Cathedral, London. Personal photograph by author. 7 Mar. 2003.

See 5.9.9d for paintings, sculptures, and photographs online or on CD-ROM.

5.8.7. An Interview

For purposes of documentation, there are three kinds of interviews:

- Published or recorded interviews
- Interviews broadcast on television or radio
- Interviews conducted by the researcher

Begin with the name of the person interviewed. If the interview is part of a publication, recording, or program, enclose the title of the interview, if any, in quotation marks; if the interview was published independently, underline the title. If the interview is untitled, use the descriptive label *Interview*, neither underlined nor enclosed in quotation marks. The interviewer's name may be added if known and pertinent to your paper (see the sample entries for Breslin and Wiesel). Conclude with the appropriate bibliographic information.

> Breslin, Jimmy. Interview with Neal Conan. Talk of the Nation. Natl. Public Radio. WBUR, Boston. 26 Mar. 2002.

Fellini, Federico. "The Long Interview." Juliet of the Spirits. Ed. Tullio Kezich. Trans. Howard Greenfield. New York: Ballantine, 1966. 17-64.

Gordimer, Nadine. Interview. New York Times 10 Oct. 1991, late ed.: C25.

Lansbury, Angela. Interview. Off-Camera: Conversations with the Makers of Prime-Time Television. By Richard Levinson and William Link. New York: Plume-NAL, 1986. 72-86.

Wiesel, Elie. Interview with Ted Koppel. Nightline. ABC. WABC, New York. 18 Apr. 2002.

Wolfe, Tom. Interview. The Wrong Stuff: American Architecture. Dir. Tom Bettag. Videocassette. Carousel, 1983.

To cite an interview that you conducted, give the name of the person interviewed, the kind of interview (*Personal interview, Telephone interview, E-mail interview*), and the date or dates.

Pei, I. M. Personal interview. 22 July 1993.

Poussaint, Alvin F. Telephone interview. 10 Dec. 1998.

Rowling, J. K. E-mail interview. 8-12 May 2002.

See 5.9.9e for interviews online.

5.8.8. A Map or Chart

In general, treat a map or chart like an anonymous book (5.6.11), but add the appropriate descriptive label (*Map, Chart*).

Japanese Fundamentals. Chart. Hauppauge: Barron, 1992.

Michigan. Map. Chicago: Rand, 2000.

See 5.9.9f for maps and charts online. For guidance on how to cite such sources as dioramas, flash cards, games, globes, kits, and models, see Eugene B. Fleischer, *A Style Manual for Citing Microform and Nonprint Media* (Chicago: ALA, 1978).

5.8.9. A Cartoon or Comic Strip

To cite a cartoon or comic strip, state the artist's name; the title of the cartoon or comic strip (if any), in quotation marks; and the descriptive label *Cartoon* or *Comic strip*, neither underlined nor enclosed in quotation marks. Conclude with the usual publication information.

Chast, Roz. Cartoon. New Yorker 4 Feb. 2002: 53.

Trudeau, Garry. "Doonesbury." Comic strip. Star-Ledger [Newark] 4 May 2002: 26.

See 5.9.9g for cartoons and comic strips online.

5.8.10. An Advertisement

To cite an advertisement, state the name of the product, company, or institution that is the subject of the advertisement, followed by the descriptive label *Advertisement*, neither underlined nor enclosed in quotation marks. Conclude with the usual publication information.

Air Canada. Advertisement. CNN. 15 May 1998.

The Fitness Fragrance by Ralph Lauren. Advertisement. GQ Apr. 1997: 111-12.

See 5.9.9h for advertisements online.

5.8.11. A Lecture, a Speech, an Address, or a Reading

In a citation of an oral presentation, give the speaker's name; the title of the presentation (if known), in quotation marks; the meeting and the sponsoring organization (if applicable); the location; and the date. If there is no title, use an appropriate descriptive label (*Address*, *Lecture*, *Keynote speech*, *Reading*), neither underlined nor enclosed in quotation marks.

Atwood, Margaret. "Silencing the Scream." Boundaries of the Imagination Forum. MLA Convention. Royal York Hotel, Toronto. 29 Dec. 1993.

Hyman, Earle. Reading of Shakespeare's Othello. Symphony Space, New York. 28 Mar. 1994.

Terkel, Studs. Address. Conf. on Coll. Composition and Communication Convention. Palmer House, Chicago. 22 Mar. 1990.

5.8.12. A Manuscript or Typescript

To cite a manuscript or a typescript, state the author, the title or a description of the material (e.g., *Notebook*), the form of the material (*ms.* for a manuscript, *ts.* for a typescript), and any identifying number assigned to it. Give the name and location of any library or other research institution housing the material.

> Chaucer, Geoffrey. The Canterbury Tales. Harley ms. 7334. British Lib., London.
>
> Octovian. Ms. 91. Dean and Chapter Lib., Lincoln, Eng.
>
> Salviati, Lionardo. Poetica d'Aristotile parafrasata e comentata. Ms. 2.2.11. Biblioteca Nazionale Centrale, Firenze.
>
> Smith, Sonia. "Shakespeare's Dark Lady Revisited." Unpublished essay, 2002.
>
> Twain, Mark. Notebook 32, ts. Mark Twain Papers. U of California, Berkeley.

See 5.9.9i for manuscripts and working papers online.

5.8.13. A Letter or Memo

As bibliographic entries, letters fall into three general categories:

- Published letters
- Unpublished letters in archives
- Letters received by the researcher

Treat a published letter like a work in a collection (see 5.6.7), adding the date of the letter and the number (if the editor assigned one).

> Woolf, Virginia. "To T. S. Eliot." 28 July 1920. Letter 1138 of The Letters of Virginia Woolf. Ed. Nigel Nicolson and Joanne Trautmann. Vol. 2. New York: Harcourt, 1976. 437-38.

If you use more than one letter from a published collection, however, provide a single entry for the entire work and cite the letters individually in the text, following the form recommended for cross-references in works-cited lists (see 5.6.10).

In citing an unpublished letter, follow the guidelines for manuscripts and typescripts (see 5.8.12).

> Benton, Thomas Hart. Letter to Charles Fremont. 22 June 1847. John Charles Fremont Papers. Southwest Museum Lib., Los Angeles.

Cite a letter that you received as follows:

Morrison, Toni. Letter to the author. 17 May 2001.

Treat memos similarly: give the name of the writer of the memo, a description of the memo that includes the recipient, and the date of the document. Any title of the memo should be enclosed in quotation marks and placed immediately after the writer's name.

Cahill, Daniel J. Memo to English dept. fac., Brooklyn Technical High School, New York. 1 June 2000.

See 5.9.9j for e-mail communications.

5.8.14. A Legal Source

The citation of legal documents and law cases may be complicated. If your paper requires many such references, consult the most recent edition of *The Blue Book: A Uniform System of Citation* (Cambridge: Harvard Law Rev. Assn.), an indispensable guide in this field.

In general, do not underline or enclose in quotation marks the titles of laws, acts, and similar documents in either the text or the list of works cited (Declaration of Independence, Constitution of the United States, Taft-Hartley Act). Such titles are usually abbreviated, and the works are cited by sections. The years are added if relevant. No entry in the works-cited list is needed for familiar historical documents and the United States Code (USC), since references to them can be documented with brief parenthetical citations in the text: "(US Const., art. 1, sec. 1)," "(17 USC 304, 1976)." Note that references to the United States Code begin with the title number. For example, in the citation "(21 USC 1401a, 1988)," *21* refers to title 21, which contains laws concerned with food and drugs.

If you are citing an act in the works-cited list, state the name of the act, its Public Law number, the date it was enacted, and its Statutes at Large cataloging number. Use the abbreviations *Pub. L.* for Public Law and *Stat.* for Statutes at Large.

Aviation and Transportation Security Act. Pub. L. 107-71. 19 Nov. 2001. Stat. 115.597.

Names of law cases are similarly abbreviated ("Brown v. Board of Ed.," for the case of Oliver Brown versus the Board of Education of

Topeka, Kansas), but the first important word of each party's name is always spelled out. Names of cases, unlike those of laws, are underlined in the text but not in bibliographic entries. In citing a case, include, in addition to the names of the first plaintiff and the first defendant, the number of the case, the name of the court that decided the case, and the date of the decision. Once again, considerable abbreviation is the norm. The following citation, for example, refers to the decision on the case of the New York Times Company and others against Jonathan Tasini and others, which was decided by the United States Supreme Court on 25 June 2001.

New York Times Co. v. Tasini. No. 00-201. Supreme Ct. of the US. 25 June 2001.

To cite a patent issued by the United States Patent and Trademark Office, give the following information: the name of the inventor; the title of the patent, neither underlined nor enclosed in quotation marks; the name of the assignee, if any, followed by a comma and the word *assignee*; the patent number, preceded by the word *Patent*; and the issue date.

Guha, Aloke. Method and System for Efficiently Storing Web Pages for Quick Downloading at a Remote Device. Storage Technology Corp., assignee. Patent 6,272,534. 7 Aug. 2001.

To cite a government publication, see 5.6.21.

5.9. CITING ELECTRONIC PUBLICATIONS

5.9.1. The Basic Entry: A Document from an Internet Site

Citations of electronic sources and those of print sources should accomplish the same ends and have analogous formats. Both types of citations identify a source and give sufficient information to allow a reader to locate it. Yet each type requires a different kind and amount of information to fulfill these objectives. Print culture has developed standard reference tools (library catalogs, bibliographies, and so on) for locating published works. Electronic media, in contrast, so far lack agreed-on means of organizing works. Moreover, electronic texts are not as fixed and stable as their print counterparts.

References to electronic works therefore must provide more information than print citations generally offer.

The recommendations in this section mostly treat sources for which a considerable amount of relevant publication information is available. In truth, though, many sources do not supply all desired information, for few standards currently govern the presentation of electronic publications—for instance, many texts do not include reference markers, such as paragraph numbers, so it is difficult if not impossible to direct a reader to the exact location of the material you are citing. Thus, while aiming for comprehensiveness, writers must often settle for citing whatever information is available to them.

These recommendations are aimed not at specialists in academic computing but primarily at students who use ideas and facts from electronic sources to complement those derived from traditional print sources. Moreover, since this section cannot possibly cover all materials available in electronic form, its emphasis, like that of the rest of this handbook, is on refereed, authoritative sources (see 1.6) as well as on historical texts. This edition's recommendations on citing electronic works are necessarily not definitive and will doubtless change as technology, scholarly uses of electronic materials, and electronic publication practices evolve.

Whereas the basic entry for print publications, like books and articles in periodicals, typically has three main divisions—*author's name*, *title*, and *publication information* (see 5.6.1 and 5.7.1)—a citation for an electronic publication, such as a document from an Internet site, may have as many as five divisions:

> Author's name. "Title of the document." Information about print publication. Information about electronic publication. Access information.

Author's Name

In general, follow the recommendations for citing the names of authors of books (5.6.1). Take the author's name directly from the document; it normally appears at the beginning or the end of the document (see fig. 30). Reverse the name for alphabetizing, and put a period after it.

> Zeki, Semir.

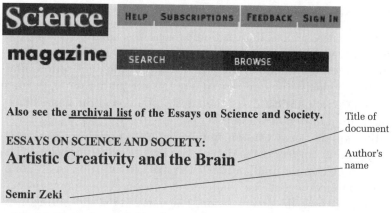

Fig. 30. The author and title of an article in a periodical on the Web.

Title of the Document

In general, follow the recommendations for titles given in 3.6. State the full title of the document, enclosed in quotation marks (unless you are citing an entire Internet site [see 5.9.2] or an online book [see 5.9.3]). (See fig. 30.)

Zeki, Semir. "Artistic Creativity and the Brain."

If no author's name is available, begin the entry with the title of the document.

"Catalán."

Information about Print Publication

If the document gives information pertaining to a previous or simultaneous print publication (see fig. 31), state that information, as indicated in the document, following the recommendations for print publications (see 5.6 for books and 5.7 for articles in periodicals).

Zeki, Semir. "Artistic Creativity and the Brain." Science 6 July 2001: 51-52.

⌐ **ESSAYS ON SCIENCE AND SOCIETY:**
Artistic Creativity and the Brain
Semir Zeki
Science 2001 July 6; 293: 51-52. (in Essays on Science and Society)
[Summary] [Full Text]

Fig. 31. Information about the print publication of an article in a periodical on the Web.

Information about Electronic Publication

Internet sites, such as information databases, scholarly projects, professional Web sites, and online periodicals, vary significantly in the publication information they provide. Electronic publication information typically includes the title of the site (underlined), the date of electronic publication or the latest update, and the name of any institution or organization that sponsors the site (see fig. 32). If an editor's name or a version number is stated, give that information directly following the title of the site (see examples below). The date of electronic publication is required in addition to a date of print publication because the Internet version of the document may well differ from the print version. The name of the sponsoring institution or organization normally appears at the bottom of the site's home page.

Zeki, Semir. "Artistic Creativity and the Brain." Science 6 July 2001: 51-52.

Science Magazine. 2002. Amer. Assn. for the Advancement of Science.

If no print publication is stated, cite only the electronic publication, following the author's name and the title of the document.

Ross, Don. "Game Theory." 11 Sept. 2001. Stanford Encyclopedia of

Philosophy. Ed. Edward N. Zalta. Fall 2002 ed. Center for the Study of

Lang. and Information, Stanford U.

Fig. 32. Sections of the home page of a periodical on the Web, showing the site's main title and, at the bottom, the organization responsible for the site. At this site, the copyright date can be taken as the date of the latest update of the article.

If no author is stated, begin the entry with the title of the document and proceed with the remaining information.

"Catalán." Sí, España. Ed. José Félix Barrio. Vers. 3.0. May 2002. Embassy of Spain, Ottawa.

Access Information

- **Date of access.** Most bibliographic references to printed works contain only one date, the date of publication. A citation of an electronic work, however, normally requires two and sometimes more dates to be identified fully. Since electronic texts can be readily altered, an online source must be considered unique each time it is accessed. Typically, then, a citation for an online text contains the date assigned to the document in the source as well as the date of access—that is, the date on which you viewed the document. If you accessed the document more than once, give the last date on which you viewed it. For a work with a prior or simultaneous print existence, it may be necessary, then, to give three dates—the date of print publication, if provided; the date of electronic publication; and the date of access—for the document may have been different at each stage. (On citing dates for publications on CD-ROM, diskette, and magnetic tape, see 5.9.5.)

- **URL.** The most efficient way to find an online publication at present is through its network address, or URL (uniform resource locator). This edition of the *MLA Handbook* recommends including URLs in citations of online works. Since addresses can change, however, and their length and complexity can result in transcription errors, it is crucial to be as accurate as possible in supplying not only URLs but also other identifying information (e.g., author's name, title of document, name of site), so that the reader who cannot locate the material through the stated address might be able to find it with a network searching tool. Moreover, since Internet sites and resources sometimes disappear altogether, you should download or print out the material you use, so that you can verify it if it is inaccessible later. Give the URL immediately following the date of access. Enclose URLs in angle brackets. If a URL must be divided between two lines, break it only after a slash; do not introduce a hyphen at the break or allow your word-processing program to do so. In most instances, give the complete address, including the access-mode identifier (*http, ftp, gopher, telnet,* *news*), for the specific document you are citing, but see below for exceptions.

"Catalán." Sí, España. Ed. José Félix Barrio. Vers. 3.0. May 2002. Embassy of Spain, Ottawa. 10 May 2002 <http://www.SiSpain.org/spanish/language/language/catalan.html>.

Ross, Don. "Game Theory." 11 Sept. 2001. Stanford Encyclopedia of Philosophy. Ed. Edward N. Zalta. Fall 2002 ed. Center for the Study of Lang. and Information, Stanford U. 1 Oct. 2002 <http://plato.stanford.edu/entries/game-theory/>.

Zeki, Semir. "Artistic Creativity and the Brain." Science 6 July 2001: 51-52. Science Magazine. 2002. Amer. Assn. for the Advancement of Science. 24 Sept. 2002 <http://www.sciencemag.org/cgi/content/full/293/5527/51>.

Ideally, the URL of the exact document you consulted should be given. Sometimes, however, the URL of a document is so long and complicated that reproducing it would invite transcription errors or would at least cause inconvenience. In such instances, it is preferable to give instead the URL of the site's search page, if such a page exists. Once there, the reader can readily access the document by keying in other publication facts recorded in the citation (e.g., author's name, title). For example, *JSTOR* assigns the following URL to a 1998 article by Nancy Tolson in *African American Review*:

http://links.jstor.org/sici?sici=1062-4783%28199821%2932%3A1%3C9%3AM BATRO%3E2.0.CO%3B2-2

Rather than try to reproduce such a URL, simply give the URL of the database's search page.

Tolson, Nancy. "Making Books Available: The Role of Early Libraries, Librarians, and Booksellers in the Promotion of African American Children's Literature." African American Review 32 (1998): 9-16. JSTOR. 1 Oct. 2002 <http://www.jstor.org/search>.

If an Internet site does not assign a specific URL to each document and if citing a search page is not appropriate, give the URL of the site's home page. If a reader can proceed from the home page to the document by clicking on a sequence of links, follow the URL with the word *Path* and a colon, and then specify the sequence of links. Use semicolons to separate the names of the links (see fig. 33).

Nastali, Dan, and Phil Boardman. "Searching for Arthur: Literary Highways, Electronic Byways, and Cultural Back Roads." Arthuriana 11.4 (2001): 108-22. Abstract. 1 Oct. 2002 <http://www.smu.edu/arthuriana/>. Path: Abstracts; K-O.

URLs are often omitted in entries for material obtained from a library or personal subscription service (see 5.9.7).

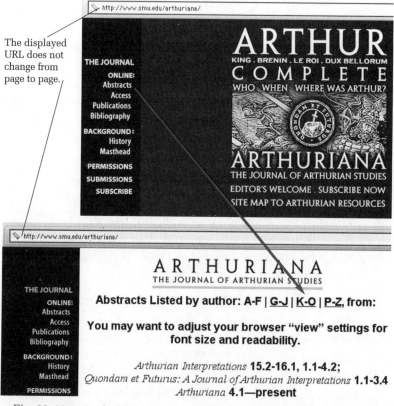

Fig. 33. No specific URL. At some Web sites, visitors do not see specific URLs for individual documents. For example, the entry for an abstract posted at *Arthuriana* could end "<http://www.smu.edu/arthuriana/>. Path: Abstracts; K–O."

Here are additional examples of the basic entry for documents from Internet sites:

"City Profile: San Francisco." CNN.com. 2002. Cable News Network. 14
    May 2002 <http://www.cnn.com/TRAVEL/atevo/city/SanFrancisco/
    intro.html>.

"Fresco Painting." Encyclopaedia Britannica Online. 2002. Encyclopaedia
    Britannica. 8 May 2002 <http://search.eb.com/>.

Hoffmann, Heinrich. "Struwwelpeter." Trans. Mark Twain. Nineteenth-
    Century German Stories. Ed. Robert Godwin-Jones. 22 Feb. 1999.
    Foreign Lang. Dept., Virginia Commonwealth U. 10 Jan. 2002
    <http://www.fln.vcu.edu/struwwel/twpete.html>.

"Reebok International Ltd." Hoover's Online. 2002. Hoover's, Inc. 19 June
    2002 <http://www.hoovers.com/co/capsule/6/0,2163,11266,00.html>.

"Selected Seventeenth-Century Events." Romantic Chronology. Ed. Laura
    Mandell and Alan Liu. 1999. U of California, Santa Barbara. 22 June
    2002 <http://english.ucsb.edu:591/rchrono/>.

Stowe, Harriet Beecher. "Sojourner Truth, the Libyan Sibyl." Atlantic Monthly
    Apr. 1863: 473-81. Electronic Text Center. Ed. David Seaman. 2002.
    Alderman Lib., U of Virginia. 19 June 2002 <http://
    etext.lib.virginia.edu/toc/modeng/public/StoSojo.html>.

"Symbiosis." UCMP Glossary. Ed. Allen Collins et al. 1 May 2002. U of
    California Museum of Paleontology, Berkeley. 15 May 2002 <http://
    www.ucmp.berkeley.edu/glossary/gloss5ecol.html>.

"This Day in Technology History: August 20." History Channel.com. 2002.
    History Channel. 14 May 2002 <http://historychannel.com/>. Path:
    Technology History; This Day in Technology History.

Sometimes additional information is required. This list shows most of the possible components of an entry for an Internet publication and the order in which they are normally arranged (see 5.9.5 for publications on CD-ROM, diskette, or magnetic tape).

1. The name of the author, editor, compiler, or translator of the source (if given), reversed for alphabetizing and, if appropriate, followed by an abbreviation, such as *ed.*

2. Title of an article, poem, short story, or similar short work in the Internet site (enclosed in quotation marks). Or title of a posting to a discussion list or forum (taken from the subject

line and put in quotation marks), followed by the description *Online posting* (see 5.9.9k)

3. Title of a book (underlined; see esp. 5.9.3)
4. Name of the editor, compiler, or translator of the text (if relevant and if not cited earlier), preceded by the appropriate abbreviation, such as *Ed.*
5. Publication information for any print version of the source
6. Title of the Internet site (e.g., scholarly project, database, online periodical, or professional or personal site [underlined]) or, for a professional or personal site with no title, a description such as *Home page*
7. Name of the editor of the site (if given)
8. Version number of the source (if not part of the title) or, for a journal, the volume number, issue number, or other identifying number
9. Date of electronic publication, of the latest update, or of posting
10. For a work from a subscription service, the name of the service and—if a library or a consortium of libraries is the subscriber—the name and geographic location (e.g., city, state abbreviation) of the subscriber (see 5.9.7)
11. For a posting to a discussion list or forum, the name of the list or forum (see 5.9.9k)
12. The number range or total number of pages, paragraphs, or other sections, if they are numbered
13. Name of any institution or organization sponsoring the site (if not cited earlier)
14. Date when the researcher accessed the source
15. URL of the source or, if the URL is impractically long and complicated, the URL of the site's search page. Or, for a document from a subscription service, the URL of the service's home page, if known (see 5.9.7a); or the keyword assigned by the service, preceded by *Keyword*; or the sequence of links followed, preceded by *Path* (see 5.9.7b).

The rest of 5.9 explains how to cite the following kinds of electronic publications:

• Entire Internet sites (e.g., online scholarly projects, information databases, professional and personal sites; 5.9.2)
• Online books (5.9.3)
• Articles in online periodicals (5.9.4)

- Publications on CD-ROM, diskette, and magnetic tape (5.9.5)
- Works published in more than one medium (5.9.6)
- Works from online subscription services (5.9.7)
- Publications in an indeterminate medium (5.9.8)
- Other electronic sources (e.g., audiovisual materials, manuscripts and working papers, e-mail communications, online postings; 5.9.9).

5.9.2. An Entire Internet Site

The typical entry for an entire online scholarly project, information database, journal, or professional site consists of the following items:

1. Title of the site (underlined)
2. Name of the editor of the site (if given)
3. Electronic publication information, including version number (if relevant and if not part of the title), date of electronic publication or of the latest update, and name of any sponsoring institution or organization
4. Date of access and URL

If you cannot find some of this information, cite what is available.

Bartleby.com: Great Books Online. Ed. Steven van Leeuwen. 2002. 5 May
    2002 <http://www.bartleby.com/>.

The Cinderella Project. Ed. Michael N. Salda. Vers. 1.1. Dec. 1997. De
    Grummond Children's Lit. Research Collection, U of Southern
    Mississippi. 15 May 2002 <http://www-dept.usm.edu/~engdept/
    cinderella/cinderella.html>.

CNN.com. 2002. Cable News Network. 15 May 2002 <http://www.cnn.com/>.

Electronic Text Center. Ed. David Seaman. 2002. Alderman Lib., U of
    Virginia. 19 June 2002 <http://etext.lib.virginia.edu/>.

Encyclopaedia Britannica Online. 2002. Encyclopaedia Britannica. 15 May
    2002 <http://www.britannica.com/>.

History Channel.com. 2002. History Channel. 14 May 2002 <http://
    historychannel.com/>.

Hoover's Online. 2002. Hoover's, Inc. 19 June 2002 <http://
    www.hoovers.com/>.

Jane Austen Information Page. Ed. Henry Churchyard. 6 Sept. 2000. 15 June
2002 <http://www.pemberley.com/janeinfo/janeinfo.html>.

Nineteenth-Century German Stories. Ed. Robert Godwin-Jones. 1999.
Foreign Lang. Dept., Virginia Commonwealth U. 10 Jan. 2002 <http://
www.fln.vcu.edu/menu.html>.

Postmodern Culture. Ed. Lisa Brawley and James F. English. 2002. 1 Oct.
2002 <http://www.iath.virginia.edu/pmc/>.

Romantic Chronology. Ed. Laura Mandell and Alan Liu. 1999. U of California,
Santa Barbara. 22 June 2002 <http://english.ucsb.edu:591/rchrono/>.

Sí, España. Ed. José Félix Barrio. Vers. 3.0. May 2002. Embassy of Spain,
Ottawa. 10 May 2002 <http://www.SiSpain.org/>.

Thomas: Legislative Information on the Internet. 19 June 2001. Lib. of
Congress, Washington. 18 May 2002 <http://thomas.loc.gov/>.

UCMP Glossary. Ed. Allen Collins et al. May 2002. U of California Museum of
Paleontology, Berkeley. 19 July 2002 <http://www.ucmp.berkeley.edu/
glossary/>.

Victorian Women Writers Project. Ed. Perry Willett. May 2000. Indiana U. 26
June 2002 <http://www.indiana.edu/~letrs/vwwp/>.

a. A Home Page for a Course

To cite a home page for a course, begin the entry with the name of
the instructor, reversed for alphabetizing and followed by a period,
and the title of the course, neither underlined nor in quotation marks
(see 3.6.5 on course titles). Continue with a description such as
Course home page (neither underlined nor in quotation marks), the
dates of the course, the names of the department and the institution,
the date of access, and the URL.

Cuddy-Keane, Melba. Professing Literature. Course home page. Sept. 2000-
Apr. 2001. Dept. of English, U of Toronto. 4 Oct. 2002 <http://
www.chass.utoronto.ca/~mcuddy/ENG9900H/Index.htm>.

b. A Home Page for an Academic Department

To cite a home page for an academic department, give the name
of the department, a description such as *Dept. home page* (neither

underlined nor in quotation marks), the name of the institution, the date of access, and the URL.

Microbiology and Immunology. Dept. home page. Stanford U School of
Medicine. 4 Oct. 2002 <http://cmgm.stanford.edu/micro/>.

c. A Personal Home Page

To document a personal home page, begin the entry with the name of the person who created it, reversed for alphabetizing and followed by a period. Continue with the title of the site (underlined) or, if there is no title, with the description *Home page* (neither underlined nor in quotation marks); the date of the last update, if given; the date of access; and the URL.

Lancashire, Ian. Home page. 28 Mar. 2002. 15 May 2002 <http://
www.chass.utoronto.ca:8080/~ian/>.

5.9.3. An Online Book

The texts of some printed books are available online, independently or as part of Internet sites. In general, follow the recommendations in 5.6 for citing books, modifying them as appropriate to the electronic source.

a. An Entire Online Book

The typical entry for a complete online book consists of the following items:

1. Author's name (if given). If only an editor, a compiler, or a translator is identified, cite that person's name, followed by the appropriate abbreviation (*ed., comp., trans.*).
2. Title of the work (underlined)
3. Name of the editor, compiler, or translator of the book (if relevant); see, for example, the entries for Austen, Hawthorne, and Pascal
4. Publication information for the original print version, if given in the source (e.g., city of publication, name of publisher, year of publication). You may add in brackets relevant information not stated in the source; see the entry for Pascal.

5. Electronic publication information (e.g., title of the Internet site [underlined], editor of site, version number, date of electronic publication, name of any sponsoring institution or organization)
6. Date of access and URL for the book

If you cannot find some of this information, cite what is available. See 5.9.3c for citing a government publication.

Austen, Jane. Pride and Prejudice. Ed. Henry Churchyard. 1996. Jane Austen Information Page. 6 Sept. 2002 <http://www.pemberley.com/janeinfo/ pridprej.html>.

Cinderella. New York: Wrigley, [c. 1800-25]. The Cinderella Project. Ed. Michael N. Salda. Vers. 1.1. Dec. 1997. De Grummond Children's Lit. Research Collection, U of Southern Mississippi. 15 Apr. 2002 <http:// www-dept.usm.edu/~engdept/cinderella/cind2.html>.

Douglass, Frederick. Narrative of the Life of Frederick Douglass, an American Slave, Written by Himself. Boston, 1845. 30 Jan. 1997 <gopher://gopher.vt.edu:10010/02/73/1>.

Emerson, Ralph Waldo. Essays: First Series. 1841. 12 Feb. 1997 <ftp:// ftp.books.com/ebooks/NonFiction/Philosophy/Emerson/history.txt>.

Hawthorne, Nathaniel. Twice-Told Tales. Ed. George Parsons Lathrop. Boston: Houghton, 1883. 16 May 2002 <http://209.11.144.65/ eldritchpress/nh/ttt.html>.

Keats, John. Poetical Works. 1884. Bartleby.com: Great Books Online. Ed. Steven van Leeuwen. 2002. 5 May 2002 <http://www.bartleby.com/ 126/>.

Menzel, Peter, and Faith D'Aluisio. Robo Sapiens: Evolution of a New Species. Cambridge: MIT P, 2000. MIT Press. 8 May 2002 <http:// robosapiens.mit.edu/>.

Nagata, Linda. Goddesses. 2000. Scifi.com. 2002. 4 Oct. 2002 <http:// www.scifi.com/originals/originals_archive/nagata/>.

Nesbit, E[dith]. Ballads and Lyrics of Socialism. London, 1908. Victorian Women Writers Project. Ed. Perry Willett. May 2000. Indiana U. 26 June 2002 <http://www.indiana.edu/~letrs/vwwp/nesbit/ballsoc.html>.

Ovid. Metamorphoses. Trans. Arthur Golding. London, 1567. The Perseus Digital Library. Ed. Gregory Crane. Apr. 2001. Tufts U. 16 May 2002 <http://www.perseus.tufts.edu/cgi-bin/ptext?lookup=Ov.+Met.+1.1>.

Pascal, Blaise. Pensées. Trans. W. F. Trotter. [1910.] 29 Apr. 1997 <gopher://
   gopher.vt.edu:10010/02/130/1>.

Robinson, Mary. Sappho and Phaon. London, 1796. Electronic Text Center.
   Ed. David Seaman. 2002. Alderman Lib., U of Virginia. 19 June 2002
   <http://etext.lib.virginia.edu/britpo/sappho/sappho.html>.

b. A Part of an Online Book

If you are citing a part of an online book, place the title or name of
the part between the author's name and the title of the book. If the
part is a work like a poem or an essay, place its title in quotation
marks. If the part is a standard division of the book, such as an introduction or a preface, do not place the title in quotation marks or
underline it; see the entry for Menzel and D'Aluisio. Give the URL of
the specific part instead of that of the book if they differ.

Emerson, Ralph Waldo. "Self-Reliance." Essays: First Series. 1841. 12 Feb.
   1997 <ftp://ftp.books.com/ebooks/NonFiction/Philosophy/Emerson/
   history.txt>.

Hawthorne, Nathaniel. "Dr. Heidegger's Experiment." Twice-Told Tales. Ed.
   George Parsons Lathrop. Boston: Houghton, 1883. 16 May 2002
   <http:// 209.11.144.65/eldritchpress/nh/dhe.html>.

Keats, John. "Ode on a Grecian Urn." Poetical Works. 1884. Bartleby.com:
   Great Books Online. Ed. Steven van Leeuwen. 2002. 5 May 2002
   <http://www.bartleby.com/126/41.htm>.

Menzel, Peter, and Faith D'Aluisio. Introduction. Robo Sapiens: Evolution of
   a New Species. Cambridge: MIT P, 2000. MIT Press. 8 May 2002
   <http://robosapiens.mit.edu/intro.htm>.

Nesbit, E[dith]. "Marching Song." Ballads and Lyrics of Socialism. London,
   1908. Victorian Women Writers Project. Ed. Perry Willett. May 2000.
   Indiana U. 26 June 2002 <http://www.indiana.edu/~letrs/vwwp/nesbit/
   ballsoc.html#p9>.

c. An Online Government Publication

To cite an online government publication, begin with the same facts
given for printed government works (see 5.6.21), and conclude with
information appropriate to the electronic source.

United States. Dept. of Justice. Office of Juvenile Justice and Delinquency Prevention. Law Enforcement and Juvenile Crime. By Howard N. Snyder. Dec. 2001. 29 June 2002 <http://www.ncjrs.org/pdffiles1/ojjdp/191031.pdf>.

5.9.4. An Article in an Online Periodical

Periodical publications online include scholarly journals, newspapers, and magazines; works and other materials within such publications include articles, reviews, editorials, and letters to the editor. In general, follow the recommendations in 5.7 for citing parts of print periodicals, modifying them as appropriate to the electronic source. See 5.9.7 for citing articles derived from subscription services. The typical entry for a work in an online periodical consists of the following items:

1. Author's name (if given)
2. Title of the work or material (if any; a review or letter to the editor may be untitled), in quotation marks
3. Name of the periodical (underlined)
4. Volume number, issue number, or other identifying number
5. Date of publication
6. The number range or total number of pages, paragraphs, or other sections, if they are numbered (see fig. 34)
7. Date of access and URL

If you cannot find some of this information, cite what is available.

24. Although C.F.E. Spurgeon fails to identify a pattern of subject of Shakespeare's story (Spurgeon 346).[11] Or references to time.[12] Because of the simmering di Julian calendar, Julius Caesar's association with time highly topical subject in 1599.

25. Caesar had imposed his Julian calendar by decree on Roman Republican calendar (reformed 153 B.C.E.) w a calendar is too short or too long, the date on whicl

Fig. 34. Numbered paragraphs. Pages, paragraphs, or other sections are sometimes numbered in electronic documents. Such numbers should be included in the works-cited list and in text citations (see 6.4.2). This example shows portions of paragraphs 24 and 25 of the article by Steve Sohmer documented in 5.9.4a.

a. An Article in a Scholarly Journal (cf. 5.7.1–4)

Scholarly journals are available online independently (see, e.g., the entry below for Dane) or as part of an archival database of journals (see the entries below for Chan and Tolson). If the journal is included within a database, state the name of the database (underlined) after the print information for the article; follow with the date of access and the relevant URL within the database.

Butler, Darrell L., and Martin Sellbom. "Barriers to Adopting Technology for Teaching and Learning." Educause Quarterly 25.2 (2002): 22-28. Educause. 3 Aug. 2002 <http://www.educause.edu/ir/library/pdf/eqm0223.pdf>.

Chan, Evans. "Postmodernism and Hong Kong Cinema." Postmodern Culture 10.3 (2000). Project Muse. 20 May 2002 <http://muse.jhu.edu/journals/pmc/v010/10.3chan.html>.

Dane, Gabrielle. "Reading Ophelia's Madness." Exemplaria 10.2 (1998). 22 June 2002 <http://web.english.ufl.edu/english/exemplaria/danefram.htm>.

Sengers, Phoebe. "Cultural Informatics: Artificial Intelligence and the Humanities." Surfaces 8.107 (1999): 58 pp. 3 Aug. 2002 <http://pum12.pum.umontreal.ca/revues/surfaces/sgml/vol8/sengers.sgm>.

Sohmer, Steve. "12 June 1599: Opening Day at Shakespeare's Globe." Early Modern Literary Studies 3.1 (1997): 46 pars. 26 June 2002 <http://www.shu.ac.uk/emls/03-1/sohmjuli.html>.

Tolson, Nancy. "Making Books Available: The Role of Early Libraries, Librarians, and Booksellers in the Promotion of African American Children's Literature." African American Review 32 (1998): 9-16. JSTOR. 1 Oct. 2002 <http://www.jstor.org/search>.

b. An Article in a Newspaper or on a Newswire (cf. 5.7.5)

Achenbach, Joel. "America's River." Washington Post 5 May 2002. 20 May 2002 <http://www.washingtonpost.com/wp-dyn/articles/A13425-2202May1.html>.

Biersdorfer, J. D. "Religion Finds Technology." New York Times on the Web 16 May 2002. 20 May 2002 <http://www.nytimes.com/2002/05/16/technology/circuits/16CHUR.html>.

"Networks Seek Familiarity, Stability." AP Online 20 May 2002. 20 May 2002 <http://www.nytimes.com/aponline/arts/AP-TV-New-Season.html>.

c. An Article in a Magazine (cf. 5.7.6)

Brooks, David. "The Culture of Martyrdom." Atlantic Online June 2002. 24 Sept. 2002 <http://www.theatlantic.com/issues/2002/06/brooks.htm>.

Levy, Steven. "Great Minds, Great Ideas." Newsweek 27 May 2002. 20 May 2002 <http://www.msnbc.com/news/754336.asp>.

d. A Review (cf. 5.7.7)

Ebert, Roger. Rev. of Memento, dir. Christopher Nolan. Chicago Sun-Times Online 13 Apr. 2001. 18 May 2002 <http://www.suntimes.com/ebert/ebert_reviews/2001/04/041302.html>.

Gravlee, Cynthia A. Rev. of Magic in Medieval Romance from Chrétien de Troyes to Geoffrey Chaucer, by Michelle Sweeney. Medieval Review 2.03.15 (2002). 20 May 2002 <http://www.hti.umich.edu/t/tmr/>.

Kisselgoff, Anna. "A First Work with Hot and Cool Spices." Rev. of Haiku, chor. Albert Evans. New York City Ballet. New York State Theater. New York Times on the Web 18 May 2002. 20 May 2002 <http://www.nytimes.com/2002/05/18/arts/dance/18PRIS.html>.

Nickles, David Paull. "Superheroes of the Historical Profession." Rev. of Clio's Favorites: Leading Historians of the United States, 1945-2000, ed. Robert Allen Rutland. Boston Book Review June 2001. 20 May 2002 <http://www.bookwire.com/bookwire/bbr/reviews/june2001/Clios.htm>.

Rigby, Kate, and Bradley Franks. Rev. of The Mating Mind: How Sexual Choice Shaped the Evolution of Human Nature, by G. F. Miller. Psycoloquy 12.033 (2001): 17 pars. 20 May 2002 <http://cogprints.ecs.soton.ac.uk/cgi/psyc/newspsy?12.033>.

e. An Abstract (cf. 5.7.8)

Nastali, Dan, and Phil Boardman. "Searching for Arthur: Literary Highways, Electronic Byways, and Cultural Back Roads." Arthuriana 11.4 (2001): 108-22. Abstract. 1 Oct. 2002 <http://www.smu.edu/arthuriana/>. Path: Abstracts; K-O.

f. An Anonymous Article (cf. 5.7.9)

"Senior Fitness." USNews.com 27 May 2002. 20 May 2002 <http://
www.usnews.com/usnews/issue/020527/biztech/27home.b.htm>.

g. An Editorial (cf. 5.7.10)

"Keeping College Doors Open." Editorial. Christian Science Monitor:
CSMonitor.com 16 May 2002. 20 May 2002 <http://
www.csmonitor.com/2002/0516/p08s03-comv.html>.

h. A Letter to the Editor (cf. 5.7.11)

Schmidt, Christine. Letter. New York Times on the Web 20 May 2002. 20
    May 2002 <http://www.nytimes.com/2002/05/20/opinion/
    L20KIDS.html>.

i. A Serialized Article (cf. 5.7.12)

Levy, Clifford J. "For Mentally Ill, Death and Misery." New York Times on the
    Web 28 Apr. 2002. Pt. 1 of a series, Broken Homes. 20 May 2002
    <http://www.nytimes.com/2002/04/28/nyregion/28HOME.html>.
---. "Here, Life Is Squalor and Chaos." New York Times on the Web 29 Apr.
    2002. Pt. 2 of a series, Broken Homes, begun 28 Apr. 2002. 20 May
    2002 <http://www.nytimes.com/2002/04/29/nyregion/29HOME.html>.
---. "Voiceless, Defenseless, and a Source of Cash." New York Times on the
    Web 30 Apr. 2002. Pt. 3 of a series, Broken Homes, begun 28 Apr.
    2002. 20 May 2002 <http://www.nytimes.com/2002/04/30/nyregion/
    30HOME.html>.

5.9.5. A Publication on CD-ROM, Diskette, or Magnetic Tape

Citations for publications on CD-ROM, diskette, and magnetic tape
are similar to those for print sources, with the following important
differences.

Publication medium. Works are often published in more than one
format (e.g., print, online, CD-ROM), and the works may not be the
same in each. When you cite a publication on CD-ROM, diskette, or
magnetic tape, it is important to state the publication medium in

order to differentiate the source from its possible print or online counterpart.

Vendor's name. The persons or groups responsible for supplying the information in publications on CD-ROM, diskette, and magnetic tape are sometimes also the publishers of the works. But many information providers choose instead to lease the data to vendors (e.g., SilverPlatter, UMI-ProQuest) for distribution. It is important to state the vendor's name in your works-cited list, if it is given in your source, because the information provider may have leased electronic versions of the data to more than one vendor, and the versions may not be identical (see 5.9.5b).

Publication dates. Many databases published on CD-ROM, diskette, or magnetic tape are updated regularly (e.g., annually, quarterly). Updates add information and may also correct or otherwise alter information that previously appeared in the database. Therefore, a works-cited-list entry for material derived from such a database commonly contains the date of the document used, as indicated in the source, as well as the publication date (or date of the most recent updating) of the database (see 5.9.5b).

The sections below contain recommendations for citing nonperiodical publications on CD-ROM, diskette, or magnetic tape (5.9.5a), materials from periodically published databases on CD-ROM (5.9.5b), and multidisc publications (5.9.5c).

a. A Nonperiodical Publication on CD-ROM, Diskette, or Magnetic Tape

Many publications on CD-ROM, diskette, or magnetic tape are issued as books are—that is, without a plan to update or otherwise revise the work regularly. Cite a nonperiodical publication on CD-ROM, diskette, or magnetic tape as you would a book, but add a description of the medium of publication. Since the information provider and the publisher are usually the same for such publications, no vendor's name appears, and only one publication date is given. The typical works-cited-list entry for the source consists of the following items:

1. Author's name (if given). If only an editor, a compiler, or a translator is identified, cite that person's name, followed by the appropriate abbreviation (*ed., comp., trans.*).

2. Title of the publication (underlined)
3. Name of the editor, compiler, or translator (if relevant)
4. Publication medium (*CD-ROM*, *Diskette*, or *Magnetic tape*)
5. Edition, release, or version (if relevant)
6. Place of publication
7. Name of the publisher
8. Date of publication

If you cannot find some of this information, cite what is available.

Afro-Louisiana History and Genealogy, 1699-1860. Ed. Gwendolyn Midlo
    Hall. CD-ROM. Baton Rouge: Louisiana State UP, 2000.

Braunmuller, A. R., ed. Macbeth. By William Shakespeare. CD-ROM. New
    York: Voyager, 1994.

Encyclopaedia of Islam. CD-ROM. Leiden: Brill, 1999.

English Poetry Full-Text Database. Magnetic tape. Rel. 2. Cambridge, Eng.:
    Chadwyck-Healey, 1993.

Thiesmeyer, Elaine C., and John E. Thiesmeyer. Editor for the Macintosh: A
    Proofreading System for Usage, Mechanics, Vocabulary, and
    Troublesome Spelling. Diskette. New York: MLA, 2001.

If publication information for a printed source or printed analogue is
indicated, begin the citation with that information.

Aristotle. The Complete Works of Aristotle: The Revised Oxford Translation.
    Ed. Jonathan Barnes. 2 vols. Princeton: Princeton UP, 1984. CD-ROM.
    Clayton: InteLex, 1994.

The Oxford English Dictionary. 2nd ed. CD-ROM. Oxford: Oxford UP, 1992.

If you are citing only a part of the work, state which part. If the
part is a book-length work, underline the title; if the part is a shorter
work like an article, an essay, a poem, or a short story, enclose the
title in quotation marks. If the source supplies page numbers, paragraph numbers, screen numbers, or some other kind of section numbers, state their total if the numbering starts over with each part (see
the entry for Rodes), but state the range of the numbers in the part if
a single numbering encompasses all the parts.

"Albatross." The Oxford English Dictionary. 2nd ed. CD-ROM. Oxford:
    Oxford UP, 1992.

"The Chemistry of Air Pollution." Magill's Survey of Science. CD-ROM. 1998
    ed. Pasadena: Salem, 1998.
"Children's Television Workshop." Encyclopedia of Associations. Magnetic
    tape. Detroit: Gale, 1994.
Coleridge, Samuel Taylor. "Dejection: An Ode." The Complete Poetical
    Works of Samuel Taylor Coleridge. Ed. Ernest Hartley Coleridge. Vol. 1.
    Oxford: Clarendon, 1912. 362-68. English Poetry Full-Text Database.
    CD-ROM. Rel. 2. Cambridge, Eng.: Chadwyck-Healey, 1993.
"Ellison, Ralph." DiscLit: American Authors. Diskette. Boston: Hall, 1991.
"Ibn Hamdis." Encyclopaedia of Islam. CD-ROM. Leiden: Brill, 1999.
Rodes, David S. "The Language of Ambiguity and Equivocation." Macbeth.
    By William Shakespeare. Ed. A. R. Braunmuller. CD-ROM. New York:
    Voyager, 1994. 5 pp.

b. Material from a Periodically Published Database on CD-ROM

Many periodicals (journals, magazines, newspapers) and periodically published reference works, such as annual bibliographies and
collections of abstracts, are published both in print and on CD-ROM
as databases or as parts of databases. To cite such a work, begin with
the publication data for the printed source or printed analogue, as
identified in the CD-ROM publication. If the print version is a book
or a pamphlet, follow the guidelines in 5.6; if the print version is an
article in a periodical, follow 5.7. The typical works-cited-list entry
consists of the following items:

1. Author's name (if given)
2. Publication information for the printed source or printed
   analogue (including title and date of print publication)
3. Title of the database (underlined)
4. Publication medium (*CD-ROM*)
5. Name of the vendor (if relevant)
6. Electronic publication date

If you cannot find some of this information, cite what is available.

Krach, Peg. "Myth and Facts about Alcohol Abuse in the Elderly." Nursing
    Feb. 1998: 25+. Abstract. Periodical Abstracts Ondisc. CD-ROM. UMI-
    ProQuest. Feb. 1998.
Reese, Elaine, Catherine A. Haden, and Robyn Fivush. "Mothers, Fathers,
    Daughters, Sons: Gender Differences in Autobiographical Reminiscing."

Research on Language and Social Interaction 29 (1996): 27-56.
Abstract. Sociofile. CD-ROM. SilverPlatter. Dec. 1996.
United States. Cong. House. Committee on the Judiciary. Report on the Fair
Use of Copyrighted Works. 11 Aug. 1992. 102nd Cong. 1st sess.
Congressional Masterfile 2. CD-ROM. Congressional Information
Service. Dec. 1996.

c. A Multidisc Publication

If you are documenting a CD-ROM publication of more than one
disc, follow the publication medium (*CD-ROM*) either with the total
number of discs or with a specific disc number if you use material
from only one.

Perseus 2.0: Interactive Sources and Studies on Ancient Greece. CD-ROM. 4
discs. New Haven: Yale UP, 1996.
United States. Dept. of State. Patterns of Global Terrorism. 1994. National
Trade Data Bank. CD-ROM. Disc 2. US Dept. of Commerce. Dec. 1996.

5.9.6. A Work in More Than One Publication Medium

If the work you are citing is published in various media (e.g., a CD-
ROM and a diskette), specify all the media that constitute the publication or cite only the media you used.

Lancashire, Ian, et al. Using TACT with Electronic Texts: A Guide to Text-
Analysis Computing Tools. Book, CD-ROM. Vers. 2.1. New York: MLA,
1996.
Perseus 1.0: Interactive Sources and Studies on Ancient Greece. CD-ROM,
laser disc. New Haven: Yale UP, 1992.
Poetry Speaks: Hear Great Poets Read Their Work, from Tennyson to Plath.
Ed. Elise Paschen and Rebekah Presson Mosby. Book, CD-ROM. 3
discs. Naperville: Sourcebooks Media Fusion, 2001.

or

Mann, Thomas. Tonio Kröger. Ed. Barry Joe. Using TACT with Electronic
Texts: A Guide to Text-Analysis Computing Tools. By Ian Lancashire et
al. CD-ROM. Vers. 2.1. New York: MLA, 1996.

Tennyson, Alfred. "Ulysses." Poetry Speaks: Hear Great Poets Read Their
Work, from Tennyson to Plath. Ed. Elise Paschen and Rebekah Presson
Mosby. CD-ROM. Disc 1. Naperville: Sourcebooks Media Fusion, 2001.

5.9.7. A Work from a Library or Personal Subscription Service

Two common types of online subscription services are those to
which libraries or library systems typically subscribe (e.g., EBSCO,
Gale, Lexis-Nexis) and those to which individual users tend to subscribe personally (e.g., America Online). To document material from
either type of service, begin the entry as shown in 5.9.2–4. The format of the entry will vary depending on whether the material is an
item in an information database, an online book, an article from a
periodical, and so on. For material that originally appeared in print,
begin with standard facts about the print publication, omitting data
not given by the online service.

If possible, conclude with the URL of the specific document or, if
the URL is impractically long and complicated, the URL of the site's
search page. Often, however, these services supply material without
a URL or with a URL that is unique to the subscribing institution or
valid only during the current session (see 1.4.6d). For such services,
conclude the entry as described below.

a. A Work from a Library Subscription Service

To cite material from a service to which a library or library system
subscribes, complete the citation by stating the name of the database
used (underlined), if known; the name of the service; the name of the
library or library system (with a city, a state abbreviation, or both if
useful); and the date of access. If you know the URL of the service's
home page, give it, in angle brackets, immediately after the date of
access, or you may simply end with the date of access. If the service
provides only the starting page number of an article's original print
publication (e.g., "p192"), give the number followed by a hyphen, a
space, and a period: "192– ."

"Cooling Trend in Antarctica." Futurist May-June 2002: 15. Academic Search
Premier. EBSCO. City U of New York, Graduate Center Lib. 22 May
2002 <http://www.epnet.com/>.

Koretz, Gene. "Economic Trends: Uh-Oh, Warm Water." Business Week 21

July 1997: 22. Electric Lib. Sam Barlow High School Lib., Gresham, OR.
17 Oct. 1997 <http://www.elibrary.com/>.

McMichael, Anthony J. "Population, Environment, Disease, and Survival:
Past Patterns, Uncertain Futures." Lancet 30 Mar. 2002: 1145-48.
Academic Universe: Medical. Lexis-Nexis. California Digital Lib. 22 May
2002 <http://web.lexis-nexis.com/>.

Youakim, Sami. "Work-Related Asthma." American Family Physician 64
(2001): 1839-52. Health Reference Center. Gale. Bergen County
Cooperative Lib. System, NJ. 12 Jan. 2002 <http://
www.galegroup.com/>.

b. A Work from a Personal Subscription Service

If you are using a source from a personal subscription service that
allows you to retrieve material by entering a keyword or similar designation, complete the citation by writing *Keyword*, with a colon,
and the word itself following the name of the service and the date of
access.

"Table Tennis." Compton's Encyclopedia Online. Vers. 2.0. 1997. America
Online. 4 July 1998. Keyword: Compton's.

If instead of entering a keyword the user follows a series of topic
labels, write the word *Path*, with a colon, and specify the sequence
of topics you followed to obtain the material; use semicolons to separate topics.

"Cloning." BioTech's Life and Science Dictionary. 30 June 1998. Indiana U.
America Online. 4 July 1998. Path: Research and Learning; Science;
Biology; Biotechnology Dictionary.

5.9.8. A Work in an Indeterminate Medium

If you cannot determine the medium of a source—for example, if you
access material through a local network and cannot tell whether the
work is stored on the central computer's hard drive (where the
contents would be subject to revision) or on a CD-ROM—use the designation *Electronic* for the medium. Give whatever relevant publication information you can, as well as the name of the network or of its
sponsoring organization and the date of access.

Bartlett, John. Familiar Quotations. 9th ed. Boston: Little, 1901. New York: Columbia U, Academic Information Systems, 1995. Electronic. ColumbiaNet, Columbia U Lib. 2 July 1998.

Lubiano, Wahneema. "Toni Morrison." African American Writers. Valerie Smith, gen. ed. 2nd ed. Vol. 2. New York: Scribner's, 1999. 321-33. Electronic. Gale, 2001. Alabama Virtual Lib. 24 Apr. 2001.

5.9.9. Other Electronic Sources

In general, to document other electronic sources, follow the recommendations in 5.8 on citing miscellaneous print and nonprint sources, modifying the guidelines as appropriate (cf. 5.9.2–8). Some kinds of works need identifying labels (*Interview, Map, Online posting*), neither underlined nor enclosed in quotation marks. In documenting a source such as an online posting or a synchronous communication, try to cite an archival version, if one exists, so that the reader can more easily consult the work.

a. A Television or Radio Program (cf. 5.8.1)

Keillor, Garrison. A Prairie Home Companion. With Ledward Ka'apana and Owana Salazar. 12 Oct. 2002. Minnesota Public Radio. 18 Oct. 2002 <http://phc.mpr.org/ri/smil/021012.ram>.

Komando, Kim. "Password Security." WCBS News Radio. WCBS, New York. 20 May 2002. Transcript. 23 May 2002 <http://wcbs880.com/komando/StoryFolder/story_1002173851_html>.

"The Threat of Commercial Fishing." Earth Matters. CNN. 18 Jan. 1998. Transcript. Broadcast News. CD-ROM. Primary Source Media. Jan. 1998. 22 screens.

b. A Sound Recording or Sound Clip (cf. 5.8.2)

Edelman, Lee, Sara Suleri Goodyear, and Stephen Nichols. "Love Poetry, II." What's the Word? 2001. Modern Language Association. 20 Sept. 2002. MLA. 17 Oct. 2002 <http://www.mla.org/>. Path: MLA Radio Show; Browse Shows and Listen; 2001.

McFerrin, Bobby. "Kalimba Suite." Beyond Words. Blue Note, 2002. 21 May
2002 <http://www.liquid.com/promo/fulfill?key=3e9d38799614>.

Roosevelt, Franklin D. "Americanism." 1920. American Leaders Speak:
Recordings from World War I and the 1920 Election. 1996. American
Memory. Lib. of Congress, Washington. 19 Mar. 2002 <http://
lcweb2.loc.gov/mbrs/nforum/9000024.ram>.

c. A Film or Film Clip (cf. 5.8.3)

Kurosawa, Akira, dir. Throne of Blood. 1957. Macbeth. By William
Shakespeare. Ed. A. R. Braunmuller. CD-ROM. New York: Voyager,
1994.

Murnau, F. W., dir. Nosferatu. 1922. The Sync. 16 June 2002 <http://
www.thesync.com/ram/nosferatu.ram>.

d. A Painting, Sculpture, or Photograph (cf. 5.8.6)

Delacroix, Eugène. Death of Ophelia. 1853. Louvre, Paris. Shakespeare
Illustrated. Ed. Harry Rusche. 13 Sept. 2000. Emory U. 1 Oct. 2002
<http://www.emory.edu/ENGLISH/classes/Shakespeare_Illustrated/
Delacroix.Ophelia.html>.

Evans, Walker. Penny Picture Display. 1936. Museum of Mod. Art, New York.
30 May 2002 <http://www.moma.org/collection/photography/pages/
evans.penny.html>.

Holbein, Hans. The Ambassadors. 1533. Microsoft Art Gallery: The
Collection of the National Gallery, London. CD-ROM. Redmond:
Microsoft, 1994.

e. An Interview (cf. 5.8.7)

Ackroyd, Peter. Interview. Bold Type. Nov. 2001. 25 June 2002 <http://
www.randomhouse.com/boldtype/1101/ackroyd/interview.html>.

f. A Map (cf. 5.8.8)

"Phoenix, Arizona." Map. U.S. Gazetteer. US Census Bureau. 24 Sept. 2002
<http://factfinder.census.gov/servlet/
ReferenceMapFramesetServlet?_lang=en>.

g. A Cartoon or Comic Strip (cf. 5.8.9)

Ohman, Jack. "One Final Carrier Landing Attempt." Cartoon. USNews.com
8 Apr. 2002. 29 May 2002 <http://www.usnews.com/usnews/issue/
020408/opinion/8cartoon.html>.

h. An Advertisement (cf. 5.8.10)

Lee Mood Ring. Advertisement. 29 June 1998 <http://www.leejeans.com/
features/moodring.html>.

i. A Manuscript or Working Paper (cf. 5.8.12)

Cacicedo, Al. "Private Parts: Preliminary Notes for an Essay on Gender
Identity in Shakespeare." Working paper, 12 Mar. 1997. 24 Sept. 2002
<http://www.shaksper.net/archives/files/private.parts.html>.

Guaman Poma de Ayala, Felipe. El primer nueva corónica y buen gobierno.
1615. Ms. Gl. kgl. s. 2232, 4°. Det Kongelige Bibliotek, Köbenhavn
[Copenhagen]. 31 July 2002 <http://www.kb.dk/elib/mss/poma/
index-en.htm>.

Whitman, Walt. Notebooks. Thomas Bigg Harned Walt Whitman Collection.
Ms. Div., Lib. of Congress. American Memory. Lib. of Congress,
Washington. 29 May 2002 <http://memory.loc.gov/ammem/wwhtml/
wwcoll.html>.

j. An E-Mail Communication (cf. 5.8.13)

To cite electronic mail, give the name of the writer; the title of the
message (if any), taken from the subject line and enclosed in quotation marks; a description of the message that includes the recipient
(e.g., *E-mail to the author*); and the date of the message.

Boyle, Anthony T. "Re: Utopia." E-mail to Daniel J. Cahill. 21 June 1997.
Harner, James L. E-mail to the author. 20 Aug. 2002.

k. An Online Posting

To cite a posting to an e-mail discussion list, begin with the author's
name and the title of the document (in quotation marks), as given in
the subject line, followed by the description *Online posting*, the date
when the material was posted, the name of the forum (if known; e.g.,

Humanist Discussion Group), the date of access, and, in angle brackets, the online address of the list's Internet site or, if no Internet site is known, the e-mail address of the list's moderator or supervisor. Whenever feasible, cite an archival version of the posting, so that your readers can more easily consult your source.

> Chu, Michael. "Bellini Style." Online posting. 20 May 2002. Opera-L. 21
>
> May 2002 <http://lists.cuny.edu/archives/opera-l.html>.
>
> Lavagnino, John. "OCR and Handwriting." Online posting. 7 May 2002.
>
> Humanist Discussion Group. 24 May 2002 <http://
>
> lists.village.virginia.edu/lists_archive/Humanist/v16/0001.html>.
>
> Merrian, Joanne. "Spinoff: Monsterpiece Theatre." Online posting. 30 Apr.
>
> 1994. Shaksper: The Global Electronic Shakespeare Conf. 23 Sept.
>
> 2002 <http://www.shaksper.net/archives/1994/0380.html>.

To cite a posting to a World Wide Web forum, begin with the author's name and the title of the posting (if there is one), in quotation marks, followed by the description *Online posting*, the date when the material was posted, the name of the forum, the date of access, and, in angle brackets, the URL.

> Valentine, Mike Banks. Online posting. 16 May 2002. Online Privacy. 30 May
>
> 2002 <http://forums.nytimes.com/webin/WebX?50@.f2b7b9a?7>.

To cite a posting to a Usenet news group, begin with the author's name and the title of the document (in quotation marks), as given in the subject line, followed by the description *Online posting*, the date when the material was posted, the date of access, and, in angle brackets, the name of the news group, with the prefix *news:*.

> Menegatos, Tom. "Re: Amsterdam." Online posting. 2 Apr. 2002. 4 May
>
> 2002 <news:humanities.misc>.

To cite a document forwarded within a posting, begin with the name of the writer, the title, and the date of the document. Then give the name of the person who forwarded it, preceded by *Fwd. by*. Conclude the entry with the description *Online posting*, the date of the posting in which the material was forwarded, and the appropriate remaining information for a posting to a discussion list, an online forum, or a news group.

> Chessid, Estelle. "Women Authors: A New List Now Available." 29 June

1997. Fwd. by Kevin Berland. Online posting. 2 July 1997. C18-L:
Resources for Eighteenth-Century Studies across the Disciplines. 5 May
2002 <http://lists.psu.edu/cgi-bin/wa?S1=C18-1>.

l. A Synchronous Communication

To cite a synchronous communication posted in a forum such as a
MUD (multiuser domain) or MOO (multiuser domain, object-oriented),
give the name of the speaker (if you are citing just one), a description
of the event, the date of the event, the forum for the communication
(e.g., LinguaMOO), the date of access, and the URL, with the prefix
telnet://.

> Grigar, Dene. Online defense of dissertation "Penelopeia: The Making of
> Penelope in Homer's Story and Beyond." 25 July 1995. LinguaMOO. 25
> July 1995 <telnet://lingua.utdallas.edu:8888>.

Whenever feasible, cite an archival version of the communication, so
that your readers can more readily consult your source.

> Grigar, Dene. Online defense of dissertation "Penelopeia: The Making of
> Penelope in Homer's Story and Beyond." 25 July 1995. LinguaMOO. 1
> June 2002 <http://lingua.utdallas.edu/~cynthiah/lingua_archive/
> phd-defense.txt>.

m. Downloaded Computer Software

> MacCase. Vers. 1.0. 1 Aug. 1998 <ftp://ftp.adfa.oz.au/pub/mac/
> MacCASE/>.
> TACT: Text-Analysis Computing Tools. Vers. 2.1. 24 Sept. 2002 <http://
> www.chass.utoronto.ca/cch/tact.html>.

⑥ Documentation: Citing Sources in the Text

6.1. PARENTHETICAL DOCUMENTATION AND THE LIST OF WORKS CITED

The list of works cited at the end of your research paper plays an important role in your acknowledgment of sources (see ch. 5), but the list does not in itself provide sufficiently detailed and precise documentation. You must indicate to your readers not only what works you used in writing the paper but also exactly what you derived from each source and exactly where in the work you found the material. The most practical way to supply this information is to insert a brief parenthetical acknowledgment in your paper wherever you incorporate another's words, facts, or ideas. Usually the author's last name and a page reference are enough to identify the source and the specific location from which you borrowed material.

> Medieval Europe was a place both of "raids, pillages, slavery, and extortion" and of "traveling merchants, monetary exchange, towns if not cities, and active markets in grain" (Townsend 10).

The parenthetical reference "(Townsend 10)" indicates that the quotations come from page 10 of a work by Townsend. Given the author's last name, your readers can find complete publication information for the source in the alphabetically arranged list of works cited that follows the text of your paper.

> Townsend, Robert M. The Medieval Village Economy. Princeton: Princeton UP, 1993.

The sample references in 6.4 offer recommendations for documenting many other kinds of sources.

6.2. INFORMATION REQUIRED IN PARENTHETICAL DOCUMENTATION

In determining the information needed to document sources accurately, keep the following guidelines in mind.

References in the text must clearly point to specific sources in the list of works cited. The information in your parenthetical references in the text must match the corresponding information in the entries in your list of works cited. For a typical works-cited-list entry, which begins with the name of the author (or editor, translator, or narrator), the parenthetical reference begins with the same name. When the list contains only one work by the author cited, you need give only the author's last name to identify the work: "(Patterson 183–85)." If your list contains more than one author with the same last name, you must add the first initial—"(A. Patterson 183–85)" and "(L. Patterson 230)"—or, if the initial is shared too, the full first name. If two or three names begin the entry, give the last name of each person listed: "(Rabkin, Greenberg, and Olander vii)." If the work has more than three authors, follow the form in the bibliographic entry: either give the first author's last name followed by *et al.*, without any intervening punctuation—"(Lauter et al. 2425–33)"—or give all the last names. If there is a corporate author, use its name, shortened or in full (see 6.4.5). If the work is listed by title, use the title, shortened or in full; if two or more anonymous works have the same title, add a publication fact, such as a date, that distinguishes the works (see 6.4.4). If the list contains more than one work by the author, add the cited title, shortened or in full, after the author's last name (see 6.4.6).

Identify the location of the borrowed information as specifically as possible. For a printed source, give the relevant page number or numbers in the parenthetical reference (see esp. 6.4.2) or, if you cite from more than one volume of a multivolume work, the volume and page numbers (see 6.4.3). In a reference to a literary work or to the Bible, it is helpful to give information other than, or in addition to, the page number—for example, the chapter, book, or stanza number or the numbers of the act, scene, and line (see 6.4.8). You may omit page numbers when citing complete works (see 6.4.1). A page reference is similarly unnecessary if, for example, you use a passage from a one-page work. Of course, nonprint sources such as films, television programs, recordings, and performances and electronic sources with no pagination or other type of reference markers cannot be cited by page number. Such works are usually cited in their entirety (see 6.4.1) and often by title (see 6.4.4). (See 6.4.2 for electronic publications with paragraph numbers or other kinds of reference numbers.)

6.3. READABILITY

Keep parenthetical references as brief—and as few—as clarity and accuracy permit. Give only the information needed to identify a source, and do not add a parenthetical reference unnecessarily. Identify sources by author and, if necessary, title; do not use abbreviations such as *ed.*, *trans.*, and *comp.* after the name. If you are citing an entire work, for example, rather than a specific part of it, the author's name in the text may be the only documentation required. The statement "Booth has devoted an entire book to the subject" needs no parenthetical documentation if the list of works cited includes only one work by Booth. If, for the reader's convenience, you wish to name the book in your text, you could recast the sentence: "Booth has devoted an entire book, *The Rhetoric of Fiction*, to the subject."

Remember that there is a direct relation between what you integrate into your text and what you place in parentheses. If, for example, you include an author's name in a sentence, you need not repeat the name in the parenthetical page citation that follows, provided that the reference is clearly to the work of the author you mention. The paired sentences below illustrate alternative ways of identifying authors. Note that sometimes one version is more concise than the other.

AUTHOR'S NAME IN TEXT

Tannen has argued this point (178-85).

AUTHOR'S NAME IN REFERENCE

This point has already been argued (Tannen 178-85).

AUTHORS' NAMES IN TEXT

Others, like Jakobson and Waugh (210-15), hold the opposite point of view.

AUTHORS' NAMES IN REFERENCE

Others hold the opposite point of view (e.g., Jakobson and Waugh 210-15).

AUTHOR'S NAME IN TEXT

Only Daiches has seen this relation (2: 776-77).

AUTHOR'S NAME IN REFERENCE

Only one scholar has seen this relation (Daiches 2: 776-77).

AUTHOR'S NAME IN TEXT

It may be true, as Robertson maintains, that "in the appreciation of medieval art the attitude of the observer is of primary importance . . ." (136).

AUTHOR'S NAME IN REFERENCE

It may be true that "in the appreciation of medieval art the attitude of the observer is of primary importance . . ." (Robertson 136).

To avoid interrupting the flow of your writing, place the parenthetical reference where a pause would naturally occur (preferably at the end of a sentence), as near as possible to the material documented. The parenthetical reference precedes the punctuation mark that concludes the sentence, clause, or phrase containing the borrowed material.

In his Autobiography, Benjamin Franklin states that he prepared a list of thirteen virtues (135-37).

A reference directly after a quotation follows the closing quotation mark.

In the late Renaissance, Machiavelli contended that human beings were by nature "ungrateful" and "mutable" (1240), and Montaigne thought them "miserable and puny" (1343).

If the quotation, whether of poetry or prose, is set off from the text (see 3.7.2–4), type a space after the concluding punctuation mark of the quotation and insert the parenthetical reference.

John K. Mahon adds a further insight to our understanding of the War of 1812:

> Financing the war was very difficult at the time. Baring Brothers, a banking firm of the enemy country, handled routine accounts for the United States overseas, but the firm would take on no loans. The loans were in the end absorbed by wealthy Americans at great hazard--also, as it turned out, at great profit to them. (385)

Elizabeth Bishop's "In the Waiting Room" is rich in evocative detail:

> It was winter. It got dark
>
> early. The waiting room
>
> was full of grown-up people,
>
> arctics and overcoats,
>
> lamps and magazines. (6-10)

For guidelines on citing literary works, see 6.4.8.

If you need to document several sources for a statement, you may cite them in a note to avoid unduly disrupting the text (see 6.5.2). If you quote more than once from the same page within a single paragraph—and no quotation from another source intervenes—you may give a single parenthetical reference after the last quotation.

6.4. SAMPLE REFERENCES

Each of the following sections concludes with a list of the works cited in the examples. Note that the lists for the first five sections (6.4.1–5) do not include more than one work by the same author. On citing two or more works by an author, see 6.4.6.

6.4.1. Citing an Entire Work, Including a Work with No Page Numbers

If you wish to cite an entire work—whether a print source; a nonprint source such as a film, television program, or performance; or an electronic publication that has no pagination or other type of reference markers—it is usually preferable to include in the text, rather than in a parenthetical reference, the name of the person (e.g., author, editor, director, performer) that begins the corresponding entry in the works-cited list. (See 6.4.4 for citing a work by title.)

BOOKS (cf. 5.6)

Fukuyama's <u>Our Posthuman Future</u> includes many examples of this trend.

Paul Lauter and his coeditors have provided a useful anthology of American literature.

Gilbert and Gubar broke new ground on the subject.

ARTICLES IN PERIODICALS (cf. 5.7)

But Katie Trumpener has offered another view.

Diction, according to Anthony Tommasini, is more important than vocal prowess in a singer of Gilbert and Sullivan.

MISCELLANEOUS NONPRINT SOURCES (cf. 5.8)

Kurosawa's Rashomon was one of the first Japanese films to attract a Western audience.

Diana Rigg gave a memorable interpretation of Medea.

Margaret Atwood's remarks drew an enthusiastic response.

ELECTRONIC SOURCES (cf. 5.9)

William J. Mitchell's City of Bits discusses architecture and urban life in the context of the digital telecommunications revolution.

Stempel has tried to develop a "historical sociology" of sport in nineteenth-century America.

Michael Joyce was among the first to write fiction in hypertext.

Joanne Merrian reported on a parody of Shakespeare performed by the Muppets.

Works Cited

Atwood, Margaret. "Silencing the Scream." Boundaries of the Imagination Forum. MLA Convention. Royal York Hotel, Toronto. 29 Dec. 1993.

Fukuyama, Francis. Our Posthuman Future: Consequences of the Biotechnology Revolution. New York: Farrar, 2002.

Gilbert, Sandra M., and Susan Gubar. The Madwoman in the Attic: The Woman Writer and the Nineteenth-Century Literary Imagination. New Haven: Yale UP, 1979.

Joyce, Michael. Afternoon: A Story. Diskette. Watertown: Eastgate, 1987.

Kurosawa, Akira, dir. Rashomon. Perf. Toshiro Mifune. Daiei, 1950.

Lauter, Paul, et al., eds. The Heath Anthology of American Literature. 4th ed. 2 vols. Boston: Houghton, 2002.

Merrian, Joanne. "Spinoff: Monsterpiece Theatre." Online posting. 30 Apr. 1994. Shaksper: The Global Electronic Shakespeare Conf. 23 Sept. 2002 <http://www.shaksper.net/archives/1994/0380.html>.

Mitchell, William J. City of Bits: Space, Place, and the Informationbahn. Cambridge: MIT P, 1995. MIT Press. 23 Sept. 2002 <http://mitpress2.mit.edu/e-books/City_of_Bits/>.

Rigg, Diana, perf. Medea. By Euripides. Trans. Alistair Elliot. Dir. Jonathan Kent. Longacre Theatre, New York. 7 Apr. 1994.

Stempel, Carl William. "Towards a Historical Sociology of Sport in the United States, 1825-1875." DAI 53 (1993): 3374A. U of Oregon, 1992. Dissertation Abstracts Ondisc. CD-ROM. UMI-ProQuest. Sept. 1993.

Tommasini, Anthony. "In G. and S., Better to Have More Words, Less Voice." Rev. of The Mikado, by William S. Gilbert and Arthur Sullivan. New York City Opera. New York State Theater, New York. New York Times 10 Mar. 1997, late ed.: C22.

Trumpener, Katie. "Memories Carved in Granite: Great War Memorials and Everyday Life." PMLA 115 (2000): 1096-103.

6.4.2. Citing Part of a Work

If you quote, paraphrase, or otherwise use a specific passage in a book or an article, give the relevant page or section (e.g., paragraph) number or numbers. When the author's name is in your text, give only the number reference in parentheses, but if the context does not clearly identify the author, add the author's last name before the reference. Leave a space between them, but do not insert punctuation or, for a page reference, the word *page* or *pages* or the abbreviation *p.* or *pp.* If you used only one volume of a multivolume work and included the volume number in the bibliographic entry, you need give only page numbers in the reference (see the Lauter et al. example), but if you used more than one volume of the work, you must cite both volume and page numbers (see 6.4.3).

If your source uses paragraph numbers rather than page numbers—as, for example, some electronic journals do (see fig. 34, in 5.9.4)—give the relevant number or numbers preceded by the abbreviation *par.* or *pars.* (see the Sohmer example); if the author's name begins such a citation, place a comma after the name. If another kind of section is numbered in the source (e.g., screens), either write out the word for the section or use a standard abbreviation (see ch. 7); if the author's name begins such a citation, place a comma after the name (see the Gardiner example). When a source has no page numbers or any other kind of reference numbers, no number can be given in the parenthetical reference. The work must be cited in its entirety (see 6.4.1).

BOOKS (cf. 5.6)

Brian Taves suggests some interesting conclusions regarding the philosophy and politics of the adventure film (153-54, 171).

The anthology by Lauter and his coeditors contains Stowe's "Sojourner Truth, the Libyan Sibyl" (2530-38).

Among intentional spoonerisms, the "punlike metathesis of distinctive features may serve to weld together words etymologically unrelated but close in their sound and meaning" (Jakobson and Waugh 304).

Although writings describing utopia have always seemed to take place far from the everyday world, in fact "all utopian fiction whirls contemporary actors through a costume dance no place else but here" (Rabkin, Greenberg, and Olander vii).

Another engaging passage is the opening of Isabel Allende's story "Toad's Mouth" (83).

In Hansberry's play A Raisin in the Sun, the rejection of Lindner's tempting offer permits Walter's family to pursue the new life they had long dreamed about (274-75).

ARTICLES IN PERIODICALS (cf. 5.7)

Between 1968 and 1988, television coverage of presidential elections changed dramatically (Hallin 5).

Repetitive strain injury, or RSI, is reported to be "the fastest-growing occupational hazard of the computer age" (Taylor A1).

ELECTRONIC SOURCES (cf. 5.9)

"The study of comparative literature," Bill Readings wrote, "takes off from the idea of humanity" (6).

Beethoven has been called the "first politically motivated composer," for he was "caught up in the whole ferment of ideas that came out of the French Revolution" (Gardiner, screens 2-3).

"The debut of Julius Caesar," according to Sohmer, "proclaimed Shakespeare's Globe a theater of courage and ideas, a place where an audience must observe with the inner eye, listen with the inner ear" (par. 44).

Works Cited

Allende, Isabel. "Toad's Mouth." Trans. Margaret Sayers Peden. A Hammock beneath the Mangoes: Stories from Latin America. Ed. Thomas Colchie. New York: Plume, 1992. 83-88.

Gardiner, John Eliot. "The Importance of Beethoven." Interview. Charlie Rose. PBS. 25 July 1996. Transcript. Broadcast News. CD-ROM. Primary Source Media. July 1996. 23 screens.

Hallin, Daniel C. "Sound Bite News: Television Coverage of Elections, 1968-1988." Journal of Communication 42.2 (1992): 5-24.

Hansberry, Lorraine. A Raisin in the Sun. Black Theater: A Twentieth-Century Collection of the Work of Its Best Playwrights. Ed. Lindsay Patterson. New York: Dodd, 1971. 221-76.

Jakobson, Roman, and Linda R. Waugh. The Sound Shape of Language. Bloomington: Indiana UP, 1979.

Lauter, Paul, et al., eds. The Heath Anthology of American Literature. 4th ed. Vol. 1. Boston: Houghton, 2002.

Rabkin, Eric S., Martin H. Greenberg, and Joseph D. Olander. Preface. No Place Else: Explorations in Utopian and Dystopian Fiction. Ed. Rabkin, Greenberg, and Olander. Carbondale: Southern Illinois UP, 1983. vii-ix.

Readings, Bill. "Translatio and Comparative Literature: The Terror of European Humanism." Surfaces 1.11 (1991): 19 pp. 23 Sept. 2002 <http://www.pum.umontreal.ca/revues/surfaces/vol1/readin-a.html>.

Sohmer, Steve. "12 June 1599: Opening Day at Shakespeare's Globe." Early Modern Literary Studies 3.1 (1997): 46 pars. 26 June 2002 <http://www.shu.ac.uk/emls/03-1/sohmjuli.html>.

Taves, Brian. The Romance of Adventure: The Genre of Historical Adventure Movies. Jackson: UP of Mississippi, 1993.

Taylor, Paul. "Keyboard Grief: Coping with Computer-Caused Injuries." Globe and Mail [Toronto] 27 Dec. 1993: A1+.

6.4.3. Citing Volume and Page Numbers of a Multivolume Work

When citing a volume number as well as a page reference for a multivolume work, separate the two by a colon and a space: "(Wellek 2: 1–10)." Use neither the words *volume* and *page* nor their abbreviations. The functions of the numbers in such a citation are understood. If, however, you wish to refer parenthetically to an entire volume of a multivolume work, there is no need to cite pages. Place a comma after the author's name and include the abbreviation *vol.*: "(Wellek, vol. 2)." If you integrate such a reference into a sentence, spell out *volume*: "In volume 2, Wellek deals with. . . ."

The anthology by Lauter and his coeditors contains both Stowe's "Sojourner Truth, the Libyan Sibyl" (1: 2530-38) and Gilman's "The Yellow Wall-Paper" (2: 606-19).

Between the years 1945 and 1972, the political-party system in the United States underwent profound changes (Schlesinger, vol. 4).

Wellek admits in the middle of his multivolume history of modern literary criticism, "An evolutionary history of criticism must fail. I have come to this resigned conclusion" (5: xxii).

Works Cited

Lauter, Paul, et al., eds. The Heath Anthology of American Literature. 4th ed. 2 vols. Boston: Houghton, 2002.

Schlesinger, Arthur M., Jr., gen. ed. History of U.S. Political Parties. 4 vols. New York: Chelsea, 1973.

Wellek, René. A History of Modern Criticism, 1750-1950. 8 vols. New Haven: Yale UP, 1955-92.

6.4.4. Citing a Work Listed by Title

In a parenthetical reference to a work alphabetized by title in the list of works cited, the full title (if brief) or a shortened version precedes the page or section number or numbers (if any; see 6.2), unless the title appears in your text. When abbreviating the title, begin with the word by which it is alphabetized. Do not, for example, shorten *Glossary of Terms Used in Heraldry* to *Heraldry*, since this abbreviation would lead your reader to look for the bibliographic entry under *h* rather than *g*. If you are citing two or more anonymous works that have the same title, find a publication fact that distinguishes the works in their works-cited-list entries, and add it to their parenthetical references. For a book or other print source, this fact could be the year of publication. For an article or an Internet document, it could be the title of the periodical or of the overall Web site (see the "Snowy Owl" example under "Electronic Sources"). If you wish to cite a specific definition in a dictionary entry, give the relevant designation (e.g., number, letter) after the abbreviation *def.* (see the "Noon" example under "Electronic Sources").

BOOKS (cf. 5.6)

A presidential commission reported in 1970 that recent campus protests had focused on "racial injustice, war, and the university itself" (Report 3).

The nine grades of mandarins were "distinguished by the color of the button on the hats of office" ("Mandarin").

ARTICLES IN PERIODICALS (cf. 5.7)

International espionage was as prevalent as ever in the 1990s ("Decade").

A New York Times editorial called Ralph Ellison "a writer of universal reach" ("Death").

MISCELLANEOUS NONPRINT SOURCES (cf. 5.8)

Even Sixty Minutes launched an attack on modern art, in a segment entitled "Yes . . . but Is It Art?"

The classical Greek tragedy Medea, one of the most successful Broadway plays of the 1990s, made a lasting impression on me.

ELECTRONIC SOURCES (cf. 5.9)

The database Duecento is an invaluable source for texts of medieval Italian poetry.

Perseus 1.0 revolutionized the way scholars conduct research on ancient civilizations.

In fresco painting, "the pigments are completely fused with a damp plaster ground to become an integral part of the wall surface" ("Fresco Painting").

In winter the snowy owl feeds primarily on small rodents ("Snowy Owl," Hinterland), but in spring it also feeds on the eggs of much larger waterfowl, such as geese and swans ("Snowy Owl," Arctic).

Milton's description of the moon at "her highest noon" signifies the "place of the moon at midnight" ("Noon," def. 4b).

Voice of the Shuttle has links to many helpful resources.

Works Cited

"Death of a Writer." Editorial. New York Times 20 Apr. 1994, late ed.: A18.

"Decade of the Spy." Newsweek 7 Mar. 1994: 26-27.

Duecento: La poesia italiana dalle origini a Dante. Ed. Francesco Bonomi. 2000. Si.Lab, Firenze. 19 June 2002 <http://www.silab.it/frox/200/>.

"Fresco Painting." Encyclopaedia Britannica Online. 2002. Encyclopaedia Britannica. 8 May 2002 <http://search.eb.com>.

"Mandarin." The Encyclopedia Americana. 1994 ed.

Medea. By Euripides. Trans. Alistair Elliot. Dir. Jonathan Kent. Perf. Diana Rigg. Longacre Theatre, New York. 7 Apr. 1994.

"Noon." The Oxford English Dictionary. 2nd ed. CD-ROM. Oxford: Oxford UP, 1992.

Perseus 1.0: Interactive Sources and Studies on Ancient Greece. CD-ROM, laser disc. New Haven: Yale UP, 1992.

Report of the President's Commission on Campus Unrest. New York: Arno, 1970.

"Snowy Owl." Arctic Studies Center. 2002. Natl. Museum of Natural History of the Smithsonian Inst. 8 Aug. 2002 <http://www.mnh.si.edu/arctic/html/owl.html>.

"Snowy Owl." Hinterland Who's Who. 15 May 2002. Canadian Wildlife Service. 8 Aug. 2002 <http://www.cws-scf.ec.gc.ca/hww-fap/index_e.cfm>.

Voice of the Shuttle. 2002. U of California, Santa Barbara. 8 July 2002 <http://vos.ucsb.edu/>.

"Yes . . . but Is It Art?" Narr. Morley Safer. Sixty Minutes. CBS. WCBS, New York. 19 Sept. 1993.

6.4.5. Citing a Work by a Corporate Author

To cite a work by a corporate author, you may use the author's name followed by a page reference: "(United Nations, Economic Commission for Africa 79–86)." It is better, however, to include a long name in the text, so that the reading is not interrupted with an extended parenthetical reference. When giving the name of a corporate author in parentheses, shorten terms that are commonly abbreviated (see 7.4): "(Natl. Research Council 15)."

According to a study sponsored by the National Research Council, the population of China around 1990 was increasing by more than fifteen million annually (15).

By 1992 it was apparent that the American health care system, though impressive in many ways, needed "to be fixed and perhaps radically modified" (Public Agenda Foundation 4).

A study prepared by the United States Department of State defined terrorism as "premeditated, politically motivated violence against noncombatant targets by subnational groups or clandestine agents, usually intended to influence an audience" (lines 14-16).

In 1963 the United Nations Economic Commission for Africa predicted that Africa would evolve into an advanced industrial economy within fifty years (1-2, 4-6).

Works Cited

National Research Council. China and Global Change: Opportunities for
    Collaboration. Washington: Natl. Acad., 1992.

Public Agenda Foundation. The Health Care Crisis: Containing Costs,
    Expanding Coverage. New York: McGraw, 1992.

United Nations. Economic Commission for Africa. Industrial Growth in Africa.
    New York: United Nations, 1963.

United States. Dept. of State. Patterns of Global Terrorism. 1994. National
    Trade Data Bank. CD-ROM. Disc 2. US Dept. of Commerce. Dec. 1996.

6.4.6. Citing Two or More Works by the Same Author or Authors

In a parenthetical reference to one of two or more works by the same author, put a comma after the author's last name and add the title of the work (if brief) or a shortened version and the relevant page reference: "(Frye, *Double Vision* 85)," "(Durant and Durant, *Age* 214–48)." If you state the author's name in the text, give only the title and page reference in parentheses: "(*Double Vision* 85)," "(*Age* 214–48)." If you include both the author's name and the title in the text, indicate only the pertinent page number or numbers in parentheses: "(85)," "(214–48)."

PRINT SOURCES

Dreiser's universe, according to E. L. Doctorow, "is composed of merchants, workers, club-men, managers, actors, salesmen, doormen, cops, derelicts--a Balzacian population unified by the rules of commerce and the ideals of property and social position" (Introduction ix).

The brief but dramatic conclusion of chapter 13 of Doctorow's Welcome to Hard Times constitutes the climax of the novel (206-09).

In The Age of Voltaire, the Durants portray eighteenth-century England as a minor force in the world of music and art (214-48).

To Will and Ariel Durant, creative men and women make "history forgivable by enriching our heritage and our lives" (Dual Autobiography 406).

Shakespeare's King Lear has been called a "comedy of the grotesque" (Frye, Anatomy 237).

For Northrop Frye, one's death is not a unique experience, for "every moment we have lived through we have also died out of into another order" (Double Vision 85).

ELECTRONIC SOURCES

Moulthrop sees the act of reading hypertext as "struggle": "a chapter of chances, a chain of detours, a series of revealing figures in commitment out of which come the pleasures of the text" ("Traveling").

Hypertext, as one theorist puts it, is "all about connection, linkage, and affiliation" (Moulthrop, "You Say," par. 19).

Works Cited

Doctorow, E. L. Introduction. Sister Carrie. By Theodore Dreiser. New York: Bantam, 1982. v-xi.

---. Welcome to Hard Times. 1960. New York: Vintage-Random, 1988.

Durant, Will, and Ariel Durant. The Age of Voltaire. New York: Simon, 1965. Vol. 9 of The Story of Civilization. 11 vols. 1933-75.

---. A Dual Autobiography. New York: Simon, 1977.

Frye, Northrop. Anatomy of Criticism: Four Essays. Princeton: Princeton UP, 1957.

---. The Double Vision: Language and Meaning in Religion. Toronto: U of Toronto P, 1991.

Moulthrop, Stuart. "Traveling in the Breakdown Lane: A Principle of Resistance for Hypertext." Mosaic 28.4 (1995): 55-77. Home page. 12 July 2002 <http://iat.ubalt.edu/moulthrop/essays/breakdown.html>.

---. "You Say You Want a Revolution? Hypertext and the Laws of Media." Postmodern Culture 1.3 (1991): 53 pars. 12 July 2002 <http:// muse.jhu.edu/journals/postmodern_culture/v001/ 1.3moulthrop.html>.

6.4.7. Citing Indirect Sources

Whenever you can, take material from the original source, not a secondhand one. Sometimes, however, only an indirect source is available—for example, someone's published account of another's spoken remarks. If what you quote or paraphrase is itself a quotation, put the abbreviation *qtd. in* ("quoted in") before the indirect source you cite in your parenthetical reference. (You may document the original source in a note; see 6.5.1.)

Samuel Johnson admitted that Edmund Burke was an "extraordinary man" (qtd. in Boswell 2: 450).

The commentary of the sixteenth-century literary scholars Bernardo Segni and Lionardo Salviati shows them to be less-than-faithful followers of Aristotle (qtd. in Weinberg 1: 405, 616-17).

Works Cited

Boswell, James. <u>The Life of Johnson</u>. Ed. George Birkbeck Hill and L. F. Powell. 6 vols. Oxford: Clarendon, 1934-50.

Weinberg, Bernard. <u>A History of Literary Criticism in the Italian Renaissance</u>. 2 vols. Chicago: U of Chicago P, 1961.

6.4.8. Citing Literary and Religious Works

In a reference to a classic prose work, such as a novel or play, that is available in several editions, it is helpful to provide more information than just a page number from the edition used; a chapter number, for example, would help readers to locate a quotation in any copy of a novel. In such a reference, give the page number first, add a semicolon, and then give other identifying information, using appropriate abbreviations: "(130; ch. 9)," "(271; bk. 4, ch. 2)."

> Raskolnikov first appears in <u>Crime and Punishment</u> as a man contemplating a terrible act but frightened of meeting his talkative landlady on the stairs (Dostoevsky 1; pt. 1, ch. 1).

> In one version of the William Tell story, the son urges the reluctant father to shoot the arrow (Sastre 315; sc. 6).

> In <u>A Vindication of the Rights of Woman</u>, Mary Wollstonecraft recollects many "women who, not led by degrees to proper studies, and not permitted to choose for themselves, have indeed been overgrown children" (185; ch. 13, sec. 2).

When you cite an unpaginated source, the chapter number or similar designation may be the only identifying information you can give.

> Douglass notes that he had "no accurate knowledge" of his date of birth, "never having had any authentic record containing it" (ch. 1).

In citing classic verse plays and poems, omit page numbers altogether and cite by division (act, scene, canto, book, part) and line, with periods separating the various numbers—for example, "*Iliad* 9.19" refers to book 9, line 19, of Homer's *Iliad*. If you are citing only line numbers, do not use the abbreviation *l.* or *ll.*, which can be confused with numerals. Instead, initially use the word *line* or *lines* and then, having established that the numbers designate lines, give the numbers alone (see fig. 35).

In general, use arabic numerals rather than roman numerals for division and page numbers. Although you must use roman numerals when citing pages of a preface or other section that are so numbered, designate volumes, parts, books, and chapters with arabic numerals even if your source does not. Some instructors prefer roman numerals, however, for citations of acts and scenes in plays (*King Lear* IV.i), but if your instructor does not require this practice, use arabic numerals (*King Lear* 4.1; see fig. 35). On numbers, see 3.5.

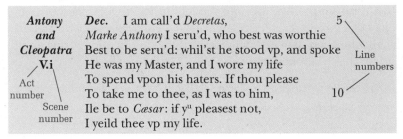

Fig. 35. A literary work with numbered divisions. Unless instructed otherwise, use arabic numbers for citations of acts, scenes, and other numbered divisions of literary works; titles of famous works are often abbreviated: "(*Ant.* 5.1.5–12)."

When included in parenthetical references, the titles of the books of the Bible and of famous literary works are often abbreviated (1 Chron. 21.8, Rev. 21.3, *Oth.* 4.2.7–13, *FQ* 3.3.53.3). The most widely used and accepted abbreviations for such titles are listed in 7.7. Follow prevailing practices for other abbreviations (*Troilus* for Chaucer's *Troilus and Criseyde*, "Nightingale" for Keats's "Ode to a Nightingale," etc.).

In Ballads and Lyrics of Socialism, Nesbit declares, "Our arms and hearts are strong for all who suffer wrong" ("Marching Song" 11).

Like the bard who made the Ballad of Sir Patrick Spence, Coleridge sees the "new-moon winter bright" with the "old Moon in her lap, foretelling / The coming on of rain and squally blast" (1.9, 13-14).

The Dean and Chapter Library manuscript version of Octovian, as edited
by Frances McSparran, has a more formal ending than other versions do:
"And thus endis Octouean, / That in his tym was a doghety man . . ."
(1629-30).

One Shakespearean protagonist seems resolute at first when he asserts,
"Haste me to know't, that I, with wings as swift / As meditation . . . / May
sweep to my revenge" (Ham. 1.5.35-37), but he soon has second
thoughts; another tragic figure, initially described as "too full o' th' milk of
human kindness" (Mac. 1.5.17), quickly descends into horrific slaughter.

In one of the most vivid prophetic visions in the Bible, Ezekiel saw "what
seemed to be four living creatures," each with the faces of a man, a lion,
an ox, and an eagle (New Jerusalem Bible, Ezek. 1.5-10). John of Patmos
echoes this passage when describing his vision (Rev. 4.6-8).

Works Cited

Coleridge, Samuel Taylor. "Dejection: An Ode." The Complete Poetical
Works of Samuel Taylor Coleridge. Ed. Ernest Hartley Coleridge. Vol. 1.
Oxford: Clarendon, 1912. 362-68. English Poetry Full-Text Database.
CD-ROM. Rel. 2. Cambridge, Eng.: Chadwyck-Healey, 1993.

Dostoevsky, Feodor. Crime and Punishment. Trans. Jessie Coulson. Ed.
George Gibian. New York: Norton, 1964.

Douglass, Frederick. Narrative of the Life of Frederick Douglass, an
American Slave, Written by Himself. Boston, 1845. 30 Jan. 1997
<gopher://gopher.vt.edu:10010/02/73/1>.

Nesbit, E[dith]. Ballads and Lyrics of Socialism. London, 1908. Victorian
Women Writers Project. Ed. Perry Willett. May 2000. Indiana U. 26
June 2002 <http://www.indiana.edu/~letrs/vwwp/nesbit/
ballsoc.html>.

The New Jerusalem Bible. Henry Wansbrough, gen. ed. New York:
Doubleday, 1985.

Octovian. Ed. Frances McSparran. Early English Text Soc. 289. London:
Oxford UP, 1986. Electronic Text Center. Ed. David Seaman. May 1995.
Alderman Lib., U of Virginia. 24 Feb. 2002 <http://
etext.lib.virginia.edu/mideng.browse.html>.

Sastre, Alfonso. Sad Are the Eyes of William Tell. Trans. Leonard Pronko. The
New Wave Spanish Drama. Ed. George Wellwarth. New York: New York
UP, 1970. 165-321.

Shakespeare, William. Hamlet. Ed. Barbara A. Mowat and Paul Werstine.
New York: Washington Square-Pocket, 1992.

---. Macbeth. Ed. Barbara A. Mowat and Paul Werstine. New York:
Washington Square-Pocket, 1992.

Wollstonecraft, Mary. A Vindication of the Rights of Woman. Ed. Carol H.
Poston. New York: Norton, 1975.

6.4.9. Citing More Than One Work in a Single Parenthetical Reference

If you wish to include two or more works in a single parenthetical
reference, cite each work as you normally would in a reference, and
use semicolons to separate the citations.

(Fukuyama 42; McRae 101-33)

(Natl. Research Council 25-35; Fitzgerald 330-43)

(Rabkin, Greenberg, and Olander vii; Boyle 96-125)

(Craner 308-11; Moulthrop, pars. 39-53)

(Gilbert and Gubar, Madwoman 1-25; Murphy 39-52)

(Gilbert and Gubar, Norton; Manning)

(Guidelines; Hallin 18-24)

(Lauter et al., vol. 1; Crane)

Keep in mind, however, that a long parenthetical reference such as
the following example may prove intrusive and disconcerting to
your reader:

(Taylor A1; Moulthrop, pars. 39-53; Armstrong, Yang, and Cuneo 80-82;
Craner 308-11; Fukuyama 42; Frank; Alston)

To avoid an excessive disruption, cite multiple sources in a note
rather than in parentheses in the text (see 6.5.2).

Works Cited

Alston, Robin. "Bodley CD-ROM." Online posting. 15 June 1994. ExLibris. 8
July 2002 <http://palimpsest.stanford.edu/byform/mailing-lists/
exlibris/1994/06/msg00170.html>.

Armstrong, Larry, Dori Jones Yang, and Alice Cuneo. "The Learning Revolution: Technology Is Reshaping Education--at Home and at School." Business Week 28 Feb. 1994: 80-88.

Boyle, Anthony T. "The Epistemological Evolution of Renaissance Utopian Literature, 1516-1657." Diss. New York U, 1983.

Crane, Stephen. The Red Badge of Courage: An Episode of the American Civil War. 1895. Ed. Fredson Bowers. Charlottesville: UP of Virginia, 1975.

Craner, Paul M. "New Tool for an Ancient Art: The Computer and Music." Computers and the Humanities 25 (1991): 303-13.

Fitzgerald, John. "The Misconceived Revolution: State and Society in China's Nationalist Revolution, 1923-26." Journal of Asian Studies 49 (1990): 323-43.

Frank, Holly. Negative Space: A Computerized Video Novel. Vers. 1.0. Diskette, videocassette. Prairie Village: Diskotech, 1990.

Fukuyama, Francis. Our Posthuman Future: Consequences of the Biotechnology Revolution. New York: Farrar, 2002.

Gilbert, Sandra M., and Susan Gubar. The Madwoman in the Attic: The Woman Writer and the Nineteenth-Century Literary Imagination. New Haven: Yale UP, 1979.

---, eds. The Norton Anthology of Literature by Women: The Tradition in English. 2nd ed. New York: Norton, 1996.

Guidelines for Family Television Viewing. Urbana: ERIC Clearinghouse on Elementary and Early Childhood Educ., 1990. ERIC. CD-ROM. SilverPlatter. Oct. 1993.

Hallin, Daniel C. "Sound Bite News: Television Coverage of Elections, 1968-1988." Journal of Communication 42.2 (1992): 5-24.

Lauter, Paul, et al., eds. The Heath Anthology of American Literature. 4th ed. 2 vols. Boston: Houghton, 2002.

Manning, Anita. "Curriculum Battles from Left and Right." USA Today 2 Mar. 1994: 5D.

McRae, Murdo William, ed. The Literature of Science: Perspectives on Popular Science Writing. Athens: U of Georgia P, 1993.

Moulthrop, Stuart. "You Say You Want a Revolution? Hypertext and the Laws of Media." Postmodern Culture 1.3 (1991): 53 pars. 12 July

2002 <http://muse.jhu.edu/journals/postmodern_culture/v001/
1.3moulthrop.html>.

Murphy, Cullen. "Women and the Bible." Atlantic Monthly Aug. 1993: 39-
64.

National Research Council. China and Global Change: Opportunities for
Collaboration. Washington: Natl. Acad., 1992.

Rabkin, Eric S., Martin H. Greenberg, and Joseph D. Olander. Preface. No
Place Else: Explorations in Utopian and Dystopian Fiction. Ed. Rabkin,
Greenberg, and Olander. Carbondale: Southern Illinois UP, 1983. vii-ix.

Taylor, Paul. "Keyboard Grief: Coping with Computer-Caused Injuries."
Globe and Mail [Toronto] 27 Dec. 1993: A1+.

6.5. USING NOTES WITH PARENTHETICAL DOCUMENTATION

Two kinds of notes may be used with parenthetical documentation:

- Content notes offering the reader comment, explanation, or information that the text cannot accommodate
- Bibliographic notes containing either several sources or evaluative
comments on sources

In providing this sort of supplementary information, place a
superscript arabic numeral at the appropriate place in the text and
write the note after a matching numeral either at the end of the text
(as an endnote) or at the bottom of the page (as a footnote). See the
examples in 6.5.1–2. For more information on using notes for documentation, see appendix B.

6.5.1. Content Notes

In your notes, avoid lengthy discussions that divert the reader's
attention from the primary text. In general, comments that you cannot fit into the text should be omitted unless they provide essential
justification or clarification of what you have written. You may use a
note, for example, to give full publication facts for an original source
for which you cite an indirect source and perhaps to explain why
you worked from secondary material.

The commentary of the sixteenth-century literary scholars Bernardo Segni and Lionardo Salviati shows them to be less-than-faithful followers of Aristotle.[1]

Note

[1] Examples are conveniently available in Weinberg. See Segni, Rettorica et poetica d'Aristotile (Firenze, 1549) 281, qtd. in Weinberg 1: 405, and Salviati, Poetica d'Aristotile parafrasata e comentata, 1586, ms. 2.2.11, Biblioteca Nazionale Centrale, Firenze, 140v, qtd. in Weinberg 1: 616-17.

Work Cited

Weinberg, Bernard. A History of Literary Criticism in the Italian Renaissance. 2 vols. Chicago: U of Chicago P, 1961.

6.5.2. Bibliographic Notes

Use notes for evaluative comments on sources and for references containing numerous citations.

Many observers conclude that health care in the United States is inadequate.[1]

Technological advancements have brought advantages as well as unexpected problems.[2]

Notes

[1] For strong points of view on different aspects of the issue, see Public Agenda Foundation 1-10 and Sakala 151-88.

[2] For a sampling of materials that reflect the range of experiences related to recent technological changes, see Taylor A1; Moulthrop, pars. 39-53; Armstrong, Yang, and Cuneo 80-82; Craner 308-11; Fukuyama 42; Frank; and Alston.

Works Cited

Alston, Robin. "Bodley CD-ROM." Online posting. 15 June 1994. ExLibris. 8 July 2002 <http://palimpsest.stanford.edu/byform/mailing-lists/exlibris/1994/06/msg00170.html>.

Armstrong, Larry, Dori Jones Yang, and Alice Cuneo. "The Learning Revolution: Technology Is Reshaping Education--at Home and at School." Business Week 28 Feb. 1994: 80-88.

Craner, Paul M. "New Tool for an Ancient Art: The Computer and Music." Computers and the Humanities 25 (1991): 303-13.

Frank, Holly. Negative Space: A Computerized Video Novel. Vers. 1.0. Diskette, videocassette. Prairie Village: Diskotech, 1990.

Fukuyama, Francis. Our Posthuman Future: Consequences of the Biotechnology Revolution. New York: Farrar, 2002.

Moulthrop, Stuart. "You Say You Want a Revolution? Hypertext and the Laws of Media." Postmodern Culture 1.3 (1991): 53 pars. 12 July 2002 <http://muse.jhu.edu/journals/postmodern_culture/v001/ 1.3moulthrop.html>.

Public Agenda Foundation. The Health Care Crisis: Containing Costs, Expanding Coverage. New York: McGraw, 1992.

Sakala, Carol. "Maternity Care Policy in the United States: Toward a More Rational and Effective System." Diss. Boston U, 1993.

Taylor, Paul. "Keyboard Grief: Coping with Computer-Caused Injuries." Globe and Mail [Toronto] 27 Dec. 1993: A1+.

7 Abbreviations

7.1. INTRODUCTION

Abbreviations are used regularly in the list of works cited and in tables but rarely in the text of a research paper (except within parentheses). In choosing abbreviations, keep your audience in mind. While economy of space is important, clarity is more so. Spell out a term if the abbreviation may puzzle your readers.

When abbreviating, always use accepted forms. In appropriate contexts, you may abbreviate the names of days, months, and other measurements of time (see 7.2); the names of states and countries (see 7.3); terms and reference words common in scholarship (see 7.4); publishers' names (see 7.5); and the titles of well-known literary and religious works (see 7.7).

The trend in abbreviation is to use neither periods after letters nor spaces between letters, especially for abbreviations made up of all capital letters.

BC	MA	S
NJ	CD-ROM	US

The chief exception to this trend continues to be the initials used for personal names: a period and a space ordinarily follow each initial.

J. R. R. Tolkien

Most abbreviations that end in lowercase letters are followed by periods.

assn.	fig.	Mex.
Eng.	introd.	prod.

In most abbreviations made up of lowercase letters that each represent a word, a period follows each letter, but no space intervenes between letters.

a.m.	i.e.
e.g.	n.p.

But there are numerous exceptions.

mph	os
ns	rpm

7.2. TIME DESIGNATIONS

Spell out the names of months in the text but abbreviate them in the list of works cited, except for May, June, and July. Whereas words denoting units of time are also spelled out in the text (*second, minute, week, month, year, century*), some time designations are used only in abbreviated form (*a.m., p.m., AD, BC, BCE, CE*).

AD	after the birth of Christ (from the Latin *anno Domini* 'in the year of the Lord'; used before numerals ["AD 14"] and after references to centuries ["twelfth century AD"])
a.m.	before noon (from the Latin *ante meridiem*)
Apr.	April
Aug.	August
BC	before Christ (used after numerals ["19 BC"] and references to centuries ["fifth century BC"])
BCE	before the common era (used after numerals and references to centuries)
CE	common era (used after numerals and references to centuries)
cent.	century
Dec.	December
Feb.	February
Fri.	Friday
hr.	hour
Jan.	January
Mar.	March
min.	minute
mo.	month
Mon.	Monday
Nov.	November
Oct.	October
p.m.	after noon (from the Latin *post meridiem*)
Sat.	Saturday
sec.	second
Sept.	September
Sun.	Sunday
Thurs.	Thursday
Tues.	Tuesday
Wed.	Wednesday
wk.	week
yr.	year

7.3. GEOGRAPHIC NAMES

Spell out the names of states, territories, and possessions of the
United States in the text, except usually in addresses and sometimes
in parentheses. Likewise, spell out in the text the names of countries, with a few exceptions (e.g., USSR). In documentation, however, abbreviate the names of states, provinces, and countries.

AB	Alberta	Gr.	Greece
Afr.	Africa	Gt. Brit.	Great Britain
AK	Alaska	GU	Guam
AL	Alabama	HI	Hawaii
Alb.	Albania	Hung.	Hungary
Ant.	Antarctica	IA	Iowa
AR	Arkansas	ID	Idaho
Arg.	Argentina	IL	Illinois
Arm.	Armenia	IN	Indiana
AS	American Samoa	Ire.	Ireland
Aus.	Austria	Isr.	Israel
Austral.	Australia	It.	Italy
AZ	Arizona	Jap.	Japan
BC	British Columbia	KS	Kansas
Belg.	Belgium	KY	Kentucky
Braz.	Brazil	LA	Louisiana
Bulg.	Bulgaria	Leb.	Lebanon
CA	California	MA	Massachusetts
Can.	Canada	MB	Manitoba
CO	Colorado	MD	Maryland
CT	Connecticut	ME	Maine
CZ	Canal Zone	Mex.	Mexico
DC	District of Columbia	MI	Michigan
DE	Delaware	MN	Minnesota
Den.	Denmark	MO	Missouri
Ecua.	Ecuador	MS	Mississippi
Eng.	England	MT	Montana
Eur.	Europe	NB	New Brunswick
FL	Florida	NC	North Carolina
Fr.	France	ND	North Dakota
GA	Georgia	NE	Nebraska
Ger.	Germany	Neth.	Netherlands

NH	New Hampshire	Russ.	Russia
NJ	New Jersey	SC	South Carolina
NL	Newfoundland and	Scot.	Scotland
	Labrador	SD	South Dakota
NM	New Mexico	SK	Saskatchewan
No. Amer.	North America	So. Amer.	South America
Norw.	Norway	Sp.	Spain
NS	Nova Scotia	Swed.	Sweden
NT	Northwest Territories	Switz.	Switzerland
NV	Nevada	TN	Tennessee
NY	New York	Turk.	Turkey
NZ	New Zealand	TX	Texas
OH	Ohio	UK	United Kingdom
OK	Oklahoma	US, USA	United States, United
ON	Ontario		States of America
OR	Oregon	USSR	Union of Soviet
PA	Pennsylvania		Socialist Republics
Pan.	Panama	UT	Utah
PE	Prince Edward Island	VA	Virginia
Pol.	Poland	VI	Virgin Islands
Port.	Portugal	VT	Vermont
PR	Puerto Rico	WA	Washington
PRC	People's Republic of	WI	Wisconsin
	China	WV	West Virginia
QC	Québec	WY	Wyoming
RI	Rhode Island	YT	Yukon Territory

7.4. COMMON SCHOLARLY ABBREVIATIONS

The following list includes abbreviations commonly used in humanities research studies in English. Abbreviations within parentheses are alternative but not recommended forms. Most of the abbreviations listed would replace the spelled forms only in parentheses, tables, and documentation.

abbr.	abbreviation, abbreviated
abr.	abridgment, abridged, abridged by
acad.	academy

adapt.	adapter, adaptation, adapted by
adj.	adjective
adv.	adverb
Amer.	America, American
anon.	anonymous
app.	appendix
arch.	archaic
art.	article
assn.	association
assoc.	associate, associated
attrib.	attributed to
aux.	auxiliary
b.	born
BA	bachelor of arts
bib.	biblical
bibliog.	bibliographer, bibliography, bibliographic
biog.	biographer, biography, biographical
bk.	book
BL	British Library, London
BM	British Museum, London (now British Library)
BS	bachelor of science
bull.	bulletin
©	copyright ("© 2003")
c. (ca.)	circa, *or* around (used with approximate dates: "c. 1796")
cap.	capital, capitalize
CD	compact disc
CD-ROM	compact disc read-only memory
cf.	compare (not "see"; from the Latin *confer*)
ch. (chap.)	chapter
chor.	choreographer, choreographed by
col.	column
coll.	college
colloq.	colloquial
com	commercial (used as a suffix in Internet domain names: "www.nytimes.com")
comp.	compiler, compiled by
compar.	comparative
cond.	conductor, conducted by
conf.	conference
Cong.	Congress

Cong. Rec.	*Congressional Record*
conj.	conjunction
Const.	Constitution
cont.	contents; continued
(contd.)	continued
d.	died
DA	doctor of arts
DA, DAI	*Dissertation Abstracts, Dissertation Abstracts International*
DAB	*Dictionary of American Biography*
def.	definition; definite
dept.	department
dev.	development, developed by
dict.	dictionary
dir.	director, directed by
diss.	dissertation
dist.	district
distr.	distributor, distributed by
div.	division
DNB	*Dictionary of National Biography*
doc.	document
DVD	originally *digital videodisc* but now used to describe discs containing a wide range of data
ed.	editor, edition, edited by
EdD	doctor of education
edu	educational (used as a suffix in Internet domain names: "www.indiana.edu")
educ.	education, educational
e.g.	for example (from the Latin *exempli gratia*; rarely capitalized; set off by commas, unless preceded by a different punctuation mark)
e-mail	electronic mail
encyc.	encyclopedia
enl.	enlarged (as in "rev. and enl. ed.")
esp.	especially
et al.	and others (from the Latin *et alii, et aliae*)
etc.	and so forth (from the Latin *et cetera*; like most abbreviations, not appropriate in text)
ex.	example
fac.	faculty
facsim.	facsimile

fig.	figure
fl.	flourished, *or* reached greatest development or influence (from the Latin *floruit*; used before dates of historical figures when birth and death dates are not known: "fl. 1200")
fr.	from
front.	frontispiece
FTP	File Transfer Protocol ("ftp" at the beginning of an Internet address)
fut.	future
fwd.	foreword, foreword by; forwarded (as in "fwd. by")
gen.	general (as in "gen. ed.")
gov	government (used as a suffix in Internet domain names: "www.census.gov")
govt.	government
GPO	Government Printing Office, Washington, DC
H. Doc.	House of Representatives Document
hist.	historian, history, historical
HMSO	Her (His) Majesty's Stationery Office, London
HR	House of Representatives
H. Rept.	House of Representatives Report
H. Res.	House of Representatives Resolution
HTML	Hypertext Markup Language
HTTP	Hypertext Transfer Protocol ("http" at the beginning of an Internet address)
i.e.	that is (from the Latin *id est*; rarely capitalized; set off by commas, unless preceded by a different punctuation mark)
illus.	illustrator, illustration, illustrated by
inc.	including; incorporated
infin.	infinitive
inst.	institute, institution
intl.	international
introd.	introduction, introduced by
ips	inches per second (used in reference to tape recordings)
irreg.	irregular
JD	doctor of law (from the Latin *juris doctor*)
jour.	journal
Jr.	Junior

KB	kilobyte
(l., ll.)	line, lines (avoided in favor of *line* and *lines* or, if clear, numbers only)
lang.	language
LC	Library of Congress
leg.	legal
legis.	legislator, legislation, legislature, legislative
lib.	library
lit.	literally; literature, literary
LLB	bachelor of laws (from the Latin *legum baccalaureus*)
LLD	doctor of laws (from the Latin *legum doctor*)
LLM	master of laws (from the Latin *legum magister*)
LP	long-playing phonograph record
ltd.	limited
MA	master of arts
mag.	magazine
MB	megabyte
MD	doctor of medicine (from the Latin *medicinae doctor*)
misc.	miscellaneous
mod.	modern
MOO	multiuser domain, object-oriented (cf. *MUD*)
MS	master of science
ms., mss.	manuscript, manuscripts (as in "Bodleian ms. Tanner 43"; cf. *ts., tss.*)
MUD	multiuser domain (cf. *MOO*)
n, nn	note, notes (used immediately after the number of the page containing the text of the note or notes: "56n," "56n3," "56nn3–5")
n.	noun
narr.	narrator, narrated by
natl.	national
NB	take notice (from the Latin *nota bene*; always capitalized)
n.d.	no date of publication
NED	*A New English Dictionary* (cf. *OED*)
no.	number (cf. *numb.*)
nonstand.	nonstandard
n.p.	no place of publication; no publisher
n. pag.	no pagination

ns	new series
NS	New Style (calendar designation)
numb.	numbered (cf. *no.*)
obj.	object, objective
obs.	obsolete
OCLC	Online Computer Library Center
OED	*The Oxford English Dictionary* (formerly *A New English Dictionary* [*NED*])
op.	opus (work)
orch.	orchestra (also Italian *orchestra*, French *orchestre*, etc.), orchestrated by
org	organization (used as a suffix in Internet domain names: "www.mla.org")
orig.	original, originally
os	old series; original series
OS	Old Style (calendar designation)
P	Press (used in documentation; cf. *UP*)
p., pp.	page, pages (omitted before page numbers unless necessary for clarity)
par.	paragraph
part.	participle
perf.	performer, performed by
PhD	doctor of philosophy (from the Latin *philosophiae doctor*)
philol.	philological
philos.	philosophical
pl.	plate; plural
poss.	possessive
pref.	preface, preface by
prep.	preposition
pres.	present
proc.	proceedings
prod.	producer, produced by
pron.	pronoun
pronunc.	pronunciation
PS	postscript
pseud.	pseudonym
pt.	part
pub. (publ.)	publisher, publication, published by
Pub. L.	Public Law

qtd.	quoted
r.	reigned
R	Reference (used to indicate the reference section in a library)
rec.	record, recorded
Ref	Reference (used to indicate the reference section in a library)
reg.	registered; regular
rel.	release
rept.	report, reported by
res.	resolution
resp.	respectively
rev.	review, reviewed by; revision, revised, revised by (spell out *review* where *rev.* might be ambiguous)
RLIN	Research Libraries Information Network
rpm	revolutions per minute (used in reference to phonograph recordings)
rpt.	reprint, reprinted, reprinted by
S	Senate
sc.	scene (omitted when act and scene numbers are used together for verse plays: "*King Lear* 4.1")
S. Doc.	Senate Document
sec. (sect.)	section
ser.	series
sess.	session
sic	thus in the source (in square brackets as an editorial interpolation, otherwise in parentheses; not followed by an exclamation point)
sing.	singular
soc.	society
spec.	special
Sr.	Senior
S. Rept.	Senate Report
S. Res.	Senate Resolution
st.	stanza
St., Sts. (S, SS)	Saint, Saints
Stat.	Statutes at Large
subj.	subject, subjective; subjunctive
substand.	substandard

supp.	supplement
syn.	synonym
trans. (tr.)	transitive; translator, translation, translated by
ts., tss.	typescript, typescripts (cf. *ms., mss.*)
U	University (also Spanish *Universidad*, Italian *Università*, German *Universität*, French *Université*, etc.; used in documentation; cf. *UP*)
univ.	university (used outside documentation—e.g., in parentheses and tables: "Montclair State Univ.")
UP	University Press (used in documentation: "Columbia UP")
URL	uniform resource locator
usu.	usually
var.	variant
vb.	verb
vers.	version
VHS	video home system (the recording and playing standard for videocassette recorders)
vol.	volume
vs. (v.)	versus (*v.* preferred in titles of legal cases)
writ.	writer, written by
www	World Wide Web (used in the names of servers, or computers, on the Web)

7.5. PUBLISHERS' NAMES

In the list of works cited, shortened forms of publishers' names immediately follow the cities of publication, enabling the reader to locate books or to acquire more information about them. Since publications like *Books in Print*, *Literary Market Place*, and *International Literary Market Place* list publishers' addresses, you need give only enough information so that your reader can look up the publishers in one of these sources. It is usually sufficient, for example, to give "Harcourt" as the publisher's name even if the title page shows "Harcourt Brace" or one of the other earlier names of that firm (Harcourt, Brace; Harcourt, Brace, and World; Harcourt Brace Jovanovich). If you are preparing a bibliographic study, however, or if publication history is important to your paper, give the publisher's name in full.

In shortening publishers' names, keep in mind the following points:

- Omit articles (*A*, *An*, *The*), business abbreviations (*Co.*, *Corp.*, *Inc.*, *Ltd.*), and descriptive words (*Books*, *House*, *Press*, *Publishers*). When citing a university press, however, always add the abbreviation *P* (Ohio State UP) because the university itself may publish independently of its press (Ohio State U).
- If the publisher's name includes the name of one person (Harry N. Abrams, W. W. Norton, John Wiley), cite the surname alone (Abrams, Norton, Wiley). If the publisher's name includes the names of more than one person, cite only the first of the surnames (Bobbs, Dodd, Faber, Farrar, Funk, Grosset, Harcourt, Harper, Houghton, McGraw, Prentice, Simon).
- Use standard abbreviations whenever possible (*Acad.*, *Assn.*, *Soc.*, *UP*; see 7.4).
- If the publisher's name is commonly abbreviated with capital initial letters and if the abbreviation is likely to be familiar to your audience, use the abbreviation as the publisher's name (GPO, MLA, UMI). If your readers are not likely to know the abbreviation, shorten the name according to the general guidelines given above (Mod. Lang. Assn.).

Following are examples of how various types of publishers' names are shortened:

Acad. for Educ. Dev.	Academy for Educational Development, Inc.
ALA	American Library Association
Basic	Basic Books
CAL	Center for Applied Linguistics
Cambridge UP	Cambridge University Press
Eastgate	Eastgate Systems
Einaudi	Giulio Einaudi Editore
ERIC	Educational Resources Information Center
Farrar	Farrar, Straus and Giroux, Inc.
Feminist	The Feminist Press at the City University of New York
Gale	Gale Research, Inc.
Gerig	Gerig Verlag
GPO	Government Printing Office
Harper	Harper and Row, Publishers, Inc.; HarperCollins Publishers, Inc.

Harvard Law Rev. Assn.	Harvard Law Review Association
HMSO	Her (His) Majesty's Stationery Office
Houghton	Houghton Mifflin Co.
Knopf	Alfred A. Knopf, Inc.
Larousse	Librairie Larousse
Little	Little, Brown and Company, Inc.
Macmillan	Macmillan Publishing Co., Inc.
McGraw	McGraw-Hill, Inc.
MIT P	The MIT Press
MLA	The Modern Language Association of America
NCTE	The National Council of Teachers of English
NEA	The National Education Association
Norton	W. W. Norton and Co., Inc.
Planeta	Editorial Planeta Mexicana
PUF	Presses Universitaires de France
Random	Random House, Inc.
Scribner's	Charles Scribner's Sons
Simon	Simon and Schuster, Inc.
SIRS	Social Issues Resources Series
State U of New York P	State University of New York Press
St. Martin's	St. Martin's Press, Inc.
UMI	University Microfilms International
U of Chicago P	University of Chicago Press
UP of Mississippi	University Press of Mississippi

7.6. SYMBOLS AND ABBREVIATIONS USED IN PROOFREADING AND CORRECTION

7.6.1. Selected Proofreading Symbols

Proofreaders use the symbols below when correcting typeset material. Many instructors also use them in marking student papers.

˅	add an apostrophe or a single quotation mark
◠	close up (basket ball)
⋏	add a comma
℀	delete
⋀	insert

¶	begin a new paragraph
No¶	do not begin a new paragraph
⊙	add a period
⌄" ⌄"	add double quotation marks
#	add space
∿	transpose elements (usually with *tr* in margin) (th⟨ie⟩r)

7.6.2. Common Correction Symbols and Abbreviations

‖	lack of parallelism
ab	faulty abbreviation
adj	improper use of adjective
adv	improper use of adverb
agr	faulty agreement
amb	ambiguous expression or construction
awk	awkward expression or construction
cap	faulty capitalization
d	faulty diction
dgl	dangling construction
frag	fragment
lc	use lowercase
num	error in use of numbers
p	faulty punctuation
ref	unclear pronoun reference
rep	unnecessary repetition
r-o	run-on sentence
sp	error in spelling
ss	faulty sentence structure
t	wrong tense of verb
tr	transpose elements
vb	wrong verb form
wdy	wordy writing

7.7. TITLES OF LITERARY AND RELIGIOUS WORKS

In documentation, you may abbreviate the titles of works and parts of works. It is usually best to introduce an abbreviation in parentheses immediately after the first use of the full title in the text: "In *All's Well That Ends Well* (*AWW*), Shakespeare. . . ." Abbreviating titles is appropriate, for example, if you repeatedly cite a variety of works by the same author. In such a discussion, abbreviations make for more concise parenthetical documentation—"(*AWW* 3.2.100–29)," "(*MM* 4.3.93–101)"—than the usual shortened titles would: "(*All's Well* 3.2.100–29)," "(*Measure* 4.3.93–101)." For works not on the following lists, you may use the abbreviations you find in your sources, or you may devise simple, unambiguous abbreviations of your own.

7.7.1. Bible

The following abbreviations and spelled forms are commonly used for parts of the Bible (Bib.).

Old Testament (OT)

Gen.	Genesis
Exod.	Exodus
Lev.	Leviticus
Num.	Numbers
Deut.	Deuteronomy
Josh.	Joshua
Judg.	Judges
Ruth	Ruth
1 Sam.	1 Samuel
2 Sam.	2 Samuel
1 Kings	1 Kings
2 Kings	2 Kings
1 Chron.	1 Chronicles
2 Chron.	2 Chronicles
Ezra	Ezra
Neh.	Nehemiah
Esth.	Esther
Job	Job
Ps.	Psalms
Prov.	Proverbs
Eccles.	Ecclesiastes
Song Sol. (also Cant.)	Song of Solomon (also Canticles)
Isa.	Isaiah
Jer.	Jeremiah

Lam.	Lamentations
Ezek.	Ezekiel
Dan.	Daniel
Hos.	Hosea
Joel	Joel
Amos	Amos
Obad.	Obadiah
Jon.	Jonah
Mic.	Micah
Nah.	Nahum
Hab.	Habakkuk
Zeph.	Zephaniah
Hag.	Haggai
Zech.	Zechariah
Mal.	Malachi

Selected Apocryphal and Deuterocanonical Works

1 Esd.	1 Esdras
2 Esd.	2 Esdras
Tob.	Tobit
Jth.	Judith
Esth. (Apocr.)	Esther (Apocrypha)
Wisd. Sol. (also Wisd.)	Wisdom of Solomon (also Wisdom)
Ecclus. (also Sir.)	Ecclesiasticus (also Sirach)
Bar.	Baruch
Song 3 Childr.	Song of the Three Children
Sus.	Susanna
Bel and Dr.	Bel and the Dragon
Pr. Man.	Prayer of Manasseh
1 Macc.	1 Maccabees
2 Macc.	2 Maccabees

New Testament (NT)

Matt.	Matthew
Mark	Mark
Luke	Luke
John	John
Acts	Acts
Rom.	Romans
1 Cor.	1 Corinthians
2 Cor.	2 Corinthians

Gal.	Galatians
Eph.	Ephesians
Phil.	Philippians
Col.	Colossians
1 Thess.	1 Thessalonians
2 Thess.	2 Thessalonians
1 Tim.	1 Timothy
2 Tim.	2 Timothy
Tit.	Titus
Philem.	Philemon
Heb.	Hebrews
Jas.	James
1 Pet.	1 Peter
2 Pet.	2 Peter
1 John	1 John
2 John	2 John
3 John	3 John
Jude	Jude
Rev. (also Apoc.)	Revelation (also Apocalypse)

Selected Apocryphal Works

G. Thom.	Gospel of Thomas
G. Heb.	Gospel of the Hebrews
G. Pet.	Gospel of Peter

7.7.2. Shakespeare

Ado	*Much Ado about Nothing*
Ant.	*Antony and Cleopatra*
AWW	*All's Well That Ends Well*
AYL	*As You Like It*
Cor.	*Coriolanus*
Cym.	*Cymbeline*
Err.	*The Comedy of Errors*
F1	First Folio edition (1623)
F2	Second Folio edition (1632)
Ham.	*Hamlet*
1H4	*Henry IV, Part 1*
2H4	*Henry IV, Part 2*
H5	*Henry V*

1H6	*Henry VI, Part 1*
2H6	*Henry VI, Part 2*
3H6	*Henry VI, Part 3*
H8	*Henry VIII*
JC	*Julius Caesar*
Jn.	*King John*
LC	*A Lover's Complaint*
LLL	*Love's Labour's Lost*
Lr.	*King Lear*
Luc.	*The Rape of Lucrece*
Mac.	*Macbeth*
MM	*Measure for Measure*
MND	*A Midsummer Night's Dream*
MV	*The Merchant of Venice*
Oth.	*Othello*
Per.	*Pericles*
PhT	*The Phoenix and the Turtle*
PP	*The Passionate Pilgrim*
Q	Quarto edition
R2	*Richard II*
R3	*Richard III*
Rom.	*Romeo and Juliet*
Shr.	*The Taming of the Shrew*
Son.	*Sonnets*
TGV	*The Two Gentlemen of Verona*
Tim.	*Timon of Athens*
Tit.	*Titus Andronicus*
Tmp.	*The Tempest*
TN	*Twelfth Night*
TNK	*The Two Noble Kinsmen*
Tro.	*Troilus and Cressida*
Ven.	*Venus and Adonis*
Wiv.	*The Merry Wives of Windsor*
WT	*The Winter's Tale*

7.7.3. Chaucer

BD	*The Book of the Duchess*
CkT	The Cook's Tale
ClT	The Clerk's Tale

CT	*The Canterbury Tales*
CYT	The Canon's Yeoman's Tale
FranT	The Franklin's Tale
FrT	The Friar's Tale
GP	The General Prologue
HF	*The House of Fame*
KnT	The Knight's Tale
LGW	*The Legend of Good Women*
ManT	The Manciple's Tale
Mel	The Tale of Melibee
MerT	The Merchant's Tale
MilT	The Miller's Tale
MkT	The Monk's Tale
MLT	The Man of Law's Tale
NPT	The Nun's Priest's Tale
PardT	The Pardoner's Tale
ParsT	The Parson's Tale
PF	*The Parliament of Fowls*
PhyT	The Physician's Tale
PrT	The Prioress's Tale
Ret	Chaucer's Retraction
RvT	The Reeve's Tale
ShT	The Shipman's Tale
SNT	The Second Nun's Tale
SqT	The Squire's Tale
SumT	The Summoner's Tale
TC	*Troilus and Criseyde*
Th	The Tale of Sir Thopas
WBT	The Wife of Bath's Tale

7.7.4. Other Literary Works

Aen.	Vergil, *Aeneid*
Ag.	Aeschylus, *Agamemnon*
Ant.	Sophocles, *Antigone*
Bac.	Euripides, *Bacchae*
Beo.	*Beowulf*
Can.	Voltaire, *Candide*
Dec.	Boccaccio, *Decameron*
DJ	Byron, *Don Juan*

DQ	Cervantes, *Don Quixote*
Eum.	Aeschylus, *Eumenides*
FQ	Spenser, *The Faerie Queene*
Gil.	*Epic of Gilgamesh*
GT	Swift, *Gulliver's Travels*
Hept.	Marguerite de Navarre, *Heptaméron*
Hip.	Euripides, *Hippolytus*
Il.	Homer, *Iliad*
Inf.	Dante, *Inferno*
LB	Wordsworth, *Lyrical Ballads*
Lys.	Aristophanes, *Lysistrata*
MD	Melville, *Moby-Dick*
Med.	Euripides, *Medea*
Mis.	Molière, *Le misanthrope*
Nib.	*Nibelungenlied*
Od.	Homer, *Odyssey*
OR	Sophocles, *Oedipus Rex* (also called *Oedipus Tyrannus* [*OT*])
Or.	Aeschylus, *Oresteia*
OT	Sophocles, *Oedipus Tyrannus* (also called *Oedipus Rex* [*OR*])
Par.	Dante, *Paradiso*
PL	Milton, *Paradise Lost*
Prel.	Wordsworth, *The Prelude*
Purg.	Dante, *Purgatorio*
Rep.	Plato, *Republic*
SA	Milton, *Samson Agonistes*
SGGK	*Sir Gawain and the Green Knight*
Sym.	Plato, *Symposium*
Tar.	Molière, *Tartuffe*

Appendix A: Selected Reference Works by Field

Each of the sections below is divided into two parts. The first contains titles of indexes, abstracts collections, annual bibliographies, and other such periodically published reference works. Many of these works are published in print and online versions; check your library's holdings to see what is available to you. The second part of each section contains titles of dictionaries, encyclopedias, and similar reference works.

A.1. ANTHROPOLOGY

Abstracts in Anthropology. Westport: Greenwood, 1970– .
Anthropological Literature. Cambridge: Tozzer Lib., Harvard U, 1979– .

Companion Encyclopedia of Anthropology. Ed. Tim Ingold. New York: Routledge, 1994.
The Dictionary of Anthropology. Ed. Thomas J. Barfield. New York: Blackwell, 1997.
Encyclopedia of Social and Cultural Anthropology. Ed. Alan Barnard and Jonathan Spencer. New York: Routledge, 1996.

A.2. ART AND ARCHITECTURE

Art Abstracts. New York: Wilson, 1994– .
Art Index. New York: Wilson, 1929– .
Avery Index to Architectural Periodicals. Boston: Hall; Santa Monica: Getty, 1973– .
BHA: Bibliography of the History of Art / Bibliographie d'histoire de l'art. Vandoeuvre-lès-Nancy: Centre National de la Recherche Scientifique; Santa Monica: Getty, 1991– .

The Dictionary of Art. Ed. Jane Turner. 34 vols. New York: Grove, 1996.
Encyclopedia of Architecture: Design, Engineering, and Construction. Ed. Joseph A. Wilkes. 5 vols. New York: Wiley, 1988.
Encyclopedia of World Art. 17 vols. New York: McGraw, 1959–87.
An International Dictionary of Architects and Architecture. Ed. Randall J. Van Vynckt. 2 vols. Detroit: St. James, 1993.

The *Oxford Dictionary of Art*. Ed. Ian Chilvers and Harold Osborne. 2nd ed. New York: Oxford UP, 1997.
The Penguin Dictionary of Architecture and Landscape Architecture. By John Fleming, Hugh Honour, and Nikolaus Pevsner. 5th ed. New York: Penguin, 1998.
The Yale Dictionary of Art and Artists. By Erika Langmuir and Norbert Lynton. New Haven: Yale UP, 2000.

A.3. BIOLOGY

Biological Abstracts. Philadelphia: BioSciences Information Service, 1926– . Online version incorporated into *BIOSIS*.
Biological and Agricultural Index. New York: Wilson, 1964– .

Chambers Biology Dictionary. Ed. Peter Walker. 4th ed. New York: Cambridge UP, 1989.
Encyclopedia of Bioethics. Ed. Warren T. Reich. Rev. ed. 5 vols. New York: Macmillan-Simon, 1995.
Encyclopedia of Human Biology. Ed. Renato Dulbecco. 2nd ed. 9 vols. San Diego: Academic, 1997.
Henderson's Dictionary of Biological Terms. Ed. Eleanor Lawrence. 12th ed. New York: Prentice, 2000.
The Penguin Dictionary of Biology. Ed. Michael Thain and Michael Hickman. 10th ed. New York: Penguin, 2000.

A.4. BUSINESS

ABI/Inform. Ann Arbor: UMI, 1971– .
Business Abstracts. New York: Wilson, 1995– .
Business Periodicals Index. New York: Wilson, 1958– .
EconLit. Nashville: Amer. Economic Assn., 1969– .
PAIS. New York: Public Affairs Information Service, 1972– .
Predicasts F and S Indexes. Cleveland: Predicasts, 1968– .

Companion Encyclopedia of Marketing. Ed. Michael J. Baker. New York: Routledge, 1995.
Dictionary of Business and Management. Ed. Jerry M. Rosenberg. 3rd ed. New York: Wiley, 1992.

Encyclopedia of Management. Ed. Marilyn M. Helms. 4th ed. Detroit: Gale, 2000.

McGraw-Hill Encyclopedia of Economics. Ed. Douglas Greenwald. 2nd ed. New York: McGraw, 1993.

The MIT Dictionary of Modern Economics. Ed. David Pearce. 4th ed. Cambridge: MIT P, 1992.

Oxford Dictionary of Economics. Ed. John Black. 2nd ed. New York: Oxford UP, 2002.

The Routledge Dictionary of Economics. Ed. Donald Rutherford. 2nd ed. New York: Routledge, 2002.

A.5. CHEMISTRY

Chemical Abstracts. Columbus: Amer. Chemical Soc., 1907– . Online version incorporated into *SciFinder Scholar.*

Hawley's Condensed Chemical Dictionary. Ed. Richard J. Lewis. 14th ed. New York: Wiley, 2001.

Lange's Handbook of Chemistry. Ed. John A. Dean. 15th ed. New York: McGraw, 1998.

Macmillan Encyclopedia of Chemistry. Ed. Joseph J. Lagowski. 4 vols. New York: Macmillan, 1996.

Van Nostrand Reinhold Encyclopedia of Chemistry. Ed. Douglas M. Considine. 8th ed. New York: Van Nostrand, 1995.

A.6. COMPUTER SCIENCE

ACM Guide to Computing Literature. New York: Assn. for Computing Machinery, 1977– .

Computer Abstracts. London: Technical Information, 1957– .

Computer Literature Index. Phoenix: Applied Computer Research, 1980– .

Dictionary of Computing. Ed. Valerie Illingsworth. 4th ed. Oxford: Oxford UP, 1997.

Encyclopedia of Computers and Computer History. Ed. Raúl Rojas. 2 vols. Chicago: Fitzroy, 2001.

Encyclopedia of Computer Science. Ed. Anthony Ralston, Edwin D. Riley, and David Hemmendinger. Rev. 4th ed. New York: Grove, 2000.

A.7. EDUCATION

CIJE: Current Index to Journals in Education. Phoenix: Oryx, 1969– .
Online version incorporated into *ERIC.*
Education Abstracts. New York: Wilson, 1994– .
Education Index. New York: Wilson, 1929– .
ERIC: Educational Resources Information Center. Washington: GPO,
1966– .
Resources in Education. Washington: GPO, 1967– . Online version
incorporated into *ERIC.*

Dictionary of Education. Ed. Fred Goodman. Phoenix: Oryx, 1998.
The Encyclopedia of Education. Ed. Lee C. Deighton. 10 vols. New
York: Free, 1971.
Encyclopedia of Educational Research. Ed. Marvin C. Alkin. 6th ed.
4 vols. New York: Macmillan, 1992.
Encyclopedia of Special Education. Ed. Cecil R. Reynolds and Elaine
Fletcher-Janzen. 2nd ed. 3 vols. New York: Wiley, 2000.
The Oryx Dictionary of Education. Ed. William J. Russell. Westport:
Greenwood, 2002.
World Education Encyclopedia. Ed. Chris Lopez. 2nd ed. 3 vols.
Detroit: Gale, 2001.

A.8. ENVIRONMENTAL SCIENCES

Ecology Abstracts. Bethesda: Cambridge Scientific Abstracts, 1975– .
Environment Abstracts. New York: Environment Information Center,
1971– .
Environmental Periodicals Bibliography. Santa Barbara: Environ-
mental Studies Inst., 1972– .
Environment Index. New York: Environment Information Center,
1971– .
Pollution Abstracts. Bethesda: Cambridge Scientific Abstracts, 1970– .

A Dictionary of Ecology. Ed. Michael Allaby. 2nd ed. New York:
Oxford UP, 1998.
Encyclopedia of Ecology and Environmental Management. Ed. Peter
Calow. New York: Blackwell, 1997.

Environment Dictionary. Ed. David Kemp. New York: Routledge, 1998.

McGraw-Hill Encyclopedia of Environmental Science and Engineering. Ed. Sybil P. Parker and Robert A. Corbitt. 3rd ed. New York: McGraw, 1993.

A.9. GEOGRAPHY

Geographical Abstracts. Norwich, Eng.: Geo Abstracts, 1972– . Online version incorporated into *Geobase.*

Companion Encyclopedia of Geography. Ed. Ian Douglas, Richard J. Huggett, and M. E. Robinson. New York: Routledge, 1996.

A Dictionary of Geography. Ed. Susan Mayhew. 2nd ed. New York: Oxford UP, 1997.

Encyclopedia of Geographic Information Sources. Ed. Jennifer Mossman. 4th ed. 2 vols. Detroit: Gale, 1986.

Modern Geography: An Encyclopedic Survey. Ed. Gary S. Dunbar. New York: Garland, 1991.

The Penguin Dictionary of Geography. Ed. Audrey N. Clark. 2nd ed. New York: Penguin, 1999.

A.10. GEOLOGY

Bibliography and Index of Geology. Alexandria: Amer. Geological Inst., 1933– . Online version incorporated into *GeoRef.*

Challinor's Dictionary of Geology. Ed. Anthony Wyatt. 6th ed. New York: Oxford UP, 1986.

The Encyclopedia of Field and General Geology. Ed. Charles W. Finkl. New York: Van Nostrand, 1988.

McGraw-Hill Dictionary of Geology and Mineralogy. Ed. Sybil P. Parker. New York: McGraw, 1997.

McGraw-Hill Encyclopedia of the Geological Sciences. Ed. Sybil P. Parker. 2nd ed. New York: McGraw, 1988.

The New Penguin Dictionary of Geology. Ed. Philip Kearey. New York: Viking, 1996.

A.11. HISTORY

America: History and Life. Santa Barbara: ABC-Clio, 1964– .
Historical Abstracts. Santa Barbara: ABC-Clio, 1955– .

Dictionary of American History. Ed. James T. Adams. Rev. ed. 8 vols. New York: Scribner's, 1976.
A Dictionary of Ancient History. Ed. Graham Speake. Cambridge, Eng.: Blackwell, 1994.
Encyclopedia of African American Culture and History. Ed. Jack Salman, David L. Smith, and Cornel West. 5 vols. New York: Macmillan, 1996.
Encyclopedia of American History. Ed. Richard B. Morris. 7th ed. New York: Harper, 1996.
Encyclopedia of European Social History from 1350 to 2000. Ed. Peter N. Stearns. 6 vols. Detroit: Scribner's, 2001.
The Encyclopedia of World History. Ed. Peter N. Stearns. 6th ed. Boston: Houghton, 2001.
Larousse Dictionary of World History. Ed. Bruce Lenman. New York: Larousse, 1995.

A.12. LANGUAGE AND LITERATURE

L'année philologique: Bibliographie critique et analytique de l'antiquité gréco-latine. Paris: Belles Lettres, 1924– .
Bibliographie linguistique / Linguistic Bibliography. Dordrecht: Kluwer, 1949– .
LLBA: Linguistics and Language Behavior Abstracts. San Diego: Sociological Abstracts, 1974– .
MLA International Bibliography. New York: MLA, 1921– .

The Cambridge Encyclopedia of Language. Ed. David Crystal. 2nd ed. New York: Cambridge UP, 1997.
The Cambridge Guide to Literature in English. Ed. Ian Ousby. 2nd ed. New York: Cambridge UP, 1994.
The Cambridge Guide to Theatre. Ed. Martin Banham. Rev. ed. New York: Cambridge UP, 1995.

Dictionary of Italian Literature. Ed. Peter Bondanella, Julia C. Bondanella, and Jody R. Shiffman. Rev. ed. Westport: Greenwood, 1996.

Dictionary of the Literature of the Iberian Peninsula. By Germán Bleiberg, Maureen Ihrie, and Janet Pérez. 2 vols. Westport: Greenwood, 1993.

An Encyclopaedia of Language. Ed. N. E. Collinge. New York: Routledge, 1990.

Encyclopedia of Latin American Literature. Ed. Verity Smith. Chicago: Fitzroy, 1997.

International Encyclopedia of Linguistics. Ed. William Bright. 4 vols. New York: Oxford UP, 1992.

The Johns Hopkins Guide to Literary Theory and Criticism. Ed. Michael Groden and Martin Kreisworth. Baltimore: Johns Hopkins UP, 1994.

Literary Research Guide. By James L. Harner. 4th ed. New York: MLA, 2002.

The New Oxford Companion to Literature in French. Ed. Peter France. New York: Oxford UP, 1995.

The New Princeton Encyclopedia of Poetry and Poetics. Ed. Alex Preminger and T. V. F. Brogan. Princeton: Princeton UP, 1993.

The Oxford Classical Dictionary. Ed. Simon Hornblower and Antony Spawforth. 3rd ed. Oxford: Oxford UP, 1996.

The Oxford Companion to African American Literature. Ed. William L. Andrews, Frances S. Foster, and Trudier Harris. New York: Oxford UP, 1997.

The Oxford Companion to American Literature. Ed. James D. Hart and Phillip Leininger. 6th ed. New York: Oxford UP, 1995.

The Oxford Companion to Canadian Literature. Ed. Eugene Benson and William Toye. 2nd ed. New York: Oxford UP, 1998.

The Oxford Companion to Classical Literature. Ed. M. C. Howatson. 2nd ed. New York: Oxford UP, 1989.

The Oxford Companion to English Literature. Ed. Margaret Drabble. 6th ed. New York: Oxford UP, 2000.

The Oxford Companion to German Literature. Ed. Henry Garland and Mary Garland. 3rd ed. New York: Oxford UP, 1997.

The Oxford Companion to Italian Literature. Ed. Peter Hainsworth and David Robey. New York: Oxford UP, 2001.

A.13. LAW

Criminal Justice Abstracts. Monsey: Willow Tree, 1977– .
Criminal Justice Periodical Index. Ann Arbor: UMI, 1975– .
Index to Legal Periodicals and Books. New York: Wilson, 1908– .

Black's Law Dictionary. Ed. Bryan A. Garner. 7th ed. St. Paul: West, 1999.
A Dictionary of Modern Legal Usage. Ed. Bryan A. Garner. 2nd ed. New York: Oxford UP, 1991.
Encyclopedia of Crime and Justice. Ed. Joshua Dressler. 2nd ed. 4 vols. Detroit: Gale, 2001.

A.14. MATHEMATICS

Mathematical Reviews. Providence: Amer. Mathematical Soc., 1940– . Online version incorporated into *MathSciNet.*

Companion Encyclopedia of the History and Philosophy of the Mathematical Sciences. Ed. Ivor Gratten-Guinness. New York: Routledge, 1993.
Encyclopedic Dictionary of Mathematics. Ed. Kiyosi Itô. 2nd ed. 4 vols. Cambridge: MIT P, 1987.
The HarperCollins Dictionary of Mathematics. Ed. E. J. Borowski and Jonathan M. Borwein. New York: Harper, 1991.
McGraw-Hill Dictionary of Mathematics. Ed. Sybil P. Parker. New York: McGraw, 1997.

A.15. MEDICINE

Cumulative Index to Nursing and Allied Health Literature. Glendale: CINAHL Information Systems, 1977– .
Index Medicus. Bethesda: US Natl. Lib. of Medicine, 1960– . Online version incorporated into *Medline.*

The American Medical Association Encyclopedia of Medicine. By Amer. Medical Assn. Ed. Charles B. Clayman. New York: Random, 1989.

Dorland's Illustrated Medical Dictionary. 29th ed. Philadelphia:
Saunders, 2000.
Melloni's Illustrated Medical Dictionary. Ed. Ida Dox et al. 4th ed.
Boca Raton: Parthenon, 2002.
Stedman's Medical Dictionary. 27th ed. Philadelphia: Lippincott,
2000.

A.16. MUSIC

The Music Index. Detroit: Information Coordinators, 1949– .
RILM Abstracts of Musical Literature. New York: RILM, 1967– .

The HarperCollins Dictionary of Music. Ed. Christine Ammer. 3rd
ed. New York: Harper, 1995.
The New Grove Dictionary of American Music. Ed. H. Wiley Hitchcock and Stanley Sadie. 4 vols. London: Macmillan, 1986.
The New Grove Dictionary of Music and Musicians. Ed. Stanley
Sadie and John Tyrell. 2nd ed. 29 vols. New York: Macmillan,
2001.
The New Grove Dictionary of Opera. 4 vols. New York: Macmillan,
1992.
The New Harvard Dictionary of Music. Ed. Don M. Randel. Cambridge: Harvard UP, 1986.
The Oxford Companion to Music. Ed. Alison Latham. Rev. ed. Ox-
ford: Oxford UP, 2002.

A.17. PHILOSOPHY

The Philosopher's Index. Bowling Green: Bowling Green State U,
1967– .

The Cambridge Dictionary of Philosophy. Ed. Robert Audi. 2nd ed.
New York: Cambridge UP, 1999.
The Companion Encyclopedia of Asian Philosophy. Ed. Brian Carr
and Indira Mahalingam. New York: Routledge, 1997.
A Companion to Feminist Philosophy. Ed. Alison M. Jaggar and Iris
M. Young. Malden: Blackwell, 1998.
A Dictionary of Philosophy. Ed. Alan R. Lacey. 3rd ed. New York:
Routledge, 1996.

Encyclopedia of Classical Philosophy. Ed. Donald J. Zeyl. Westport: Greenwood, 1997.

Encyclopedia of Ethics. Ed. Lawrence C. Becker and Charlotte B. Becker. 2nd ed. 3 vols. New York: Routledge, 2001.

The Encyclopedia of Philosophy. Ed. Paul Edwards. 8 vols. New York: Free, 1967.

The HarperCollins Dictionary of Philosophy. Ed. Peter A. Angeles. 2nd ed. New York: Harper, 1992.

The Oxford Companion to Philosophy. Ed. Ted Honderich. New York: Oxford UP, 1995.

Routledge Encyclopedia of Philosophy. Ed. Edward Craig. 10 vols. New York: Routledge, 1998.

A.18. PHYSICS

Physics Abstracts. Surrey: Inst. of Electrical Engineers, 1898– . Online version incorporated into *Inspec.*

Encyclopedia of Applied Physics. Ed. George L. Trigg. 23 vols. New York: VCH, 1991–99.

Encyclopedia of Physics. Ed. Rita G. Lerner and George L. Trigg. 2nd ed. New York: VCH, 1991.

McGraw-Hill Encyclopedia of Physics. Ed. Sybil P. Parker. 2nd ed. New York: McGraw, 1993.

A.19. PSYCHOLOGY

Psychological Abstracts. Washington: Amer. Psychological Assn., 1927– . Online version incorporated into *PsycINFO.*

Companion Encyclopedia of Psychology. Ed. Andrew M. Colman. 2 vols. New York: Routledge, 1994.

The Corsini Encyclopedia of Psychology and Behavioral Science. Ed. W. Edward Craighead and Charles B. Nemeroff. 3rd ed. 4 vols. New York: Wiley, 2001.

A Dictionary of Psychology. Ed. Andrew M. Colman. New York: Oxford UP, 2001.

Encyclopedia of Psychology. Ed. Alan E. Kazdin. 8 vols. Washington: Amer. Psychological Assn., 2000.
The International Dictionary of Psychology. Ed. Stuart Sutherland. 2nd ed. New York: Crossroad, 1996.

A.20. RELIGION

Religion Index. Chicago: Amer. Theological Lib. Assn., 1977– .
Religious and Theological Abstracts. Myerstown: Religious and Theological Abstracts, 1958– .

The Anchor Bible Dictionary. Ed. David Noel Freedman et al. 6 vols. New York: Doubleday, 1992.
The Dictionary of Bible and Religion. Ed. William H. Gentz. Nashville: Abingdon, 1986.
Eerdmans Dictionary of the Bible. Ed. David N. Freeman. Grand Rapids: Eerdmans, 2000.
The Encyclopedia of Religion. Ed. Mircea Eliade. 16 vols. New York: Macmillan, 1987.
The HarperCollins Dictionary of Religion. Ed. Jonathan Z. Smith et al. New York: Harper, 1995.
The International Standard Bible Encyclopedia. Ed. Geoffrey W. Bromiley et al. 4 vols. Grand Rapids: Eerdmans, 1979–88.

A.21. SCIENCE AND TECHNOLOGY

Applied Science and Technology Abstracts. New York: Wilson, 1993– .
Applied Science and Technology Index. New York: Wilson, 1958– .
Engineering Index. New York: Engineering Information, 1906– . Online version incorporated into *Ei Compendex.*
General Science Abstracts. New York: Wilson, 1993– .
General Science Index. New York: Wilson, 1978– .
Science Citation Index. Philadelphia: Inst. for Scientific Information, 1945– . Online version incorporated into *Web of Science.*

A Dictionary of Science. Ed. Alan Isaacs et al. New York: Oxford UP, 1999.

McGraw-Hill Encyclopedia of Engineering. Ed. Sybil P. Parker. 2nd ed. New York: McGraw, 1993.

McGraw-Hill Encyclopedia of Science and Technology. Ed. Sybil P. Parker. 9th ed. 20 vols. New York: McGraw, 2002.

The New Penguin Dictionary of Science. Ed. M. J. Clugston. New York: Penguin, 1998.

A.22. SOCIOLOGY

Sociological Abstracts. San Diego: Sociological Abstracts, 1953– .

Encyclopedia of Sociology. Ed. Edgar F. Borgatta et al. 2nd ed. 5 vols. Detroit: Macmillan, 2000.

The Penguin Dictionary of Sociology. Ed. Nicholas Abercrombie et al. 4th ed. New York: Penguin, 2000.

Appendix B:
Other Systems
of Documentation

This appendix describes three documentation systems other than the MLA system. The appendix ends with a selected list of specialized style manuals.

B.1. ENDNOTES AND FOOTNOTES

Some scholars in the fields of art, dance, history, music, religion, theater, and theology use endnotes or footnotes to document sources.

B.1.1. Documentation Notes versus the List of Works Cited and Parenthetical References

If you use notes for documentation, you may not need a list of works cited or a bibliography. (Check your instructor's preference.) The first note referring to a source includes the publication information found in a bibliographic entry—the author's name, the title, and the publication facts—as well as the page reference identifying the portion of the source you refer to at that point in the text. (Subsequent references to the work require less information; see B.1.9.) A bibliographic entry for a work published as part of a book or periodical usually ends with the inclusive page numbers for the entire work cited, but a documentation note, in contrast, ends with the page number or numbers only of the portion you refer to. Note form differs slightly from bibliographic form in other ways (see B.1.3), and note numbers replace parenthetical references at the points in the text where citations are necessary (see B.1.2). Documentation notes appear either at the end of the text, as endnotes, or at the bottoms of relevant pages, as footnotes (see B.1.4).

B.1.2. Note Numbers

Number notes consecutively, starting from 1, throughout a research paper, except for any notes accompanying special material, such as a figure or a table (see 4.7). Do not number them by page or designate them by asterisks or other symbols. Format note numbers as superior, or superscript, arabic numerals (i.e., raised slightly above the line, like this[1]), without periods, parentheses, or slashes. The numbers follow punctuation marks, except dashes. In general, to avoid interrupting the continuity of the text, place a note number, like a parenthetical reference, at the end of the sentence, clause, or phrase containing the material quoted or referred to.

B.1.3. Note Form versus Bibliographic Form

With some exceptions, documentation notes and bibliographic entries provide the same information but differ in form.

Bibliographic Form

A bibliographic entry has three main divisions, each followed by a period: the author's name reversed for alphabetizing, the title, and the publication data.

> Tannen, Deborah. You Just Don't Understand: Women and Men in
>   Conversation. New York: Morrow, 1990.

Note Form

A documentation note has four main divisions: the author's name in normal order, followed by a comma; the title; the publication data in parentheses; and a page reference. There is a period only at the end.

> [1] Deborah Tannen, You Just Don't Understand: Women and Men in
> Conversation (New York: Morrow, 1990) 52.

B.1.4. Endnotes versus Footnotes

In research papers, make all notes endnotes, unless you are instructed otherwise. As their name implies, endnotes appear after the text, starting on a new page numbered in sequence with the preceding page. Center the title *Notes* one inch from the top, double-space, indent one-half inch (or five spaces, if you are using a typewriter) from the left margin, and add the note number, without punctuation, slightly above the line. Type a space and then the reference. If the note extends to two or more lines, begin subsequent lines at the left margin. Type the notes consecutively, double-spaced, and number all pages.

Footnotes appear at the bottoms of pages, beginning four lines (two double spaces) below the text. Single-space footnotes, but double-space between them. Otherwise, format a footnote like an endnote. When a footnote continues on the following page, add a solid line across the new page two lines (one double space) below the last line of the text and continue the note two lines (one double space) below the solid line. Footnotes for the new page immediately follow the note continued from the previous page, after a double space.

B.1.5. Sample First Note References: Books and Other Nonperiodical Publications

For additional information on citing the following types of sources, consult the related sections on bibliographic entries, indicated in parentheses after the headings.

a. A Book by a Single Author (5.6.1)

[1] Francis Fukuyama, Our Posthuman Future: Consequences of the Biotechnology Revolution (New York: Farrar, 2002) 32.

b. An Anthology or a Compilation (5.6.2)

[2] Susan Ostrov Weisser, ed., Women and Romance: A Reader (New York: New York UP, 2001).

c. A Book by Two or More Authors (5.6.4)

[3] James W. Marquart, Sheldon Ekland Olson, and Jonathan R. Sorensen, The Rope, the Chair, and the Needle: Capital Punishment in Texas, 1923-1990 (Austin: U of Texas P, 1994) 52-57.

d. A Book by a Corporate Author (5.6.6)

[4] Public Agenda Foundation, The Health Care Crisis: Containing Costs, Expanding Coverage (New York: McGraw, 1992) 69.

e. A Work in an Anthology (5.6.7)

[5] Isabel Allende, "Toad's Mouth," trans. Margaret Sayers Peden, A Hammock beneath the Mangoes: Stories from Latin America, ed. Thomas Colchie (New York: Plume, 1992) 83.

f. An Article in a Reference Book (5.6.8)

[6] "Mandarin," The Encyclopedia Americana, 1994 ed.

g. An Introduction, a Preface, a Foreword, or an Afterword (5.6.9)

[7] J. M. Coetzee, introduction, The Confusions of Young Törless, by Robert Musil, trans. Shaun Whiteside (New York: Penguin, 2001) v-vi.

h. An Anonymous Book (5.6.11)

[8] New York Public Library American History Desk Reference (New York: Macmillan, 1997) 241-47.

i. An Edition (5.6.12)

[9] Jane Austen, Sense and Sensibility, ed. Claudia Johnson (New York: Norton, 2001) 121.

[10] Fredson Bowers, ed., The Red Badge of Courage: An Episode of the American Civil War, by Stephen Crane (1895; Charlottesville: UP of Virginia, 1975).

j. A Translation (5.6.13)

[11] Laura Esquivel, Like Water for Chocolate: A Novel in Monthly Installments, with Recipes, Romances, and Home Remedies, trans. Carol Christensen and Thomas Christensen (New York: Doubleday, 1992) 1-5.

k. A Book Published in a Second or Subsequent Edition (5.6.14)

[12] Peter Bondanella, Italian Cinema: From Neorealism to the Present, 3rd ed. (New York: Continuum, 2001) 61.

l. A Multivolume Work (5.6.15)

[13] Paul Lauter et al., eds., The Heath Anthology of American Literature, 4th ed., 2 vols. (Boston: Houghton, 2002).

[14] Arthur Conan Doyle, The Oxford Sherlock Holmes, ed. Owen Dudley Edwards, vol. 8 (New York: Oxford UP, 1993).

[15] René Wellek, A History of Modern Criticism, 1750-1950, vol. 5 (New Haven: Yale UP, 1986) 322-26.

m. A Book in a Series (5.6.16)

[16] Alfreda Murck, Poetry and Painting in Song China: The Subtle Art of Dissent, Harvard-Yenching Inst. Monograph Ser. 50 (Cambridge: Harvard UP, 2000) 62.

n. A Republished Book (5.6.17)

[17] Margaret Atwood, The Blind Assassin (2000; New York: Knopf-Random, 2001) 209-12.

o. A Publisher's Imprint (5.6.18)

[18] Phillip Lopate, ed., The Art of the Personal Essay: An Anthology from the Classical Era to the Present (New York: Anchor-Doubleday, 1994).

p. A Book with Multiple Publishers (5.6.19)

[19] J. Wight Duff, A Literary History of Rome: From the Origins to the Close of the Golden Age, ed. A. M. Duff, 3rd ed. (1953; London: Benn; New York: Barnes, 1967) 88.

q. A Pamphlet (5.6.20)

[20] Washington, DC (New York: Trip Builder, 2000).

r. A Government Publication (5.6.21)

[21] United Nations, Centre on Transnational Corporations, Foreign Direct Investment, the Service Sector, and International Banking (New York: United Nations, 1987) 4-6.

s. The Published Proceedings of a Conference (5.6.22)

[22] Steve S. Chang, Lily Liaw, and Josef Ruppenhofer, eds., Proceedings of the Twenty-Fifth Annual Meeting of the Berkeley Linguistics Society, February 12-15, 1999: General Session and Parasession on Loan Word Phenomena (Berkeley: Berkeley Linguistics Soc., 2000).

t. A Book in a Language Other Than English (5.6.23)

[23] Emanuel Poche, Prazské Palace (Praha [Prague]: Odeon, 1977) 1-5.

u. A Book Published before 1900 (5.6.24)

[24] John Dewey, The School and Society (Chicago, 1899) 104.

v. A Book without Stated Publication Information or Pagination (5.6.25)

[25] Zvi Malachi, ed., Proceedings of the International Conference on Literary and Linguistic Computing ([Tel Aviv]: [Fac. of Humanities, Tel Aviv U], n.d.).

w. An Unpublished Dissertation (5.6.26)

[26] Mary Kelly, "Factors Predicting Hospital Readmission of Normal Newborns," diss., U of Michigan, 2001, 34.

x. A Published Dissertation (5.6.27)

[27] Rudolf F. Dietze, Ralph Ellison: The Genesis of an Artist, diss., U Erlangen-Nürnberg, 1982, Erlanger Beiträge zur Sprach- und Kunstwissenschaft 70 (Nürnberg: Carl, 1982) 168.

B.1.6. Sample First Note References: Articles and Other Publications in Periodicals

For additional information on citing the following types of sources, consult the related sections on bibliographic entries, indicated in parentheses after the headings.

a. An Article in a Scholarly Journal with Continuous Pagination (5.7.1)

[1] Katie Trumpener, "Memories Carved in Granite: Great War Memorials and Everyday Life," PMLA 115 (2000): 1099.

b. An Article in a Scholarly Journal That Pages Each Issue Separately (5.7.2)

[2] Frederick Barthelme, "Architecture," Kansas Quarterly 13.3-4 (1981): 77-78.

c. An Article in a Scholarly Journal That Uses Only Issue Numbers (5.7.3)

[3] Marisa Lajolo, "The Female Reader on Trial," Brasil 14 (1995): 75-76.

d. An Article in a Scholarly Journal with More Than One Series (5.7.4)

[4] John Daniels, "Indian Population of North America in 1492," William and Mary Quarterly 3rd ser. 49 (1992): 300-02.

[5] David Berman, "Marketing Poetry," Kenyon Review ns 22.3-4 (2000): 211-12.

e. An Article in a Newspaper (5.7.5)

[6] Kenneth Chang, "The Melting (Freezing) of Antarctica," New York Times 2 Apr. 2002, late ed.: F1.

[7] Salem Alaton, "So, Did They Live Happily Ever After?" Globe and Mail [Toronto] 27 Dec. 1997: D2.

f. An Article in a Magazine (5.7.6)

[8] Annie Murphy Paul, "Self-Help: Shattering the Myths," Psychology Today Mar.-Apr. 2001: 60.

g. A Review (5.7.7)

[9] John Updike, "No Brakes," rev. of Sinclair Lewis: Rebel from Main Street, by Richard Lingeman, New Yorker 4 Feb. 2002: 77-78.

[10] Deanna L. Fassett, rev. of When Children Don't Learn: Student Failure and the Culture of Teaching, by B. M. Franklin, Communication Education 50 (2001): 85.

[11] "The Cooling of an Admiration," rev. of Pound/Joyce: The Letters of Ezra Pound to James Joyce, with Pound's Essays on Joyce, ed. Forrest Read, Times Literary Supplement 6 Mar. 1969: 239-40.

[12] Rev. of Anthology of Danish Literature, ed. F. J. Billeskov Jansen and P. M. Mitchell, Times Literary Supplement 7 July 1972: 785.

h. An Abstract in an Abstracts Journal (5.7.8)

[13] Mary Kelly, "Factors Predicting Hospital Readmission of Normal Newborns," diss., U of Michigan, 2001, DAI 62 (2001): 2283B.

i. An Anonymous Article (5.7.9)

[14] "It Barks! It Kicks! It Scores!" Newsweek 30 July 2001: 12.

j. An Editorial (5.7.10)

[15] "Death of a Writer," editorial, New York Times 20 Apr. 1994, late ed.: A18.

k. A Letter to the Editor (5.7.11)

[16] Jeffrey Mehlman, letter, Partisan Review 69 (2002): 320.

l. A Serialized Article (5.7.12)

[17] Harrison T. Meserole and James M. Rambeau, "Articles on American Literature Appearing in Current Periodicals," American Literature 52 (1981): 704-05; 53 (1981): 164-66.

[18] Deborah Sontag, "A Mexican Town That Transcends All Borders," New York Times 21 July 1998, late ed.: A1; pt. 3 of a series, Here and There: Immigration Now, begun 19 July 1998.

m. A Special Issue (5.7.13)

[19] Kwame Anthony Appiah and Henry Louis Gates, Jr., eds., Identities, spec. issue of Critical Inquiry 18.4 (1992): 625-884 (Chicago: U of Chicago P, 1995).

[20] State Autonomy, spec. issue of Critical Review 14.2-3 (2000): 139-374.

[21] Christiane Makward, "Reading Maryse Condé's Theater," Maryse Condé, ed. Delphine Perret and Marie-Denise Shelton, spec. issue of Callaloo 18.3 (1995): 681-82.

n. An Article in a Microform Collection of Articles (5.7.14)

[22] Dan Chapman, "Panel Could Help Protect Children," Winston-Salem Journal 14 Jan. 1990: 14, NewsBank: Welfare and Social Problems 12 (1990): fiche 1, grids A8-11.

o. An Article Reprinted in a Loose-Leaf Collection of Articles (5.7.15)

[23] Brad Edmondson, "AIDS and Aging," American Demographics Mar. 1990: 28+, The AIDS Crisis, ed. Eleanor Goldstein, vol. 2 (Boca Raton: SIRS, 1991) art. 24.

B.1.7. Sample First Note References: Miscellaneous Print and Nonprint Sources

For additional information on the following types of documentation, consult the related sections on bibliographic entries, indicated in parentheses after the headings.

a. A Television or Radio Program (5.8.1)

[1] "Frankenstein: The Making of the Monster," Great Books, narr. Donald Sutherland, writ. Eugenie Vink, dir. Jonathan Ward, Learning Channel, 8 Sept. 1993.

b. A Sound Recording (5.8.2)

[2] Roger Norrington, cond., Symphony no. 1 in C, op. 21, and Symphony no. 6 in F, op. 68, by Ludwig van Beethoven, London Classical Players, EMI, 1988.

[3] Billie Holiday, "God Bless the Child," rec. 9 May 1941, The Essence of Billie Holiday, Columbia, 1991.

[4] Edward Hermann, narr., John Adams, by David McCullough, audiocassette, Simon, 2001.

[5] D. K. Wilgus, Southern Folk Tales, rec. 23-25 Mar. 1965, audiotape, U of California, Los Angeles, Archives of Folklore, B.76.82.

[6] David Lewiston, liner notes, The Balinese Gamelan: Music from the Morning of the World, LP, Nonesuch, n.d.

c. A Film or Video Recording (5.8.3)

[7] It's a Wonderful Life, dir. Frank Capra, perf. James Stewart, Donna Reed, Lionel Barrymore, and Thomas Mitchell, RKO, 1946.

[8] Rudolph Nureyev, chor., Swan Lake, by Pyotr Ilich Tchaikovsky, perf. Margot Fonteyn and Nureyev, Vienna State Opera Ballet, Vienna Symphony Orch., cond. John Lanchbery, 1966, DVD, Philips, 1997.

[9] Looking at Our Earth: A Visual Dictionary, sound filmstrip, Natl. Geographic Educ. Services, 1992.

d. A Performance (5.8.4)

[10] Diana Rigg, perf., Medea, by Euripides, trans. Alistair Elliot, dir. Jonathan Kent, Longacre Theatre, New York, 7 Apr. 1994.

[11] Scott Joplin, Treemonisha, dir. Frank Corsaro, perf. Carmen Balthrop, Betty Allen, and Curtis Rayam, Houston Grand Opera Orch. and Chorus, cond. Gunther Schuller, Miller Theatre, Houston, 18 May 1975.

e. A Musical Composition (5.8.5)

[12] Ludwig van Beethoven, Symphony no. 7 in A, op. 92.

f. A Painting, Sculpture, or Photograph (5.8.6)

[13] Rembrandt van Rijn, Aristotle Contemplating the Bust of Homer, Metropolitan Museum of Art, New York.

[14] Mary Cassatt, Mother and Child, Wichita Art Museum, American Painting: 1560-1913, by John Pearce (New York: McGraw, 1964) slide 22.

g. An Interview (5.8.7)

[15] Federico Fellini, "The Long Interview," Juliet of the Spirits, ed. Tullio Kezich, trans. Howard Greenfield (New York: Ballantine, 1966) 56.

[16] Jimmy Breslin, interview with Neal Conan, Talk of the Nation, Natl. Public Radio, WBUR, Boston, 26 Mar. 2002.

[17] I. M. Pei, personal interview, 22 July 1993.

h. A Map or Chart (5.8.8)

[18] Michigan, map (Chicago: Rand, 2000).

[19] Japanese Fundamentals, chart (Hauppauge: Barron, 1992).

i. A Cartoon or Comic Strip (5.8.9)

[20] Roz Chast, cartoon, New Yorker 4 Feb. 2002: 53.

[21] Garry Trudeau, "Doonesbury," comic strip, Star-Ledger [Newark] 4 May 2002: 26.

j. An Advertisement (5.8.10)

[22] The Fitness Fragrance by Ralph Lauren, advertisement, GQ Apr. 1997: 111-12.

k. A Lecture, a Speech, an Address, or a Reading (5.8.11)

[23] Margaret Atwood, "Silencing the Scream," Boundaries of the Imagination Forum, MLA Convention, Royal York Hotel, Toronto, 29 Dec. 1993.

[24] Studs Terkel, address, Conf. on Coll. Composition and Communication Convention, Palmer House, Chicago, 22 Mar. 1990.

l. A Manuscript or Typescript (5.8.12)

[25] Mark Twain, notebook 32, ts., Mark Twain Papers, U of California, Berkeley, 50.

m. A Letter or Memo (5.8.13)

[26] Virginia Woolf, "To T. S. Eliot," 28 July 1920, letter 1138 of The Letters of Virginia Woolf, ed. Nigel Nicolson and Joanne Trautmann, vol. 2 (New York: Harcourt, 1976) 437-38.

[27] Thomas Hart Benton, letter to Charles Fremont, 22 June 1847, John Charles Fremont Papers, Southwest Museum Lib., Los Angeles.

[28] Toni Morrison, letter to the author, 17 May 2001.

[29] Daniel J. Cahill, memo to English dept. fac., Brooklyn Technical High School, New York, 1 June 2000.

n. A Legal Source (5.8.14)

[30] New York Times Co. v. Tasini, no. 00-201, Supreme Ct. of the US, 25 June 2001.

B.1.8. Sample First Note References: Electronic Publications

For additional information on citing the following types of sources, consult the related sections on bibliographic entries, indicated in parentheses after the headings.

a. A Document from an Internet Site (5.9.1)

[1] "Catalán," Sí, España, ed. José Félix Barrio, vers. 3.0, May 2002, Embassy of Spain, Ottawa, 10 May 2002 <http://www.SiSpain.org/spanish/language/language/catalan.html>.

[2] "Selected Seventeenth-Century Events," Romantic Chronology, ed. Laura Mandell and Alan Liu, 1999, U of California, Santa Barbara, 22 June 2002 <http://english.ucsb.edu:591/rchrono/>.

[3] Semir Zeki, "Artistic Creativity and the Brain," Science 6 July 2001: 51–52, Science Magazine, 2002, Amer. Assn. for the Advancement of Science, 24 Sept. 2002 <http://www.sciencemag.org/cgi/content/full/293/5527/51>.

b. An Entire Internet Site (5.9.2)

[4] Sí, España, ed. José Félix Barrio, vers. 3.0, May 2002, Embassy of Spain, Ottawa, 10 May 2002 <http://www.SiSpain.org/>.

[5] Romantic Chronology, ed. Laura Mandell and Alan Liu, 1999, U of California, Santa Barbara, 22 June 2002 <http://english.ucsb.edu:591/rchrono/>.

c. An Online Book (5.9.3)

[6] Jane Austen, Pride and Prejudice, ed. Henry Churchyard, 1996, Jane Austen Information Page, 6 Sept. 2002 <http://www.pemberley.com/janeinfo/pridprej.html>.

[7] Nathaniel Hawthorne, Twice-Told Tales, ed. George Parsons Lathrop (Boston: Houghton, 1883), 16 May 2002 <http://209.11.144.65/eldritchpress/nh/ttt.html>.

[8] E[dith] Nesbit, Ballads and Lyrics of Socialism (London, 1908), Victorian Women Writers Project, ed. Perry Willett, May 2000, Indiana U, 26 June 2002 <http://www.indiana.edu/~letrs/vwwp/nesbit/ballsoc.html>.

[9] John Keats, "Ode on a Grecian Urn," Poetical Works, 1884, Bartleby.com: Great Books Online, ed. Steven van Leeuwen, 2002, 5 May 2002 <http://www.bartleby.com/126/41.htm>.

d. An Article in an Online Periodical (5.9.4)

[10] Gabrielle Dane, "Reading Ophelia's Madness," Exemplaria 10.2 (1998), 22 June 2002 <http://web.english.ufl.edu/english/exemplaria/danefram.htm>.

[11] J. D. Biersdorfer, "Religion Finds Technology," New York Times on the Web 16 May 2002, 20 May 2002 <http://www.nytimes.com/2002/05/16/technology/circuits/16CHUR.html>.

[12] David Brooks, "The Culture of Martyrdom," Atlantic Online June 2002, 24 Sept. 2002 <http://www.theatlantic.com/issues/2002/06/brooks.htm>.

[13] Cynthia A. Gravlee, rev. of Magic in Medieval Romance from Chrétien de Troyes to Geoffrey Chaucer, by Michelle Sweeney, Medieval Review 2.03.15 (2002), 20 May 2002 <http://www.hti.umich.edu/t/tmr/>.

[14] Dan Nastali and Phil Boardman, "Searching for Arthur: Literary Highways, Electronic Byways, and Cultural Back Roads," Arthuriana 11.4 (2001): 108-22, abstract, 1 Oct. 2002 <http://www.smu.edu/arthuriana/>, path: Abstracts; K-O.

[15] "Keeping College Doors Open," editorial, Christian Science Monitor: CSMonitor.com 16 May 2002, 20 May 2002 <http://www.csmonitor.com/2002/0516/p08s03-comv.html>.

[16] Christine Schmidt, letter, New York Times on the Web 20 May 2002, 20 May 2002 <http://www.nytimes.com/2002/05/20/opinion/L20KIDS.html>.

e. A Publication on CD-ROM, Diskette, or Magnetic Tape (5.9.5)

[17] A. R. Braunmuller, ed., Macbeth, by William Shakespeare, CD-ROM (New York: Voyager, 1994).

[18] English Poetry Full-Text Database, magnetic tape, rel. 2 (Cambridge, Eng.: Chadwyck-Healey, 1993).

[19] Elaine C. Thiesmeyer and John E. Thiesmeyer, Editor for the Macintosh: A Proofreading System for Usage, Mechanics, Vocabulary, and Troublesome Spelling, diskette (New York: MLA, 2001).

[20] "Albatross," The Oxford English Dictionary, 2nd ed., CD-ROM (Oxford: Oxford UP, 1992).

[21] "Children's Television Workshop," Encyclopedia of Associations, magnetic tape (Detroit: Gale, 1994).

[22] "Ibn Hamdis," Encyclopaedia of Islam, CD-ROM (Leiden: Brill, 1999).

[23] Peg Krach, "Myth and Facts about Alcohol Abuse in the Elderly," Nursing Feb. 1998: 25+, abstract, Periodical Abstracts Ondisc, CD-ROM, UMI-ProQuest, Feb. 1998.

[24] Perseus 2.0: Interactive Sources and Studies on Ancient Greece, CD-ROM, 4 discs (New Haven: Yale UP, 1996).

f. A Work in More Than One Publication Medium (5.9.6)

[25] Perseus 1.0: Interactive Sources and Studies on Ancient Greece, CD-ROM, laser disc (New Haven: Yale UP, 1992).

g. A Work from a Library or Personal Subscription Service (5.9.7)

[26] "Cooling Trend in Antarctica," Futurist May-June 2002: 15, Academic Search Premier, EBSCO, City U of New York, Graduate Center Lib., 22 May 2002 <http://www.epnet.com/>.

[27] Sami Youakim, "Work-Related Asthma," American Family Physician 64 (2001): 1839-52, Health Reference Center, Gale, Bergen County Cooperative Lib. System, NJ, 12 Jan. 2002 <http://www.galegroup.com/>.

[28] "Table Tennis," Compton's Encyclopedia Online, vers. 2.0, 1997, America Online, 4 July 1998, keyword: Compton's.

h. A Work in an Indeterminate Medium (5.9.8)

[29] John Bartlett, Familiar Quotations, 9th ed. (Boston: Little, 1901), New York: Columbia U, Academic Information Systems, 1995, electronic, ColumbiaNet, Columbia U Lib., 2 July 1998.

i. Other Electronic Sources (5.9.9)

[30] "The Threat of Commercial Fishing," Earth Matters, CNN, 18 Jan. 1998, transcript, Broadcast News, CD-ROM, Primary Source Media, Jan. 1998, screen 10.

[31] Franklin D. Roosevelt, "Americanism," 1920, American Leaders Speak: Recordings from World War I and the 1920 Election, 1996, American Memory, Lib. of Congress, Washington, 19 Mar. 2002 <http://lcweb2.loc.gov/mbrs/nforum/9000024.ram>.

[32] F. W. Murnau, dir., Nosferatu, 1922, The Sync, 16 June 2002 <http://www.thesync.com/ram/nosferatu.ram>.

[33] Hans Holbein, The Ambassadors, 1533, Microsoft Art Gallery: The Collection of the National Gallery, London, CD-ROM (Redmond: Microsoft, 1994).

[34] Peter Ackroyd, interview, Bold Type, Nov. 2001, 25 June 2002 <http://www.randomhouse.com/boldtype/1101/ackroyd/interview.html>.

[35] "Phoenix, Arizona," map, U.S. Gazetteer, US Census Bureau, 24 Sept. 2002 <http://factfinder.census.gov/servlet/ReferenceMapFramesetServlet?_lang=en>.

[36] Al Cacicedo, "Private Parts: Preliminary Notes for an Essay on Gender Identity in Shakespeare," working paper, 12 Mar. 1997, 24 Sept. 2002 <http://www.shaksper.net/archives/files/private.parts.html>.

[37] James L. Harner, e-mail to the author, 20 Aug. 2002.

[38] John Lavagnino, "OCR and Handwriting," online posting, 7 May 2002, Humanist Discussion Group, 24 May 2002 <http://lists.village.virginia.edu/lists_archive/Humanist/v16/0001.html>.

[39] Dene Grigar, online defense of dissertation "Penelopeia: The Making of Penelope in Homer's Story and Beyond," 25 July 1995, LinguaMOO, 1 June 2002 <http://lingua.utdallas.edu/~cynthiah/lingua_archive/phd-defense.txt>.

[40] TACT: Text-Analysis Computing Tools, vers. 2.1, 24 Sept. 2002 <http://www.chass.utoronto.ca/cch/tact.html>.

B.1.9. Subsequent References

After fully documenting a work, use a shortened form in subsequent notes. As in parenthetical references (see 6.2), include enough information to identify the work. The author's last name alone, followed by the relevant page numbers, is usually adequate.

[4] Frye 345-47.

If you cite two or more works by the same author—for example, Northrop Frye's *Anatomy of Criticism* and his *The Double Vision*— include a shortened form of the title following the author's last name in each reference after the first.

[8] Frye, Anatomy 278.
[9] Frye, Double Vision 1-3.

Repeat the information even when two references in sequence refer to the same work. The abbreviations *ibid.* and *op. cit.* are not recommended.

B.2. AUTHOR-DATE SYSTEM

The author-date system, used in the social sciences and in many of the physical sciences, requires that a parenthetical reference include the author's last name, a comma, the work's year of publication, another comma, and the page reference, preceded by the abbreviation *p.* or *pp.*: "(Wilson, 1992, p. 73)." Information cited in the text is omitted from the parenthetical reference. The authoritative guide to this documentation system is the *Publication Manual of the American Psychological Association* (see the list of specialized style manuals in B.4), and the system is often called APA style.

APA and MLA bibliographic forms differ in a number of ways: in APA style, only the initials of the author's first and middle names are given; the year of publication, in parentheses, follows the author's name; for a book, only proper nouns and the first word of the title and of the subtitle are capitalized; book titles are italicized; and the names of some publishers, such as university presses and associations, are spelled out. The second and subsequent lines of the entry are indented as in MLA style.

Tannen, D. (1990). *You just don't understand: Women and men in conversation.* New York: Morrow.

If the book is edited, the abbreviation *Ed.* or *Eds.*, in parentheses, precedes the year of publication.

Tannen, D. (Ed.). (1993). *Gender and conversational interaction.* New York: Oxford University Press.

If there are two or more authors, each name is reversed, and an ampersand (&), not the word *and*, precedes the final name.

Durant, W., & Durant, A. (1977). *A dual autobiography.* New York: Simon & Schuster.

Titles of essays, book chapters, and articles in periodicals are capitalized like titles of books but are neither put in quotation marks nor italicized. Journal titles, however, are capitalized in a manner consistent with MLA capitalization style (see 3.6.1) but are italicized. The volume number, also italicized, follows the journal title and a comma; the issue number, if needed, appears in parentheses after the volume number; a comma and the inclusive page numbers for the article complete the entry.

Craner, P. M. (1991). New tool for an ancient art: The computer and music. *Computers and the Humanities, 25,* 303-313.

If the list of works cited includes more than one work by an author, the entries are arranged chronologically, and the author's name is repeated in each entry. If two or more works by the same author were published in a year, each is assigned a lowercase letter: "(1998a)," "(1998b)." For a multivolume work, the range of volume numbers is given in parentheses, preceded by the abbreviation *Vols.*: "(Vols. 1–4)."

The following parenthetical references and corresponding list of works cited demonstrate the author-date system.

Between 1968 and 1988, television coverage of presidential elections changed dramatically (Hallin, 1992, p. 5).

Eighteenth-century England was a "humble satellite" in the world of music and art (Durant & Durant, 1965, pp. 214-248).

Frye defined the *alazon* as a "self-deceiving or self-deceived character in fiction" (1957a, p. 365).

Wellek admits in the middle of his multivolume history of modern literary criticism, "An evolutionary history of criticism must fail. I have come to this resigned conclusion" (1955-1992, Vol. 5, p. xxii).

There are several excellent essays in the book *Sound and Poetry* (Frye, 1957b).

To Will and Ariel Durant, creative men and women make "history forgivable by enriching our heritage and our lives" (1977, p. 406).

References

Durant, W., & Durant, A. (1965). *The age of Voltaire*. New York: Simon & Schuster.

Durant, W., & Durant, A. (1977). *A dual autobiography*. New York: Simon & Schuster.

Frye, N. (1957a). *Anatomy of criticism: Four essays*. Princeton, NJ: Princeton University Press.

Frye, N. (Ed.). (1957b). *Sound and poetry*. New York: Columbia University Press.

Hallin, D. C. (1992). Sound bite news: Television coverage of elections, 1968-1988. *Journal of Communication, 42*(2), 5-24.

Wellek, R. (1955-1992). *A history of modern criticism, 1750-1950* (Vols. 1-8). New Haven, CT: Yale University Press.

B.3. NUMBER SYSTEM

Disciplines such as chemistry, mathematics, medicine, and physics use the number system, which varies from field to field (see the list of specialized style manuals by discipline in B.4). In the number system, arabic numerals designate entries in the list of works cited and appear in parenthetical documentation followed by commas and the relevant volume and page references, which are preceded by the appropriate abbreviations: "(13, Vol. 5, p. 259)." With this system, the year of publication remains at the end of the bibliographic entry, and the works are usually listed not in alphabetical order but in the order in which they are first cited in the text. Capitalization of titles generally follows APA style (B.2).

But Peter Scotto has offered another view (1).

Frye defined the <u>alazon</u> as a "self-deceiving or self-deceived character in fiction" (2, p. 365).

Wellek admits in the middle of his multivolume history of modern literary criticism, "An evolutionary history of criticism must fail. I have come to this resigned conclusion" (3, Vol. 5, p. xxii).

Eighteenth-century England was a "humble satellite" in the world of music and art (4, pp. 214-48).

To Will and Ariel Durant, creative men and women make "history forgivable by enriching our heritage and our lives" (5, p. 406).

Works Cited

1. Scotto, P. Censorship, reading, and interpretation: A case study from the Soviet Union. PMLA 109 (1994): 61-70.

2. Frye, N. Anatomy of criticism: Four essays. Princeton: Princeton University Press, 1957.

3. Wellek, R. A history of modern criticism, 1750-1950. 8 vols. New Haven: Yale University Press, 1955-92.

4. Durant, W., and Durant, A. The age of Voltaire. New York: Simon and Schuster, 1965.

5. Durant, W., and Durant, A. A dual autobiography. New York: Simon and Schuster, 1977.

B.4. SPECIALIZED STYLE MANUALS

Every scholarly field has its preferred style, or set of guidelines for writing. MLA style, as presented in this manual, is widely accepted in humanities disciplines. The following manuals describe the styles of other disciplines.

Biology

Council of Biology Editors. *Scientific Style and Format: The CBE Manual for Authors, Editors, and Publishers.* By Edward J. Huth. 6th ed. New York: Cambridge UP, 1994.

Chemistry

American Chemical Society. *The ACS Style Guide: A Manual for Authors and Editors.* Ed. Janet S. Dodd. 2nd ed. New York: Oxford UP, 1997.

Geology

United States. Geological Survey. *Suggestions to Authors of the Reports of the United States Geological Survey.* 7th ed. Washington: GPO, 1991.

Linguistics

Linguistic Society of America. *LSA Bulletin*, Dec. issue, annually.

Mathematics

American Mathematical Society. *AMS Author Handbook.* Providence: Amer. Mathematical Soc., 1997.

Medicine

American Medical Association. *AMA Manual of Style: A Guide for Authors and Editors.* By Cheryl Iverson et al. 9th ed. Baltimore: Williams, 1998.

Physics

American Institute of Physics. *AIP Style Manual.* 4th ed. New York: Amer. Inst. of Physics, 1990.

Psychology

American Psychological Association. *Publication Manual of the American Psychological Association.* 5th ed. Washington: Amer. Psychological Assn., 2001.

There are also style manuals that address primarily editors and concern procedures for preparing a manuscript for publication:

The Chicago Manual of Style. 14th ed. Chicago: U of Chicago P, 1993.

United States. Government Printing Office. *Style Manual.* Rev. ed. Washington: GPO, 2000.

Words into Type. By Marjorie E. Skillin, Robert M. Gay, et al. 3rd ed. Englewood Cliffs: Prentice, 1974.

For other style manuals and authors' guides, see John Bruce Howell, *Style Manuals of the English-Speaking World* (Phoenix: Oryx, 1983).

SAMPLE PAGES OF
A RESEARCH PAPER
IN MLA STYLE

First Page of a Research Paper

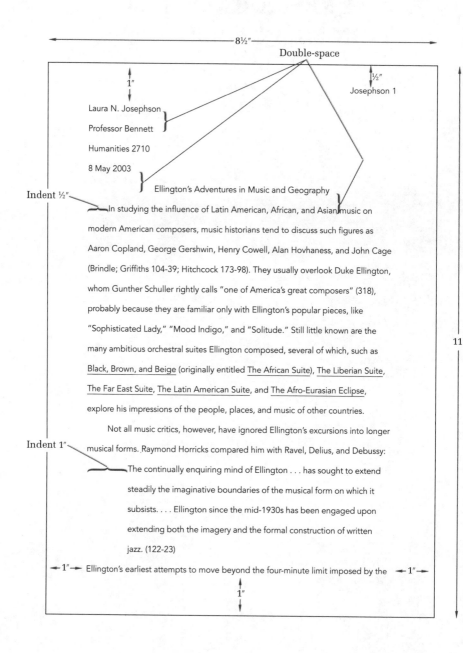

8½"

Double-space

1"

½"

Josephson 1

Laura N. Josephson

Professor Bennett

Humanities 2710

8 May 2003

Indent ½"

Ellington's Adventures in Music and Geography

In studying the influence of Latin American, African, and Asian music on

modern American composers, music historians tend to discuss such figures as

Aaron Copland, George Gershwin, Henry Cowell, Alan Hovhaness, and John Cage

(Brindle; Griffiths 104-39; Hitchcock 173-98). They usually overlook Duke Ellington,

whom Gunther Schuller rightly calls "one of America's great composers" (318),

probably because they are familiar only with Ellington's popular pieces, like

"Sophisticated Lady," "Mood Indigo," and "Solitude." Still little known are the

many ambitious orchestral suites Ellington composed, several of which, such as

Black, Brown, and Beige (originally entitled The African Suite), The Liberian Suite,

The Far East Suite, The Latin American Suite, and The Afro-Eurasian Eclipse,

explore his impressions of the people, places, and music of other countries.

Not all music critics, however, have ignored Ellington's excursions into longer

Indent 1"

musical forms. Raymond Horricks compared him with Ravel, Delius, and Debussy:

The continually enquiring mind of Ellington . . . has sought to extend

steadily the imaginative boundaries of the musical form on which it

subsists. . . . Ellington since the mid-1930s has been engaged upon

extending both the imagery and the formal construction of written

jazz. (122-23)

1"

Ellington's earliest attempts to move beyond the four-minute limit imposed by the

1"

1"

11"

First Page of a List of Works Cited

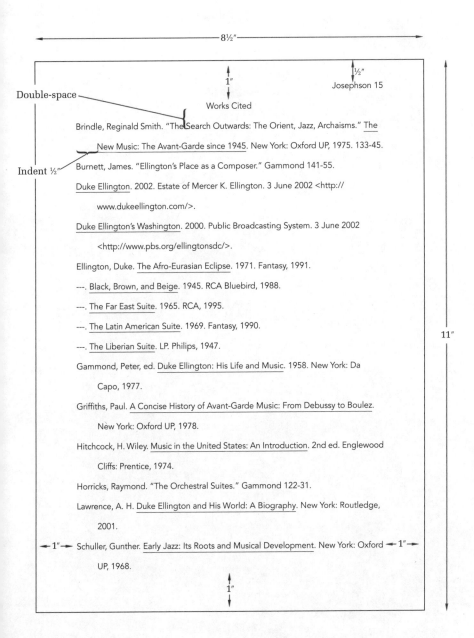

8½"

Double-space

Indent ½"

Josephson 15   ½"

1"

Works Cited

Brindle, Reginald Smith. "The Search Outwards: The Orient, Jazz, Archaisms." The

New Music: The Avant-Garde since 1945. New York: Oxford UP, 1975. 133-45.

Burnett, James. "Ellington's Place as a Composer." Gammond 141-55.

Duke Ellington. 2002. Estate of Mercer K. Ellington. 3 June 2002 <http://

www.dukeellington.com/>.

Duke Ellington's Washington. 2000. Public Broadcasting System. 3 June 2002

<http://www.pbs.org/ellingtonsdc/>.

Ellington, Duke. The Afro-Eurasian Eclipse. 1971. Fantasy, 1991.

---. Black, Brown, and Beige. 1945. RCA Bluebird, 1988.

---. The Far East Suite. 1965. RCA, 1995.

---. The Latin American Suite. 1969. Fantasy, 1990.

---. The Liberian Suite. LP. Philips, 1947.

Gammond, Peter, ed. Duke Ellington: His Life and Music. 1958. New York: Da

Capo, 1977.

Griffiths, Paul. A Concise History of Avant-Garde Music: From Debussy to Boulez.

New York: Oxford UP, 1978.

Hitchcock, H. Wiley. Music in the United States: An Introduction. 2nd ed. Englewood

Cliffs: Prentice, 1974.

Horricks, Raymond. "The Orchestral Suites." Gammond 122-31.

Lawrence, A. H. Duke Ellington and His World: A Biography. New York: Routledge,

2001.

Schuller, Gunther. Early Jazz: Its Roots and Musical Development. New York: Oxford

UP, 1968.

11"

1"

1"

1"

Index

documents, historical *See* government publications; historical documents
Don Juan, abbreviation for 7.7.4
Don Quixote, abbreviation for 7.7.4
double-spacing, of research paper
   4.4
downloading research material
   1.4.4c–d, 5.9.1
Dr. 3.4.2
drafts, of research paper 1.9
dramas *See* plays
drawings, as illustrations in
   research paper 4.7
DVDs (digital videodiscs) 7.4
   in list of works cited 5.8.3

EBSCO databases 1.4.6c
   in list of works cited 5.9.7
   in note references B.1.8g
economics, reference works for A.4
editions, documentation of
   abridged or revised
      in list of works cited 5.6.14
      in note references B.1.5k
   of newspapers 5.7.5
   no edition given 5.6.14
   of reference books 5.6.8
   scholarly
      in list of works cited 5.6.12
      in note references B.1.5i
   second or subsequent
      in list of works cited 5.6.14
      in note references B.1.5k
editions, of research sources, selecting reliable 1.6
editorials
   in list of works cited 5.7.10
      online 5.9.4g
   in note references B.1.6j
      online B.1.8d
   in parenthetical references 6.4.4
editors
   in author-date (APA) system B.2
   ed. 5.6.2, 5.6.7, 5.6.12
   in list of works cited
      of anthologies 5.6.2, 5.6.7
      in cross-references 5.6.10

editors, in list of works cited *(cont.)*
      of electronic publications
         5.9.1, 5.9.2, 5.9.3a–b, 5.9.5a
      general editors 5.6.15
      letters to 5.7.11, 5.9.4h
      of multivolume works 5.6.15
      of reference books 5.6.8
      of scholarly editions 5.6.12
      of translations 5.6.13
   in note references B.1.5b, e, i, l
      of electronic publications
         B.1.8a–c, e
   in parenthetical references
      6.4.1–3, 6.4.8–9
education, reference works for A.7
electronic, for indeterminate
   medium 5.9.8
electronic mail *See* e-mail
electronic publications
   accessing 1.4.3, 1.4.4c, 1.4.8b–e
   dates of access 1.4.8e, 5.9.1
   dates of publication 5.9.1, 5.9.5
   downloading for later verification
      5.9.1
   evaluating 1.6
   in list of works cited 5.9
      on CD-ROM, diskette, mag-
         netic tape 5.9.5; 5.9.9a, c–d
      in indeterminate medium
         5.9.8
      missing information about
         5.9.1
      in more than one medium
         5.9.1, 5.9.6
      online 5.9.1–4, 5.9.7, 5.9.9
      publication dates of 5.9.1,
         5.9.5
   network addresses for 5.9.1
   in note references B.1.8
   in parenthetical references
      corporate authors 6.4.5
      entire works 6.4.1
      listed by title 6.4.4
      literary works 6.4.8
      multiple by same author 6.4.6
      multiple in same parenthesis
         6.4.9
      no page numbers 6.2, 6.4.2